LOVE'S RETURN

LOVE'S RETURN

PSYCHOANALYTIC ESSAYS
on Childhood, Teaching, and Learning

Edited by Gail M. Boldt and Paula M. Salvio

Routledge
Taylor & Francis Group
New York   London

Routledge is an imprint of the
Taylor & Francis Group, an informa business

Published in 2006 by
Routledge
Taylor & Francis Group
270 Madison Avenue
New York, NY 10016

Published in Great Britain by
Routledge
Taylor & Francis Group
2 Park Square
Milton Park, Abingdon
Oxon OX14 4RN

© 2006 by Taylor & Francis Group, LLC
Routledge is an imprint of Taylor & Francis Group

Printed in the United States of America on acid-free paper
10 9 8 7 6 5 4 3 2 1

International Standard Book Number-10: 0-415-95205-0 (Hardcover) 0-415-95206-9 (Softcover)
International Standard Book Number-13: 978-0-415-95205-7 (Hardcover) 978-0-415-95206-4 (Softcover)
Library of Congress Card Number 2005026204

Library of Congress Cataloging-in-Publication Data

Love's return : psychoanalytic essays on childhood, teaching, and learning / edited by Gail M. Boldt
    and Paula M. Salvio with the assistance of Aimee Cheree Mapes.
        p. cm.
    Includes bibliographical references and index.
    ISBN 0-415-95205-0 (hb : alk. paper) -- ISBN 0-415-95206-9 (pb : alk. paper)
    1. Psychoanalysis and education. I. Boldt, Gail Masuchika. II.Salvio, Paula M. III. Mapes, Aimee
Cheree.

LB1092.L68 2006
370.15--dc22   2005026204

Taylor & Francis Group
is the Academic Division of Informa plc.

Visit the Taylor & Francis Web site at
http://www.taylorandfrancis.com

and the Routledge Web site at
http://www.routledge-ny.com

To my teachers.
GB

To my mother, Genevieve Bruno Salvio.
PS

To my grandmother.
AM

Contents

viii • Contents

Acknowledgments

We thank the many people and institutions that helped us to complete this book. The University of Iowa awarded us a range of funding during the last two years to support us in this work. Thanks to Dean Sandra Damico and DEO Gary Sasso for supporting our application for funding through the College of Education Research Fund and the Hazel Prehm Fund. Thanks also to Aimee Carillo-Rowe, the Project on the Rhetoric of Inquiry (POROI), and the Iowa chapters of Phi Delta Kappa and Pi Lambda Theta for support connected to the 2004 POROI conference. We express gratitude to Jennifer Beard and Burt Feintuch at the University of New Hampshire Center for the Humanities for continual support. Thanks also to the board, faculty, staff, and candidates at The Chicago Institute for Psychoanalysis for so generously and warmly welcoming Gail Boldt for a year of work and study and for the ongoing collaborations in the time since. Joe Tobin and Jim Anderson were encouraging and supportive, and Dean Michael Hoit had the vision to make this collaboration possible.

We extend our gratitude to the contributors to this volume. Each of you has provided us with tremendous insights through your scholarship and clinical practices. Your collegiality throughout this process urged us on. We thank Peter Taubman for his exacting editorial skills and keen intelligence. His work on this manuscript is invaluable and came in the nick of time. We are also grateful to Chelsea Bailey for her friendship and partnership from the very beginning and throughout this work, and to Toby Gordon and Lad Tobin for always asking the right questions. Wendy Atwell-Vasey, Madeleine Grumet, and Marta Cullberg-Weston provided invaluable support without which this book would never have come to be. Thanks to Glenn Masuchika for his steady presence and encouragement.

Catherine Bernard and Brook Cosby at Routledge have lent important editorial support. Catherine Bernard believed in this book at its inception, and we are deeply grateful for her integrity and good sense.

We thank our students and colleagues at the University of Iowa and the University of New Hampshire with whom we have deliberated on this work for many semesters. Your faith in us and in our work and your willingness to engage and to challenge us is continually gratifying. Thanks to Ryan O'Connor for marathon proofreading. Aimee Mapes deserves much of the credit for this book. She was a talented partner and collaborator throughout the months of revisions and editing.

Finally, our love and gratitude go to Kai, Alexandra, Lily, Zoë, and Una for your patience and humor particularly during those last hot and hazy days of summer.

Notes to the Text

Boldt, Gail, "Parenting and the Narcissistic Demands of Whiteness." Originally printed in *International Journal of Equity and Innovation in Early Childhood*, 2004 *1*(2), 45–60. Revised by the author and reprinted with permission from The Center for Equity and Innovation in Early Childhood at The University of Melbourne and Gail Boldt.

Eng, David, "Transnational Adoptions and Queer Diasporas." This article is a condensed version of a longer essay of the same title first published in *Social Text 76*, Fall 2003, *21*(3), 1–37. Copyright 2003 by David Eng. Reprinted with the permission of David Eng.

Grumet, Madeleine, "Romantic Research: Why We Love to Read." A longer version of this chapter was published in C. K. Kinzer and D. J. Leu (Eds.). *Literary Research, Theory, and Practice: Views from Many Perspectives* (pp. 33–48). Chicago: National Reading Conference. Reprinted with the permission of the National Reading Conference and Madeleine R. Grumet.

Powell, Linda and Barber, Margaret, "Savage Inequalities Indeed: Irrationality and Urban School Reform." This chapter was originally published in Cytrynbaum, S., & Noumair, D. (2004). *Group Dynamics, Organizational Irrationality, and Social Complexity: Group Relations Reader 3*. FL: A. K. Rice Institute for the Study of Social Systems. Reprinted with the permission of the A. K. Rice Institute and of Linda Powell and Margaret Barber.

Salvio, Paula M., "On the Vicissitudes of Love and Hate: Anne Sexton's Pedagogy of Loss and Reparation." A longer version of this text appears in *Teacher of Weird Abundance: Essays on the Teaching Life of Anne Sexton*, (2006) from State University of New York Press. Revised for this volume by Paula M. Salvio and reprinted with the permission of Paula Salvio and State University of New York Press (http://www.tandf.co.uk).

Silin, Jonathan. "Reading, Writing and the Wrath of My Father." Originally published in *Reading Research Quarterly,* April–June 2003, *38*(2), 260–267. Reprinted with permission of the International Reading Association and Jonathan Silin.

Introduction

GAIL M. BOLDT, PAULA M. SALVIO, AND PETER MAAS TAUBMAN

The book has its origins in a set of papers delivered at the annual meeting of the American Educational Research Association held in Chicago in 2004. The provocation that led Gail Boldt, Paula Salvio, Peter Taubman, and Chelsea Bailey to assemble this panel was their shared sense of the paradoxical fact that while love frequently appears in our conversations about education and relationships between adults and children, what it means as teachers to love children is rarely examined. Noting that the claim to "love children" is a nearly universal prerequisite for modern parenting, childcare, and teaching, the papers reflected a shared commitment to an examination of love. Panelists undertook to address the problem that while love is assumed in the field of education, it remains, as Roland Barthes wrote in *A Lover's Discourse*, "forsaken by the surrounding languages; ignored, disparaged, or derided by them, severed not only from authority but also from the mechanisms of authority" (1978, p. 1). What is this love that seems to be everywhere present in education?

Although the papers were offered as a session organized by the Critical Issues in Early Childhood Special Interest Group, they raised questions that spanned pedagogic relationships with the youngest children in daycare, elementary, high school, and university students, and our own children. The questions that framed the papers were these: Why as educators do we and should we care about love? What role does love play in teaching and learning? What do we require in the name of love from the children and young adults in our care? What does it mean when teachers say they love their students or when love is presented as the ground for any truly educationally transformative experience? More difficult questions were raised: What happens when our attempts to love are refracted through our difficult personal histories, the histories of our students, and the history and present climate of the educational enterprise? Does the presence of love indicate the possibility or reality of hate? If, as Freud suggested, our initial desire to learn originates in curiosity about sex, how can we understand learning as an erotic activity? In what sense, if any, are teachers and care providers seducers? How do we create ourselves as love objects for our students? How do we turn them into love objects? How do we love those students whom we hate and why do we hate those students? In what ways may love mask sadism?

To answer these questions, the presenters turned to psychoanalysis, which of all fields has offered the most valiant efforts to understand the complexity of love in human relationships. The hope was that this session would stimulate a conversation between education and psychoanalysis and that such a conversation, taking as its topic "love," would yield a deeper understanding of the relationships between adults and children, particularly those that are framed in learning and teaching.

The turn to thinking about education and love through the lens of psychoanalytic theory and clinical practice is not a new idea, but is rather a return to an old idea. Throughout the past century, the fields of education and psychoanalysis have had an ongoing if not always loving relationship. During the early and middle years of the twentieth century, educators and psychoanalysts—including a number of educators who were trained as analysts—undertook great projects to organize psychoanalytically informed education. These analyst-educators, including Anna Freud, Dorothy Burlingham, Eric Ericson, and Bruno Bettelheim, opened schools and worked to influence public practices of education both in child-care centers and in elementary and secondary schooling. Although these efforts where undertaken with great hope, they were not long-lasting. The demise of the influence of psychoanalysis in America has been well documented (see Hale, 1971, 1995). By the second half of the twentieth century, education, like the rest of American culture, was turning from the painstakingly complicated intra- and inter-subjective worlds of teaching and learning described by psychoanalysis to the promise of more efficient, cleaner—literally cleaner, turning away from the psychoanalytic emphasis on sexuality, fantasy, and the body—and empirically quantifiable outcomes (see Tobin, 2001).

This book then contributes to efforts of psychoanalytically oriented educators toward a reopening of the discussion about the potential that psychoanalytic theory holds for the field of education. Contributors to the book include psychoanalysts working with children who have many years of professional engagement with education, and educators who have undertaken a serious study of psychoanalysis. We consider this conversation to be timely because we believe that in the current educational climate in the United States, we are seeing the returns of a depersonalized empiricism—the demand, to the exclusion of all other considerations, for outcomes assessment, high-stakes testing, standards, accountability, and educational quality assurance. As these demands permeate expectations about what counts in education, educators find it increasingly difficult, even starting in children's earliest years, to make room for their own and their students' subjectivities, idiosyncrasies, creativities, and emotions. As children and teachers feel increasing alienation between their lives and the demands of education, questions of love, teaching, and learning seem both more urgent and more distant than ever before.

The title of this book, *Love's Return,* expresses this and other notions of return. In what senses does or might love return? We are, most obviously, attempting to argue persuasively for a return to collaborations between psychoanalysis and education. We use the idea of love's return to argue that regardless of how hard we may attempt to make education about the mastery of facts and knowledges, love always returns to the scene. Relationships—to teachers, peers, texts, ideas, and the self—prove to be the force that mediates between the threat and fear that inhere in the demand for learning and the possibility and willingness to learn in spite of or because of these anxieties. Finally, we are using the word "return" in the psychoanalytic sense, as in, the return of that which has been repressed. We find reports of these returns throughout this book, in the form of difficult relations among administrators, teachers, children, and families that result from our ongoing denial of the history of need and longing, conflict and failure, love and cruelty in education. These chapters also implicate psychoanalysis in the return of what it has not been able to tolerate knowing—the ways that psychoanalysis has participated in sometimes colonizing and normalizing fantasies that Deborah Britzman identifies as psychoanalysis' enlightenment project.

In presenting this book, we will not repress our awareness of the fact that it may seem anachronistic in this age of accountability, performance outcomes, and quantification, or in this postmodern moment of what Michael Hardt and Antonio Negri (2000) refer to as Empire, to speak of the place of love in psychoanalysis and its impact on teaching and learning. After all, what could be less scientific and less amenable to quantification or more modernist than psychoanalysis? If not anachronistic, then it would seem at least naïve to assume "the talking cure" or perplexing questions of love and transference might offer an intervention in the hegemony of what Peter Taubman describes in his chapter as the "new educational order," an order that has already set the terms in which education may be discussed. Those terms, established by neoliberal and conservative legislation, regulatory agencies, professional organizations, academic disciplines, and corporate agendas, reflect the larger globalization of capitalism, resist negotiation, and frame the discursive and non-discursive practices that constitute education today.

Conscious of the limitations of our effort, our goal with this collection is to explore the potential to use psychoanalysis as a method and a theory that opens within the "new educational order" a space for conscious resistance. Readers will not encounter a medicalized psychoanalysis in these chapters, one that uses its own system of labeling, pathologizing, and normalizing as a defense against its own history of dramatically radical insights. Nor will you encounter a psychoanalysis committed to honoring the conventional metaphor of the family romance that replicates the sets of binary oppositions that insistently structure sexual difference, and that unwittingly relegates psychoanalysis and education to the private relations between individuals and to a stereotypically female space.

Rather, the essays in this collection elaborate on a psychoanalysis that interrupts the symmetry of binary oppositions postulated in education today and in early psychoanalytic and feminist theory. Psychoanalytic theory as it is used in this collection addresses rather than avoids considerations of how race, gender, class, and sexuality participate in the structuring of the unconscious, the self, and social relations, including those that move between adults and children. While some of the contributors bring these issues together with a more essentialized understanding of human development, other contributors work toward a reconceptualization of psychoanalysis, arguing that we can write with and against psychoanalytic theory and clinical research to construct rich and useful descriptions of the individual's psychic experience of self as it is discursively constituted in culture. What this perspective on both psychoanalytic and poststructural discussions of identity describes is the simultaneous articulation of the social/political, and the constitution of the "individual" in a psychic-social space (Cheng, 2000) in which, as Gail Boldt argues, the self is socially compelled and bounded and is deeply felt as the day-to-day reality of one's existence. All of the contributors to this collection, regardless of their perspective on what compels the experience of psychic-social life, understand that the social and the political are inseparable from the ambivalences, needs, and desires of the adults and children who are brought together in the shared and furious space of teaching and learning.

Love with its many difficulties and vicissitudes appears in the chapters of this book. The authors share a perspective that whether or not we want or welcome the complexities of love into our relationships with children and in the spaces of our classrooms, love—or its absence—makes itself known and is, moreover, central to the educational endeavor and as Deborah Britzman explains, to our very capacity to think and to learn. Thus, readers will find that several authors raise important questions of the essential role of love and hate in our ability to learn and to refuse learning, and in the potential of love to move us toward an embrace of learning as a path to powerful and desired relationships, meanings, and identifications. In the chapters by Jonathan Silin and Michael O'Loughlin, we have accounts of what happens when children are able or unable to use classrooms and curriculum to explore fantasies and meanings and to construct usable understandings of their intra- and inter-subjective worlds. Drawing from the work of Madeleine Grumet, Silin uses a memoir of his own history with literacy to remind us that curriculum and pedagogy have the potential, although often not realized, to mediate the inevitable loses that accompany us throughout our lives. Drawing stories from his clinical practice of children who are struggling to symbolize their place in the world, Michael O'Loughlin calls on teachers to remember that play and literature are two important resources children can use to bridge the critical gap between their inner worlds and the demands of school.

Clearly, love's necessity and positive potential in the classroom and in relationships between adults and children are central to this book. However, this is not a love that is valorized or romanticized but, instead, these chapters contain difficult questions about love. Accounts of hatred, aggression, trauma, need, and desire appear as love's unwelcomed but inevitable partner. Bertram Cohler and Robert Galatzer-Levy contend that because we are unable to acknowledge that erotics underlie our drives to teach and to learn, we are forced to present a version of love in the classroom that is passionless, controlling, and desperate. Peter Taubman urges us to consider the ways that love is used to mask aggressions, hatreds, and erotics; he describes how using love as a defense against undesired knowledge plays out and in many ways structures life in classrooms. Linda Powell and Margaret Barber concur with this view, offering a reading of how the anxiety of our unacknowledged aggressions is enacted at the institutional level; they argue the outcome of this aggression is that minority students and families in school systems are positioned to be the bearers of the psychic and material weight of our failed racial history.

The difficulties continue. Contributors draw from literature, autobiography, and clinical case studies to point to the ways that we turn to love and to hate with the demand that they should repair our personal and cultural traumas. In traditional psychoanalytic accounts the blame and the burden of reparation for these traumas fall heavily on the figure of the mother. The question of this maternal object figures strongly in many of the chapters in this book, demonstrating that, as Alice Pitt (in this volume) writes, "The figure of the mother is a vexatious one in education, psychoanalysis, and feminism"; she is no less so in the pages of this book. Throughout these chapters we find a return and repetition of the psychoanalytic story of the loss of the pre-Oedipal "good" mother. This is the founding story of loss in the psychoanalytic account, and it refers to the child's loss of the fantasy of the complete emersion of the mother and child, a mother who was fantasized to be only an extension of the child's wants and desires. As Madeleine Grumet explains, in the psychoanalytic account, this fantasy is lost to the child's growing awareness that the parent and child are separate, that the child's needs and demands are not all-powerful and that the mother has desires for things that are other than the child. This loss initiates the child into subjectivity and prompts the rage-filled fantasy of the Oedipalized "bad" mother.

While the traditional psychoanalytic account tells one story of the outcomes of this trajectory, the authors in this book raise important questions about the consequences of this trajectory for women and girls, men and boys. These consequences include the ongoing production of what David Eng describes as the emergence of the white, Western heterosexual family structure as the only intelligible option; the cultural and personal alienation from women as our intellectual forebears described so aptly by Alice Pitt; and as Madeleine Grumet and Paula Salvio so poignantly argue, the alienation of women as mothers, caregivers, and teachers from their desires.

Paula Salvio's recounting of the poet Anne Sexton's terrible struggles with depression, addiction, abuse, and suicide depicts such alienation, documenting the agony and impossibility of the struggle to be a "good enough" mother. The chapters by Gail Boldt and David Eng similarly relate stories of alienation and longing, but they turn our focus to questions of how, in the privileged space of the family romance, race and sexuality are produced in the attempt to find reparation for injuries that are intimately tied to the politics of identity and economy. Boldt offers an autobiographical portrait of a mother's misplaced struggle to repair her experiences of alienation by constructing her child's racialized identity as a means to bridge the gap between "bad" and "good" mothers, which come not only in the form of the fantasy and memories of her own mother but in those of various communities in which she has lived, in the loyalties and disloyalties of identity, and in the racialized politics of sex. David Eng tells this story from the perspective of the child, a Korean adoptee into a white American family who struggles to reconcile the losses and gains of international adoption through efforts to contain her birth mother and her adoptive mother within mental categories of good mother/bad mother.

As Alice Pitt argues, the need to explain and contain the impact of mothers extends not only to our emotional or birth mothers but also to those women who are our intellectual mothers. In the chapters by Madeleine Grumet, Alice Pitt, Paula Salvio, and Deborah Britzman, we see this story of good/bad mother crossing into and structuring relationships of teaching and learning. We have known at least since the influential work of Madeleine Grumet (1998) in *Bitter Milk* and Valerie Walkerdine (1989) in "Femininity as Performance" that teaching, that ever so feminized of professions, is structured by the same fantasies, needs, and desires that structure the Western heterosexual family. As Paula Salvio and Madeline Grumet demonstrate in their chapters, the dilemmas that create impossibility of being the "good enough mother," the demand that women split themselves from their own needs and desires to serve the needs and desires of children, return in the struggle to be the "good enough teacher" or "the good enough academic."

All of these authors share David Eng's commitment to a queering up of our understandings of what is possible and desirable, a move to integrate the fantasy of the good and the bad into a portrait that gives us a full and powerful understanding of both the real and potential lives of women and men, boys and girls. In education, this means that we must question both conservative and progressive pedagogy, both the construction of classrooms as spaces wherein students are disciplined into mastery and as spaces that are "all about the kids" (see Taubman, this volume). Authors in this volume argue that we need to look instead to classrooms and curriculum as spaces wherein there is potential for both teachers and children to symbolize personal and cultural fantasies, desires, and fears in order to put these symbols to work in the service of learning. We do not mistake the classroom for the analyst's office, nor do we ignore classrooms as places wherein students work to learn those dispositions, skills, and knowledges that are important for our personal and collective well-being. However, educators must, as Britzman suggests, temper our fantasies of enlightenment and of what counts as good knowledge with the understanding that what educates is neither knowledge nor the person of the teacher but rather the emotional experiences of relationship and the child's drive to understand his or her place in these relationships and in the world.

Our call for classrooms to be places that take account of the full scope of children's and adult's intra- and inter-subjective lives as they are structured through the unconscious, fantasy, personal, and social history is not new, but it is urgent. Every contributor to this book is or has been a teacher and we share a passionate commitment to the lives of children and teachers in and out of schools. We recognize that we are in an era in education when there is little credence given to students' and teachers' needs for and experiences of subjectivity, relationship, passionate engagement, and fantasy. We therefore offer this book with the hope that its chapters will support its readers in their efforts to create and defend pedagogy, curriculum, and relationships with students that are affectively and socially rich, that support students and teachers in building, as Deborah Britzman suggests, the capacity to think, to learn, and to make lives of reparation, gratitude, work, and love.

References

Barthes, R. (1978). *A lover's discourse: Fragments*. New York: Hill & Wang.

Cheng, A. (2000). *The melancholy of race*. New York: Oxford University Press.

Grumet, M. (1998). *Bitter milk: Women and teaching*. Amherst: University of Massachusetts Press.

Hale, N. (1971). *Freud and the Americans; the beginnings of psychoanalysis in the United States, 1876–1917*. New York: Oxford University Press.

Hale, N. (1995). *The rise and crisis of psychoanalysis in the United States: Freud and the Americans, 1917–1985*. New York: Oxford University Press.

Hardt, M., & Negri, A. (2000). *Empire*. Cambridge, MA: Harvard University Press.

Tobin, J. (2001). The missing discourse of sexuality in contemporary American early childhood education. In J. Winer and J. Anderson (Eds.), *The annual of psychoanalysis*, Vol. 23: *Sigmund Freud and his impact on the modern world* (pp. 179–200). Hillsdale, NJ: Analytic Press.

Walkerdine, V. (1989). Femininity as performance. *Oxford Review of Education*, 15(3), 267–279.

The Interludes

An Introduction to Reading and Using This Book

PAULA M. SALVIO AND GAIL M. BOLDT

Readers will find that among the chapters of this text we have interspersed short essays that we have named Interludes. To create these Interludes, we began by grouping together chapters by dominant themes. Then, for each set of chapters, we chose a film that matches well with the themes we wished to highlight. We wrote the Interludes to introduce the films and explain our thinking in making these pairings.

Our decision to write these Interludes arose from the hope that through pairing chapters from this book with powerful and moving films, we could raise for the readers the very experiences of complexity that we argue are needed in discussions of learning and teaching. While contributors to this book have turned to psychoanalysis to raise difficult and complicated issues about the relationships among adults, children, experience, emotion, and culture, it is all too easy for us to fall into the reductive readings of these chapters as simple summaries, how-to-methods, or theoretical directives. We invite readers to view these films alongside of their paired chapters with the expectation that the films will work both to illuminate and to challenge the arguments of the chapters that follow. The films remind us that when seen through the vicissitudes of human lives, ideas that seem clear and direct in print are both messier than text can convey and too important to gloss over. They suggest the impossibility of education and psychoanalysis and perhaps even of love, but also remind us that there is no tidy end to the need to return to these questions.

In drawing on films, we make the decidedly psychoanalytic proposition that movies, like dreams, present the viewer with a potent mixture of private desires and public vocabularies that coalesce in a visual invitation for surrender and interpretation. At the same time, the turn to film to elucidate our discussions of psychoanalysis and education recalls other attempts to bring these fields together. It is provocative to consider that Sigmund Freud refused to have anything to do with film in spite of the fact that by the 1920s psychoanalysis had achieved such celebrity that film industries in Germany and the United States were showing an interest in the new profession. In 1925, Hollywood film producer Samuel Goldwyn offered Freud the then considerable sum of $100,000 if he would collaborate on a film about the love story between Anthony and Cleopatra. Freud not only declined, but also expressed doubts about any analysts who would become involved with the cinema. Speaking to his colleague, Sandor Ferenczi, Freud noted that, "stupid things happen in film affairs.... [F]ilming seems to be as unavoidable, it seems, as page boy haircuts, but I won't have myself trimmed that way and do not wish to be brought into personal contact with any film" (Freud and Ferenczi, 1995). Any collaboration, Freud suggested, would trivialize the work of the psychoanalyst or even psychoanalysis' power and its aims.

Freud perhaps had a point. As Taubman (this volume) points out, popular films centered on classrooms often tell stories of education that trivialize the complex work and relationships of teachers and students. Reducing classrooms to clichés of familiar storylines, films have rarely served the professional or personal interests of educators. And yet we are drawn to films, including those that do not faithfully reproduce the stories we would tell. Even Freud, while remaining critical of any involvement between psychoanalysis and the film industry, recognized that literary, cinematic, and poetic texts could be understood as collective dreams or symptoms that have their sources in unconscious desires. He also understood that artistic productions have the potential to provide a primary setting for psychoanalytic efforts to understand cultural forms of representation and the acquisition of subject identities in social beings. Throughout his writings, Freud turned to art to frame central psychic struggles, particularly because he believed that dreams and fantasy—the primary sources in analysis—have something important in common with fiction: they are all imaginary productions that have their sources in unconscious desire. Film presents the viewer with a dream, a story that is a composition of someone else's desires that are in part shaped by social and cultural forces. Cinema offers up for analysis the raw material that can illuminate, instantiate, and complicate important theoretical concepts not only in psychoanalysis, but in all disciplines. Equally important is the fact that ideologies are filtered through cinema. Cinema is indeed one of the languages through which the world communicates itself to itself.

When cinema is brought into the seminar room and placed alongside the theoretical essays we have brought together in this collection, important concepts are illuminated and compelling uses and critiques of education and of psychoanalysis are posed. The projects we outline in the Interludes of this book suggest an analysis of the reader's relationship with other subjects, images from film, language, and cultural practices.

At the same time, readers using these Interludes should not feel bound to the issues they highlight. Just as the Interludes have the capacity to expand our thinking about the chapters in this book, so too do they have the potential to limit our thinking. The themes raised in relation to one set of chapters make their appearances in other chapters. Important issues go unaccounted for in the Interludes and indeed, there are at times ideas and examples highlighted in one chapter that conflict with arguments in other chapters. Obviously, at any time we could have highlighted different themes, different movies, or made different pairings. As we know so well from psychoanalysis, that which we miss or ignore is as much a production as that which we know or discuss. Readers are therefore urged to interrogate the Interludes with the same vigor that they may apply to the chapters and the films.

Reference

Freud, S., & Ferenczi, S. (1995). Freud to Ferenczi, 14.8.1925. In E. Brabant and E. Falzeder (Eds.) and Peter T. Hoffer (Trans.), *The correspondence of Sigmund Freud and Sandor Ferenczi: 1908–1914*. Cambridge, MA: Belknap Press of Harvard University Press.

Scenes of Love and Control

Film: *Born into Brothels: Calcutta's Red Light Kids*

Paired chapters: *I Love Them to Death* by Peter Maas Taubman
*Savage Inequalities Indeed: Irrationality and Urban
School Reform* by Linda C. Powell and Margaret E.
Barber

By way of introduction to this book, we have paired the chapters written by Peter Maas Taubman and by Linda Powell and Margaret Barber to be read alongside the 2005 academy award winner for best documentary film, *Born into Brothels: Calcutta's Red Light Kids*. The two chapters address the potential dangers that surface when self-sacrifice and altruism are divorced from the acknowledgment of our feelings of aggression and anxiety and are seen as the driving forces of our efforts and desires to love our students and our disciplines. Finding the psychoanalytic concepts of splitting and projection inadequate lenses through which to explore the complex relationship shared between aggression and love, Peter Taubman turns to the writings of Jacques Lacan. Taubman explicates Lacan's concept of jouissance in an effort to consider the ways in which educators unconsciously use force and violence against their students in the name of love. Linda Powell and Margaret Barber draw on psychoanalytically informed group relations theory to elucidate the ways in which our efforts at reform, ignorant of the anxieties that underlie our structuring of schools, simply repeat the same old aggressions against the urban poor. Both chapters remind us that educators must seriously consider what we do with one another when we go about a particular relationship of trying to structure learning for our students, and the potentially dire consequences that ensue when we fail to take up this work.

We use the work of Zana Briski and Ross Kaufman in the film, *Born into Brothels,* to call attention to the consequences of just such a failure of reflexivity. Reviews of *Born into Brothels,* which is narrated primarily by Briski and presents her as the central figure, consistently describe the film as nothing less than a love story between Briski and the children she works with in Sonagchi, Calcutta. Recorded over the course of two years and edited from more than 725 hours of footage, this documentary portrays the relationships Briski develops with the children of prostitutes who work the city's dangerous maze of alleyways and are forced, as Briski tells us, "to sell affection in order to live and care for their children." Initially intending to photograph the hard, day-to-day lives of the women of India, Briski was eventually brought to the red-light district by a friend. There, she decided to photograph the lives of sex workers and their children. "The brothels are really filled with children," observes Briski. "Originally (in 1998), I went there to photograph the women and I lived in a brothel, but the children were totally fascinated by me and my camera, and they kept grabbing it and trying to play with it, and I thought it would be incredible to teach them photography."

Born into Brothels follows the relationships Briski develops with the children as she teaches them photography and explores with them the images they collect. The children's photos detail the struggles between children and their parents, sex workers and their clients. "I want to show in pictures how people live in this city," writes thirteen-year-old Gour. "I want to put across the behaviour of man." His photographs portray his friends playing cricket, his pet rabbits, and his best friend, Puja. Through this story of the children and their photography, the film turns our attention to the poverty and social stigma that they endure as the children of Calcutta's prostitutes. The film speaks to the resiliency of childhood and to the power of artistic creation.

Briski's work does not end there, however, but the film goes on to tell a second story, one that documents Briski's decision to get the children out of the brothels and into boarding schools. In this story, Briski emerges as heroic as she wrestles with the complicated desires and resistances of the children, their families, and Indian government officials in order to provide the children with a future away from prostitution. While some of the children do go to boarding school, the end of the film leaves us with the understanding that the children's problems are too big to be fixed through this well-intentioned act; many of the children leave school either voluntarily or involuntarily to return to the brothels.

While *Born into Brothels* is moving, and the creative work of the children has had a strong impact on their lives, important concerns are evident but remain largely unanalyzed and the project has its detractors. Although Briski's work brought positive change for a few children, critics note that the project has not altered the economic structures that sustain the social inequities, stigmas, and violence that diminish in an ongoing way the children's opportunities for health and well-being. In fact, Ross Kauffman wrote in an on-line interview with Wendy Mitchell that early on he was very reluctant to become involved in the project because documentary film so rarely has an impact on social structures and institutions: "I hadn't seen a lot of films that broke through and made a difference...."

Like the first two chapters of this book, *Born into Brothels* raises questions about the power of love—its influences and its limits. What forms of knowledge are transferred between Briski and her pupils? What lies on the other side of Briski's love for them? Pity? Empathy? Sentimentality? Desires to rescue and to cure? Her own history? Is it possible to read this movie for signs of aggression or even hatred? Briski has been accused by critics of being filled with a sense of colonial self-righteousness. Whether fairly or not, she has been described as a teacher who works only to make her students into "nice little British children." Her critics argue that she appears as the self-sacrificing woman who saves the children from a life of abuse and poverty. According to a review by Rachael Silvey (2005), the film promotes a colonialist view toward the poor children of India. What is lacking, argues Silvey, is a "critical, self-reflexive stance toward the discursive colonization and reification of racial/national, historical privilege that comes with such a storyline" (p. 2). What Briski does not pursue are discussions with the mothers of the children about their feelings toward their work. Nor do we gain a perspective on the availability of other low-income jobs or communities that would offer us a broader context. This is the kind of context that is provided for us in the research of Kempadoo and Doezema (1998), who argue that women move in and out of sex work depending on a range of factors, including the availability of other work, relative wage rates, and their stages in the life cycle. This research challenges the notion that sex work is worse than other forms of low-income, highly exploitative labor. Silvey notes that while Briski is busy securing her students admission to boarding schools, several of the mothers and their children want to remain together. "It is crucial," as Silvey so aptly notes, that we ask "how this film's storyline obscures, and thus unwittingly contributes to the broader global structural inequalities that silence children's voices and disenfranchise women in India.

It is interesting given that Briski is being accused of suppressing difficult knowledges, to learn that Briski's education as a documentary photographer did not take place at a distance from psychoanalysis, that great champion of self-knowledge. There is a half-spoken history associated with this film—a history that speaks of Briski's indirect relationship to Anna Freud. For five years, Briski taught at Harvard University with Robert Coles who himself had worked with Anna Freud. In an interview in which she recalled Coles's influence on her work, she remembers that "he likened photography and the interpretations they evoke to the process he and Anna Freud used when they asked children to tell them the stories of their crayoned drawings. 'Photography, like dreams, help us remember parts of ourselves,' he told us."

Dreams bridge our unconscious and conscious lives, they speak to us of our half-spoken desires, and our inner reality, the sphere where tensions, anxieties, and memory resides—not solely in linguistic form, but in the form of images, scents, texture, and sound. Dreams give expression to the unconscious and they defy easy binary categories—mother/father, rational/ irrational, male/female, truth/lies. What place does the act of remembering the elusive, vague, and half-spoken parts of ourselves have in the education of children? For educators such as Taubman, Powell, and Barber, this work is necessary precisely because we carry the impact of our early experiences and psychic lives into our work as teachers, administrators, and consultants. Whether we are conscious of such phenomena or not, these authors all demonstrate that we project what we have yet to work through with respect to authority onto our students, colleagues, and reform efforts. While no one person can solve all the problems facing any community of children, what might have been gained and lost if Briski had offered a more critical and a more psychoanalytic analysis of her investments in this work? What do we gain and lose as teachers if we undertake a more critical and psychoanalytic analysis of our investments in our work with students?

References

Kempadoo, K., & Doezema, J. (Eds.). (1998). *Global sex workers: Rights, resistance, and redefinition.* New York: Routledge.

Silvey, R. (2005). Review of *Born into Brothels*. *Children, Youth and Environments*, *15*(1) [On-line]. Available: http://www.colorado.edu/journals/cye/15_1/.

I Love Them to Death

PETER MAAS TAUBMAN

[T]he first great effort of every teacher of a large class must be to bring the will of the children into accordance with his own will. And this he can only do by an abnegation of his personal self ...

D. H. Lawrence, *The Rainbow*

She dreamed how she would make the little, ugly children love her. She would be so personal. Teachers were always so hard and impersonal. There was no vivid relationship. She would make everything personal and vivid, she would give herself, she would give, give, give all her great stores of wealth to her children, she would make them so happy, and they would prefer her to any teacher on the face of the earth.

D. H. Lawrence, *The Rainbow*

Any analyst who out of the fullness of his heart, perhaps, and his readiness to help, extends to the patient all that one human being may hope to receive from another commits [an] ... error.

Sigmund Freud, "Lines of Advance in Psycho-Analytic Therapy"

When I ask student teachers what their worst fears are about teaching, they often respond, "Losing control of the class." Some describe nightmares of literally falling apart in front of disruptive or violent students. At the same time, these aspiring teachers, when asked why they have chosen to teach, will frequently answer, "Because we love kids," and not infrequently talk about "loving them to death." This oddly constructed phrase, "loving them to death," reveals how easily aggression can take the form of love and how ambiguous the relation is between the desire to control and the desire to love. This chapter looks at that relationship as it affects teaching within schools.

In schools of education professors frequently address the fantasies student teachers have about loving and being loved and control and loss of control. If the professors are more sophisticated, they might gently point out the racial or class aspects of these fantasies about disruptive students and treat the fantasies with doses of critical pedagogy or multicultural education. They may point out the malefic generosity implicit in the desire to rescue and may encourage student teachers to see their students as in need of intellectual engagement rather than as simply desperate for love and self-esteem.

More often professors address student concerns about control with classroom management strategies, such as having clear objectives, assessments, and rubrics, having consistent standards and high expectations, and holding students accountable. The ambiguity, complexity, and emotional drain of struggling with power in the classroom can sometimes be avoided with a rigorous attention to rules of conduct and to set management procedures.

It is also not unusual for education students' fantasies about loving their students and being loved in return to be nourished by professors with encouragements to care for their students, to see their students' needs as paramount, and to locate as central to the curriculum the needs and interests of the child. Child-centered pedagogy, grounded in a psychology that makes the autonomous child the center of study and influenced by a vision of maternal care that requires the mother to sacrifice her wants for her child (Salvio, this volume), has rarely privileged the desires or passions of the teacher. In fact, one could conclude after listening to the concerns of student teachers and after reading and listening to educators, that the main focus of teaching was on controlling students' bodies and minds through discipline, set curricula, and set methods so that teachers could love them by sacrificing for them, rescuing them, nurturing them, empowering them, and as Lawrence suggests in the quote above, giving, giving, giving. The standard reply to such a description is that teacher education does not focus just on the "kids." Rather, it requires student teachers to focus on themselves through critical self-reflection and knowing how their social identities affect their teaching. This reply misses the point. The focus on oneself remains in the service of the students, the Other. While progressive educators have insisted on a critical examination of self, the word to notice is "critical," and most often the examination concludes with how student teachers may damage or shortchange their students because these student teachers haven't sacrificed—worked through—their own biases. A minor example is the National Council for Accreditation of Teacher Education's (NCATE) requirement that teacher candidates hold particular dispositions—values or attitudes—generally vaguely progressive, if they are to be recommended for certification. Implicit in such a requirement is that the student teachers sacrifice their values to comply with those deemed appropriate for working with students. Progressive approaches, in the name of love, try to control the student teachers whose fantasies of love and control continue to circulate below and on the margins of those progressive discourses and practices that purportedly attend to them. The student teacher with racist views continues to imagine helping kids and being loved by them, and the student teachers who profess their desire to save the kids continue to imagine horrible scenes of violence. Progressive discourses have done little to respect and work through these fantasies.

While fantasies about loss of control and authority and about loving and being loved swirl in the psychic life of teachers, they also circulate in the public imaginary of teaching and schooling. The success of films such as *Blackboard Jungle* (1955), *To Sir With Love* (1967), *Conrack* (1974), *Stand and Deliver* (1988), and *Dangerous Minds* (1994), where teachers initially face unmanageable students only to triumph in the end through their love of the kids, thus winning those students' love and admiration, attests to the lure of these fantasies.

Questions and fantasies about discipline and nurturance, power and love, and loss of authority and its reassertion have also increasingly come to structure the contemporary U.S. political landscape. As evidence one might consider George Lakoff's (2004) argument that has recently gained ground with Democrats. Lakoff, a well-known linguist and cognitive scientist, imagines two models of the family to describe the current split in American politics between, on one hand, neoconservatives and right-wing Evangelicals and, on the other hand, liberals and progressives. Lakoff sees conservatives as adhering to a strict father family model and liberals as acting on a nurturant parent family model.

The former positions the father or paternal substitutes, for example, teachers, as strict moral authorities who use punishment, including corporal punishment, to control inherently wild children and teach them right from wrong so they will act morally in the future (p. 8). A moral person in this model is someone who is obedient and self-reliant. A bad person has not learned discipline, cannot take care of himself or herself, and remains dependent on others. Thus "[t]his theory says that social programs are immoral because they make people dependent," and keep them from developing discipline and self-reliance.

The nurturant parent model assumes that "children are born good and can be made better. Nurturance in this model means 'empathy and responsibility'" (p. 12). According to Lakoff, this model valorizes treating children and others fairly, two-way communication, community building, and self-fulfillment through the pursuit of one's own happiness.

If applied to teaching, Lakoff's categorization of the American political landscape seems to describe the split between, on one hand, right-wing educators who preach the tonic effects of high-stakes testing or psychologists such as James Dobson, whose *Dare to Discipline* (1982) advocates corporal punishment and, on the other hand, progressive educators who rephrase discipline as classroom management or democratic spaces and talk about an ethic of care, cultural sensitivity, and empowering students. The schematization would also seem to capture the intrapsychic split student teachers feel between being friendly or "not smiling until Christmas," between being a softie or being a hard-ass.

The problem with such models, of course, is that they polarize positions and reduce more complicated social and psychic dynamics to irreconcilable differences. In fact, they often work to hide or perhaps defend against fuller understandings of the phenomena they purport to describe.

Because Lakoff's model excludes the possibility that the desire to love and be loved and the desire to control or exert power are intimately related, it keeps us from raising several questions. For example, if discipline is about imposing control and love suggests giving up control, in what way is teaching itself structured by an unexamined ambivalence about control? How might teachers be affected by the denigration and outlawing of corporal punishment or the rearticulation of their desire for control into classroom management strategies, cultural sensitivity, and critical self-reflection? If discipline and nurturance are opposite sides of the same coin, what is that coin? And why is it that one side, the side of the strict father, appears to have taken such hold on the American society? What would it mean to rethink love and power as these play out in the scene of teaching, in such a way that Lakoff's models or progressive and conservative positions could be integrated or simply superseded for a more capacious understanding of these issues? What perspective might teacher educators offer their students to help them better understand these powerful fantasies that so deeply influence classroom teaching?

These are the questions this chapter explores, and I want to explore them using various insights from psychoanalysis, which offers perhaps the most valiant attempts to understand the relationship between the desire to love and be loved and the desire to control and be controlled. In particular I'll be using the work of Jacques Lacan, who has contributed so much to our understanding of the relationship between love, altruism, and aggression.

The starting point for this exploration will be two texts, the frequently anthologized short story by William Carlos Williams (1937), entitled "A Use of Force," and a chapter from what many consider D.H. Lawrence's (1915) greatest work, *The Rainbow*. I turn to these texts because they depict individuals, a doctor and a teacher, whose idealism, apparent compassion, and desire to save the less fortunate result in and may even have required extreme violence. The naked depiction of the passions driving these characters allows us to see the relationship between love and control, nurturance and discipline, and, through a psychoanalytic lens, to gain insight into the aggression and fear that lurk in our altruism, love, and authority.

In Williams's "A Use of Force," a physician, the narrator of the story, visits a poor family, the kind one sees in Walker Evans's photos of the Great Depression, to examine the young daughter who has been running a fever. The parents seem suspicious of the doctor, nervous before a professional who may tell them what they do not want to hear—that their daughter has diphtheria. We see immediately that the doctor is struck by the girl, attracted in some primal sense, to the feral being in front of him. In his recounting of the event, he describes her as "an unusually attractive little thing, and as strong as a heifer in appearance," with "magnificent blond hair in profusion," like "[o]ne of those picture children often reproduced in advertising leaflets and the photogravure sections of the Sunday papers."

Trying to calm the girl and win her over, the doctor nevertheless fails to get the child to open her mouth. His attempts are met at first with passive resistance and then with physical resistance that grows in intensity. Straining to open the child's mouth, the narrator, helped by the father, is forced to violently pry open the girl's mouth, initially with a wooden spoon, which the girl splinters with her clenched teeth. In the struggle, the doctor grows furious but realizes he has "already fallen in love with the savage brat," who "rose to magnificent heights of insane fury of effort bred of terror of me." Finally, the doctor asks for a metal spoon.

> Get me a smooth-handled spoon of some sort, I told the mother. We're going through with this. The child's mouth was already bleeding. Her tongue was cut and she was screaming in wild

hysterical shrieks. Perhaps I should have desisted and come back in an hour or more. No doubt it would have been better. But I have seen at least two children lying dead in bed of neglect in such cases, and feeling that I must get a diagnosis now or never I went at it again. But the worst of it was that I too had got beyond reason. I could have torn the child apart in my own fury and enjoyed it. It was a pleasure to attack her. My face was burning with it.

The damned little brat must be protected against her own idiocy, one says to one's self at such times. Others must be protected against her. It is a social necessity. And all these things are true. But a blind fury, a feeling of adult shame, bred of a longing for muscular release are the operatives. One goes on to the end.

In a final unreasoning assault I overpowered the child's neck and jaws. I forced the heavy silver spoon back of her teeth and down her throat till she gagged. And there it was—both tonsils covered with membrane.

In the end the doctor's use of force has allowed for treatment in the nick of time.

The narrator's love, admiration, and hate for the girl, his contempt for the parents and the squalor of their lives, his thrill at vanquishing the wild young "thing" confronting him, his violent eroticism—what P. T. Dietrich (1966) sees as his rape of the girl, a rape aided by the father—and his drive to cure her, to save her, all seem on the surface far from the struggles of love and power that unfold in the classroom, let alone from the problem of "managing" classrooms or the proffered solutions of cultural sensitivity and antibias work. It's hard to imagine that greater sensitivity to the class, gender, and sexual dynamics of the doctor's visit would have done much to help the narrator, other than to cast his intense feelings as contemptibly sexist, classist, and misogynist. But such horrifyingly intense encounters have not always been so removed from classrooms.

When we turn to *The Rainbow*, we see that such violence has served its purposes in the classroom too. D. H. Lawrence's *The Rainbow*, considered by many to be his finest novel, and written almost a century ago, when corporal punishment in schools was the rule not the exception, contains a chapter entitled "The Man's World." The chapter describes Ursula Branwagen and her experiences teaching in a working-class school in Britain in the early part of the twentieth century.

Faced with the crushing poverty and grim patriarchal structures of the school, Ursula begins to fantasize about the effects she will have on her students. "At Christmas she would choose such fascinating Christmas cards for them, and she would give them such a happy party in one of the classrooms."

It is not only fantasies of pleasing the children that defend against the prison-like atmosphere of the school. Ursula also enjoys her imagined power.

> The prison was round her now!... But still excited, she climbed into her chair at her teacher's desk.... Here, then, she would sit in state, the queen of scholars! Here she would realise her dream of being the beloved teacher bringing light and joy to her children!

Her sense of power is fleeting. Assigned fifty-five boys and girls of ages ten to twelve, who in Lawrence's depiction range from bullies to sycophants to sneaks, she is initially overwhelmed, feeling tortured, exposed, and "naked" before their "unknown faces, watch[ing] her, hostile, ready to jeer."

Ursula comes to realize that if she is to survive she must repress her desire to nurture the children and impose her will. "She would assert herself for mastery, be only teacher. She was set now. She was going to fight and subdue." And indeed that is what she does. In the climactic scene in the chapter, Ursula thrashes a young boy who snidely torments her and refuses to obey. Using a cane, she beats the boy into a pulp. Ursula loses control in the service of gaining it.

> So she snatched her cane from the desk, and brought it down on him. He was writhing and kicking. She saw his face beneath her, white, with eyes like the eyes of a fish, stony, yet full of hate and horrible fear. And she loathed him, the hideous writhing thing that was nearly too much for her. In horror lest he should overcome her, and yet at the heart quite calm, she brought down the cane again and again, whilst he struggled making inarticulate noises, and lunging vicious kicks at her.... [A]t last ... the cane broke him, he sank with a howling yell on the floor.

She has imposed her authority, but, as Lawrence writes, "she had paid a great price out of her own soul, to do this," and she wonders why she ever became a schoolteacher.

While Ursula's violent victory provides authority, it has also, according to Lawrence, cost her. In *Bitter Milk*, Madeleine Grumet (1988) argues that Ursula Branwagen's need to exchange the "gift of maternal nurturance" for control imposed through corporal punishment reflected a feminization of teaching that at the same time required women to replicate patriarchal forms at the cost of their souls. Furthermore, Grumet suggests, the flip side of nurturance was a kind of violence. "Lawrence is able to reveal the other side of maternal love in all its sordid vigor" (p. 50). I would add that the cost also involves Ursula's own sense of self, for in this brief episode her passion for nurturance and rescue have transformed into a passion for blood.

Like Branwagen, Williams's doctor pays a price when his altruism turns to aggression. The doctor clearly wishes to save the girl, even at financial sacrifice to himself—he charges a small sum—but the success has revealed the dark underside of his Hippocratic oath and disturbed his own identity, as well as our view of the calm, kind, healing physician.

Both these pieces point to the possibility that while the raw use of force may be prohibited today, the human desires that fuel and find release in such violence remain. To understand how an apparently altruistic teacher and kind physician could in the name of love lose control as they imposed control, and transform benevolent feelings into blood lust, we can turn to the work of Jacques Lacan.

As is well known by now, Lacan postulated that our primal sense of self is already alienated because we come to form in the eyes of an Other, and our identity is from the start implicated in the desires of the other (Fink, 1995, 1998). That is why he argues our being is founded on a lack. Lack here is not the same as nothingness. Lack is a way of signaling that the pressures, drives, urges, feelings, and sensations that cannot be symbolized or even imagined preexist any self or identity or ego. Unable to be assimilated in either the imaginary ego or its elaboration in the symbolic realm, and under pressure from caretakers and society, they are absorbed into and come to constitute the unconscious, what Lacan at points calls the Real. This unconscious, a seething, tumultuous Real, cannot be approached directly. Rather it is dispersed along signifying linguistic chains and somatic symptoms and may erupt at any time in the form of over-determined actions, thoughts, and feelings that make no apparent sense.

For Lacan, the gap between our unconscious and our egos is mediated by fantasies that protect our ego integrity and our sense of reality. Our sense of reality requires a minimum of fantasy or idealization, in other words the interjection of a fantasy frame so we can maintain some distance from the Real, the horrifyingly unassimilated fragmented feelings, sensations, traumas constituting our unconscious, which is for Lacan the kernel of our being. Zizek (1998) summarizes Lacan:

> There is a gap that forever separates the ... kernel of the subject's being from the more superficial modes of his or her symbolic and/or imaginary identifications. It is never possible for me fully to assume (in the sense of symbolic integration) the ... kernel of my being. When I approach it too much, when I come too close to it, what occurs is the *aphanisis* of my subjectivity: I lose my

symbolic consistency; it disintegrates. Perhaps in this way, the forced actualization in social reality of the ... kernel of my being is the worst and most humiliating type of violence because it undermines the very basis of my identity—my "self-image." (p. 161)

We can see the effects of such violence in Ursula Branwagen's eruption and the consequent loss of her "soul," which is another way of saying that she has lost her self-image and that the hardening that ensues is a kind of suturing together of an identity that has been blown to smithereens. In Williams's story, the doctor works to preserve the fantasy that sustains his identity, not by denying the enjoyment he finds in overpowering the girl, but by constantly reminding himself that the use of force is for her own good, that she must be "protected against her own idiocy" and that it is "a social necessity." Were the fantasy frame to dissolve, he knows better than most people would know in such a situation, that he would be nothing less than a brutal sadist if not rapist.

For Lacan, then, unlike ego psychologists, our ego is not autochthonic but is conjured and shaped by the desires of others. For Lacan the ego is a necessary orthopedic device but confining and illusory. Like a patchwork coat made of imaginary identifications, it allows us to make our way through the world and shields us from madness, but it also distorts our view of ourselves and the world. It is therefore incomplete and leaves us always feeling that who we are is not really who we are. Nevertheless, we continually strive, according to Lacan, to know who we are, an impossible task, and often mistake our ego and the identifications that constitute it for our true nature. We look to others for recognition and to tell us what we really want and who we are, while failing to listen to the constant murmuring of our unconscious, wherein lie the secrets of our being.

The identity of a teacher is just one more imaginary identification layered over the originary ego. Such an identity allows us passage through the worlds of education. If we actually take ourselves for teachers in some fixed sense, as opposed to provisionally, the assumption of such an identity confines us and forces us continually to assume aspects, qualities, stances, and other identities that we take as our own but that require us to repress or deny other feelings, urges, impulses, and desires such as the desire to hurt or kill others or oneself, the desire to devour or merge with others or oneself or the desire to penetrate or to be penetrated by others or oneself. Cast beyond the pale, so to speak, these desires or urges continue to circulate, to pulse within a psyche in which the ego structures our limited understanding of ourselves and of others.

Unable to face these terrifying and repulsive feelings, desires, and impulses, we split them off and project them onto others, who emerge as, for example, murderous, dirty, wanton, seductive, aggressive, rejecting, and slothful, and who seem to remain an enigma, forever the object of scrutiny. The endless studies on children and adolescents, the majority of which either strive to humanize them or provide better ways to control them, haven't altered the talk in teacher lounges about "those animals" or reduced complaints about "out-of-control" students. As Zizek (1998) writes, "the enigma of the Other which cannot be reduced to the partner in symbolic communication ... confronts us with the enigma of that which, in ourselves, resists the universal frame of symbolic communication" (p. 155).

While the relationship between aggression and love can be approached using psychoanalytic concepts of splitting and projection, these approaches miss an important component of that relationship. It is not enough to say that the physician in "A Use of Force" may be attacking the "savage" animal in himself that his professional identity repudiates or defending against his own fear of death, or that Ursula may be brutally punishing the rebellious spirit, still undeveloped, in herself. Neither of these account for the passion with which each of these two idealistic members of helping professions lays into his patient or her student. How do we make sense of the persistence of fantasies about out-of-control students and the desire to rescue, sacrifice for, and earn the love of one's students even when progressive and mainstream approaches to teacher education, as I mentioned above, rationally address these fantasies? How can we make sense of the aggression, the sadistic or masochistic impulses, the sexual desires that seem to fuel the very actions or attitudes we take in fulfilling those duties constituting our imaginary identifications? How do we account for the authority figure, such as the doctor, who derives his own secret enjoyment from tormenting his victims for their own good or worse yet for some higher good? How do we make sense of those like Ursula who apparently want nothing more than to give, give, give to the children and receive their love but wind up devoting all their energy to disciplining the students? What accounts for the appeal of what Lakoff calls the strict father model and the seeming dullness of what he calls the nurturant parent model?

Lacan's theorization of *jouissance* can help us here. For our purposes we can focus on just a few of the many meanings of the concept. Jouissance, as Lacan defines it, exceeds pleasure or is an excess of aggressive enjoyment that is beyond pleasure and that is tied to pain. As Zizek says, "Jouissance emerges when the very reality that is the source of unpleasure, of pain, is experienced as a source of traumatic excessive pleasure" (p. 167). Jouissance can also designate a kind of ecstasy tied to loss of control and rational consciousness, and secondarily to violence, either emotional or physical. Such ecstasy can result from intense suffering—think of the mortification of the saints—or from surrender to the thrill of risk, or from the unbridled release of aggression in the service of a good. We can see these senses operative in the doctor's statement, "I could have torn the child apart in my own fury and enjoyed it. It was a pleasure to attack her. My face was burning with it." Jouissance can also be experienced by fulfilling the letter of the law in the service of one's own secret pleasures. Here Adolph Eichmann comes to mind, but on a far lesser scale so does Ursula and the teachers in her school who on some level derive enjoyment from tearing into student flesh. Ursula's release after she beats the child is akin to a near-death sexual release. Lawrence writes, "Nothing could touch her now.... She was as if violated to death."

Jouissance can also designate the pleasure that results from a transgressive act because of its transgressiveness. It is in this sense that the degree of pleasure is in direct relation to the price one must pay for it. Thus, the pleasure of the transgressive act is proportional to the punishment one risks. An example here is the perverse enjoyment experienced by students who vehemently take "politically incorrect" positions in the classroom or resignify racist, homophobic, or sexist remarks as emancipatory. Perhaps Howard Stern or Mike Savage provide the benchmark for this kind of transgressive behavior, given that they risked being fired and ultimately were fired.

Lacan, in his later writings, conceived of jouissance in relation to a particular kind of ethical behavior. Because it was beyond the pleasure principle, in other words, the normal or reasonable calculations of pleasure and pain are disregarded, one's acceptance of suffering and even death and the pursuit of an unsatisfied desire without regard for one's own safety place the pursuit in the ethical domain (see Lacan, 1992). Antigone is the primary example of such ethical behavior. The very act of sacrifice or renunciation, therefore, can provide jouissance but it must be a sacrifice that goes beyond the norm. So, for example, Lacan does not see the gesture of the good Samaritan or the saint who gives his own cloak to the naked beggar in the road as suffused with jouissance but does see as filled with jouissance the gesture of saints who, for example, drank the water in which they had washed the feet of lepers. Why? Because the former preserve their own sense of goodness by their act, and do not acknowledge the enjoyment derived from the position of superiority such an act confers. The latter form of sacrifice accepts the Real of the Other and the jouissance that accompanies such acceptance. "The ultimate problem in intersubjectivity is precisely the extent to which we are ready to accept the other— ... in the real of his or her existence" (Zizek, 1998, p. 167). The Real of the leper, the horror bursting through the skin, is exactly what must be accepted. To preach acceptance, without accepting the real of the Other is to reduce the Other is some symbolic fiction. Ursula's desire to give to the children, captured in the quote at the top of this chapter, exemplifies the former altruism, as does the physician's reduction in fee. To follow Lacan's logic, Ursula would have to beat herself in some kind of staging of the horror of the patriarchal rules of the school or the doctor would have to move into the impoverished area he visits and renounce his own security, much as the complicated heroine of David Hare's play *Skylight* moves, to friends' and family's bewilderment, into a rundown area and gives up her privileges and material wealth. Such a sacrifice is best captured at the end of Father Damien's life when after serving the lepers for years, he opens his morning sermon not with the usual, "You lepers," but with "We lepers."

What is important to understand is that jouissance is uncontrollable; it resists, subverts, and eludes control or domestication. It is beyond reason and cannot be contained by reason. I want to argue that it is exactly this jouissance, in all its unreasonableness, that is not addressed in teacher education. If we begin to take jouissance seriously it will offer greater insight into the relationship between aggression, love, and altruism and allow us to work through the very fantasies about control and love that persist in the psychic lives of teachers.

The fantasies of loss of control that haunt student teachers and perhaps all teachers hold in fact very powerful aggressive impulses that are defended against by fantasies of loving and sacrificing for the students. What the conservative strict father family model offers is the actualization of those impulses in the service of some greater good and in the day light of public legitimacy, such that the obscene supplement, for example, the doctor's pleasure, can be experienced. Thus, higher standards and high-stakes testing, corporal punishment, tough love, the end of social promotion, and the end of affirmative action, all these offer opportunities for teachers to enjoy their own aggression in the name of a greater good and actually, in some cases, to have the double enjoyment of turning such aggression into a sacrifice: "This hurts me more than it hurts you," as the punishment is meted out. There is at least a certain honesty in the sadistic conservative approach to discipline.

And we can now see how the reasonableness and conventional self-sacrificing of so much progressive education, the nurturant parent model, with its disguised control, its blindness to jouissance, its positioning of the Other as either an aseptic object of study or a victim requiring, for example, a particular cultural sensitivity can result in a social or psychic backlash, because it doesn't recognize the power of jouisssance. We can begin to understand how the emptying out of the self because "It's all about the kids," or "It's all about the love of the subject," or "It's all about empowering the students," or "Killing the oppressor in oneself," or the emptying out of the self as a kind of contemplative education, provokes transgressive responses and in fact strengthens the very ego that will, because it is inherently a defense against the Real, produce more aggression. Is it not the "spiritually enlightened," "politically correct" teachers, or the teachers who talk of nothing but their devotion to the kids or how they pass on their love of the subject, who are often the least tolerant of real differences, the most controlled, the least attuned to their students, and the least friendly to the nonteaching staff? Or conversely, are they also not the most apt to defer out of some idealization of the students to the jouissance of their own students, such that they can only regain control through the exercise of the very power they critique?

My aim here is not to consign progressives to the position of bleeding heart liberals or to elevate the right because of its more honest relation to jouissance. Rather, I am arguing for teacher educators to deepen their understanding of the jouissance, of the aggression and fear that permeate the fantasies about control and love. The only way to break the power of the fantasies of love and control that lock us into the dualism of Lakoff's political topography or that persist in the psychic lives of teachers is to confront how these fantasies and how our identities of teachers defend against and are invested with jouissance. We need to work through the misrecognition of our own egos, that is the way we take our teacher egos for who we are, and our blindness to our own jouissance and the jouissance of the Other. The working through of the misrecognition provides access to the true nature of the other and simultaneously a means to overcome our own distorted perception. Acknowledging our own and the Other's jouissance shatters the cozy, reasonable, and often, unfortunately, impotent if not counterproductive pedagogy one sees in classes where teachers reasonably discuss how best to manage classrooms, nurture students, get rid of unfair privileges, be culturally sensitive, and have the right dispositions. We need to have those discussions, but not without the difficult work of working through the fantasies of love and control.

References

Dietrich, P. (1966). The connotations of rape in the use of force. *Studies in Short Fiction, 3*(4), 44–45, 1966.

Dobson, J. (1982). *Dare to Discipline*. New York: Bantam.

Fink, B. (1995). *The Lacanian subject: Between language and jouissance*. Princeton, NJ: Princeton University Press.

Fink, B. (1998). *A clinical introduction to Lacanian psychoanalysis: Theory and technique.* Cambridge, MA: Harvard University Press.

Freud, S. (1919). Lines of advance in psycho-analytic therapy. In J. Strachey, in collaboration with Anna Freud, assisted by A. Strachey and A. Tyson. *The standard edition of the complete psychological works of Sigmund Freud* (vol. 17, pp. 159–168). London: Hogarth Press & Institute for Psychoanalysis.

Grumet, M. (1988). *Bitter milk: Women and teaching.* Amherst: University of Massachusetts Press.

Lacan, J. (1992). *The Ethics of Psychoanalysis 1959–1960 Book VII.* Jacques-Alain Miller (Ed.). Trans. by Dennis Porter. New York: WW Norton.

Lakoff, G. (2004). *Don't think of an elephant! Know your values and frame the debate.* White River Junction, VT: Chelsea Green.

Lawrence, D. H. (1915). *The rainbow.* M. Kinkead-Weekes (Ed.). Cambridge: Cambridge University Press, 1989.

Salvio, P. (2006). On the vicissitudes of love and hate: Anne Sexton's pedagogy of loss and reparation. In G. Boldt & P. Salvio (Eds.), *Love's Return: Psychoanalytic Essays on Childhood, Teaching and Learning.* New York: Routledge.

Williams, W. C. (1937, 1984). The use of force. In *The doctor stories* (pp. 56–60). New York: New Directions.

Zizek, S. (1998). "Love thy neighbor? No thanks!" In C. Lane (Ed.), *The psychoanalysis of race* (pp. 154–175). New York: Columbia University Press.

CHAPTER 2

Savage Inequalities Indeed

Irrationality and Urban School Reform

LINDA C. POWELL AND MARGARET E. BARBER

Introduction

As a culture, Americans conduct coded conversations about our future. While the manifest content is about the economy or crime, the latent conversation is about who we are and what we hope. Education is currently in fashion as the topic for displacement. Public education, especially, has reemerged loudly in our political and cultural conversation with genuine concern about its viability. Operated with public funds and described by the for-profit sector as having the market potential of more than $400 billion (Merrill Lynch, 1999), public education is under intense scrutiny by multiple stakeholders with differing agendas. For many, public schooling is an essential means of inculcating values of citizenship and democracy. For others, it is a potential source of enormous profit. For forty-five million children, public education is a critical resource for personal development, socioeconomic opportunity, and mobility.

Some districts, primarily those in urban areas, are increasingly filled with young people who are more likely to be poor, of color, and generally underserved not only by education but by health care, housing, and other social institutions. This segregation occurs as middle-class families of all colors withdraw their children from public schools and flee to private and suburban schools, taking with them financial and human capital. This purposeful flight, or export, creates a "natural-appearing" split between urban schools and suburban/private schools with the "smart" children clustered in the suburbs and the "at-risk" students left behind in the cities. Resources follow the middle-class children and are pulled away from these schools that most need them. Many poor urban students of color bring to school a variety of differing educational and developmental needs, and schools are failing to meet these needs on a massive scale. We focus increasingly on technical solutions (Heifetz, 1994) to remedy these failings, but literacy and numeracy are insufficient—even if we could guarantee even these skills for all children. Schools are failing to provide the most basic of cognitive skills, but many also damage the lives and souls of the students and adults within them (Block, 1997; Palmer, 1997; Kessler, 2000).

Our hope is to provoke and inspire an innovative but desperately needed conversation about urban educational improvement between two important audiences. We hope to paint a broad-brush portrait of the complexities of public education reform to psychologists and those in the psychoanalytic and Group Relations communities. We want simultaneously to emphasize the critical importance of social systems dynamics to the education policy, philanthropic, and school reform communities. In our experience, these communities are not commonly in communication, and yet, they have a basic relatedness. Educational reformers "know" that there is something under the surface in the intense resistance they encounter, but they do not have a systematic way to inquire or interpret the phenomenon that they confront. Psychoanalytically informed social systems theorists have a method for exploring covert processes, but they do not "know" the politics or culture of educational improvement. The authors hope that this chapter begins to build conceptual bridges between these two conceptual worlds.

As the title suggests, this chapter is written to be read "in conversation with" *Savage Inequalities: Children in America's Schools* by Kozol (1991). Kozol provided dramatic qualitative descriptions about conditions in urban schools. Although he wrote about specific cities and schools, the conditions he described are completely appropriate and endemic. Kozol was neither balanced nor dispassionate. He did not include the rare "successful" urban school. This is a book about outrage, not objectivity. *Savage Inequalities* described individual schools and critiques the systems in which they are embedded. In a sense, he provides vivid insight into the primitive processes at work in urban schools on a daily basis. Kozol challenges us to answer why the schools he describes could even exist in the wealthiest democracy in the world. Like Kozol, we intend to be provocative and heuristic. And like Kozol, we challenge our readers: Once we know what we are creating in education, how can we not act?[1]

The authors' perspective is informed by a rich and international tradition within Group Relations of interest in education. Rice (1970) wrote *The Modern University* with the hope of stretching our view of the possibilities of learning in formal institutions of education. Richardson's (1975) groundbreaking work "Environment of Learning" used Bion's (1961) basic assumption dependency group to propose a new and sophisticated level of analysis of what really happens in the classroom. Newman's (1974) classic *Groups in Schools* was the psychologically informed handbook for educators. Working from a developmental Eriksonian perspective (Erikson, 1950), Newman provided a complete framework for understanding classroom practice, leadership dynamics, and consultation technique from a psychodynamic frame.

Many theorists and practitioners continue to use eclectic variations on the Group Relations lens in a variety of ways in education. For example, they explored classroom process (Ward, 1995), schools as organizations (Alderfer, 1980; Powell, 2000), social identity and multiculturalism (Style and Powell, 1995; White, 1996, 2000), leadership development and preparation (Eisold, 1997; Powell, 2002), educational authority and leadership (White, 1996), parental involvement (Giles, 2001), and the dynamics of districts-as-a-whole (White and Bernard, 1986; Mack, 1995; Spence and Powell, 2001). In addition to the body of Group Relations work, the authors' perspective also draws on the wealth of action research directed at understanding and changing school systems (Fine, 1994a; Hess, 1995; Wasley, Fine, Gladden, Holland, King, Mosak, and Powell, 2000) as well as recent work in adult development theory (Kegan, 1995). This perspective also benefits from an understanding of the fundamental spirituality of social justice efforts (Coles, 1994; Loeb, 1999; Edelman, 2000) that underscore the moral imperative to seek out, to confront, and to set right injustice and inequity.

Additional data for this chapter came from the authors' professional orientations as a psychologist (Powell) and an educator (Barber). We work on a daily basis with teachers, administrators, researchers, and policymakers in both public and private education in urban, suburban, and rural situations. We have worked as consultants to faculties and districts, as teaching faculty at schools of education and as reform-oriented researchers in Group Relations. We have held roles within for-profit education ventures and within an education research center researching and evaluating state and federal policy. Our experiences cross the various socioeconomic, racial, and interdisciplinary divides that currently balkanize the field of education. We have used the tools of both psychology and education in these efforts.

Our viewpoint on education also benefited from our simultaneous work with a variety of noneducation clients including corporate, religious, social service, and governmental agencies. The contrast between and among these organizations has helped us identify specific characteristics that distinguish educational systems and, more specifically, urban school districts as organizations. These multiple sources of interest and theoretical grounding and vantage points have provided a unique "education-as-a-whole" view from which to develop a psychodynamic understanding of what transformation will require.

From our own experience, from Kozol, and from the work of other researchers, it seems clear that to deliver on its promise to citizens in a democracy, public education requires change that is dramatic, not gradual; disjunctive, not continuous; and transformational, not evolutionary. What follows is an initial attempt to tame and name the irrational in urban education reform. First, four fundamental and related yet under-explored ideas about American education are identified. Then, these four ideas with our primary hypothesis about consequences for transforming urban system and resistance to these efforts follow. Finally, informed by social systems theory and consultative practice, a set of nontraditional avenues for research, consultation, and service that might contribute to the transformation of urban education is identified.

Facing the Irrational in Education Reform

There are many valuable analyses of the problems facing urban schools from sociological, anthropological, and historical perspectives (Hochschild, 1984; Sizer, 1985; Banks, 1988; Sarason, 1990; Bailey, 1992, 1993; Fine, 1994a, 1994c, 1998; Delpit, 1995; Meier, 1995; Tyack and Cuban, 1995; Darling-Hammond, 1997). Two recent developments in particular created interest in the role of unconscious processes and school improvement, one from within education itself and the other from the academy. The first occurred when the true dimensions of a district's failures were illuminated, usually in the form of achievement results on standardized tests or an accurate accounting of the number of students who dropped out before graduation. Certain repetitive forms of action prevailed. Districts and foundations commissioned university studies. Community partners were sought. Individual schools and children were sensationalized for either being tremendous failures or for "beating the odds." Funds were demanded, sometimes raised, and immediately spent.

Promising programs were developed and implemented with exciting results for small numbers of students in selected schools. But, as of this writing, the country that put a human being on the moon, persuaded its citizens to wear seat belts, and reduced smoking dramatically among adults has not been able to significantly raise the achievement of all children in a single urban school district. This incredible resistance to what would seem to be much-desired change occurs despite the energy, intellect, investment of bright and capable individuals, and significant knowledge of what needs to be done. These educational systems demonstrate an alarming stability, defying genuine improvement. And when the varying forms of this resistance to change are acknowledged, some researcher or practitioner will sagely observe that the situation is "dysfunctional" or "irrational" (Cohen, 1999; Elmore, 2000; Payne, 2000).

This same thoughtful commentator will then return to the discussion of technical solutions as if he or she had not just made the observation about irrationality. If there is any attempt to explore the irrationality comment, it tends to remain at the "personality" or intrapersonal level of analysis (Wells, 1985). These explanations often inadvertently blame students for their poverty or teachers for their lack of commitment or superintendents for their leadership style. These clearly insufficient explanations comfort us momentarily, yet lead to little or no sustainable innovation. This demonstrates again the adage, "the unconscious tends to remain unconscious."

The second prod to our interest in unconscious processes in educational reform comes from our experiences as staff and members in Group Relations conferences (Rice, 1975; Rioch, 1975; Banet and Hayden, 1977; Hayden and Molenkamp, 2004). Since 1993, a series of Group Relations conferences has been conducted at graduate schools of education within courses on leadership, group dynamics, and urban education. These conferences have included a number of educators involved in school reform. The problems of innovation have been apparent at these conferences at multiple levels, as even the method of Group Relations conferences has been scrutinized for potential reform (Monroe, 2001). Many conference members have found it paralyzing to face the genuine conflicts and inequities in the schools and districts in which they are involved. It became apparent from the conference work as well as application cases that facing what is most feared offers educators the greatest opportunities for learning and substantive change.

Our attention was drawn by the simultaneity of this emerging clarity within education itself about "irrationality" and by our experiences in temporary institutions that included large numbers of reform-oriented educators. In concert, these experiences led us to identify four interrelated and fundamentally covert assumptions about American education. These are:

1. That public education has been and continues to be rooted fundamentally in conflict between competing systemic forces.
2. That because of the intensity and contradictions that characterize this conflict, as a society we have created both an individual and a collective "school-in-the-mind."
3. That as the complexity and diversity of society increase, our collective anxiety also intensifies.
4. That in response to our increasing anxiety, we employ maladaptive social defenses to avoid the underlying conflict.

These four assumptions, inherent in the history of American education, are discussed in the next section.

Four Critical Assumptions

Public Education: Conflict between Competing Systemic Forces

The history of education in America is inherently also the history of the struggle between our founding principles of equity and our failure to uphold them in the schooling of all children. An overview of schooling in the United States illustrates the internal debate that has raged over the role, tasks, and challenges that have faced the public education system since its inception. Schools, by their very definition, are containers for the social and political values of a given era and of preceding generations. Reviewing the history of education, the distinction between this social function as the actual primary task of schooling and the apparent primary task of teaching and learning was reviewed. The tension between these competing tasks has emerged over time in our struggles about whom and how to educate. Schools were originally rooted in rural communities, each developing separately under the auspices of decentralized local government and each reflecting the particular social and economic concerns of the region (Tyack, 1974). As the United States expanded west and once-rural villages developed into much larger communities filled with increasing numbers of immigrants arriving from all over the world, schools reflected the growing diversity of the population—as well as the nation's efforts to assimilate this difference.

The charge for the common school, led by Horace Mann in the mid-1800s, was regarded by many as the very foundation of public schooling for all children from all backgrounds. This movement was characterized by the development of standardized curricula and pedagogy and the advancement of a shared national ideology (Cremin, 1951). While we can regard this time of increased commitment to free public education as the growing recognition of the role of education in social and economic mobility, it is understood as a mechanism for containing different cultures and values through the inculcation of Western European, Protestant values.

These efforts can be seen in the pursuit over the past 150 years of what Tyack (1995) called the "one best system." Whether students resided in rural agricultural communities or urban industrial centers, whether they came from a family schooled in America or were first-generation immigrants just learning English, it was believed that standardized curriculum and assessment would be an appropriate and effective means of teaching all students. In the 1870s, educators developed standardized tests with the goal of classification of all students according to their demonstrated proficiency. In Portland, Oregon, schools in 1874, for example, of the twenty-one classrooms tested, seven classes of students failed. In only six of the classes were more than half of the students promoted (Tyack, 1974). In response to these poor results, teachers encouraged weaker students to drop out of school before the exam period and administrators avoided publishing the test scores to avoid criticism. More than 120 years later, these practices continue. Policymakers and educators are still trying to identify a single test that will categorize all students, and we continue to create subgroups of children stratified in school achievement and opportunities by race and socioeconomic class.

The most recent MCAS (Massachusetts Comprehensive Assessment System) scores illustrate how the public schooling system continues to use its tools to separate its students in our society by race and class at the very time that it feigns ignorance. The Massachusetts Department of Education (MA DOE) reported that in 2000, student performance revealed some distinctions by race/ethnicity. The MCAS executive summary described these results only as a "differential" outcome in all subject areas across race (MA DOE, 2001). It separated the summary descriptions by race, never noting explicitly that African American, Latino, and Native American students fail at a rate more than double that of white and Asian American students. The MCAS offered a relevant example because it is one test of many in states and communities in which there are increasingly diverse populations and in which we can see more overtly what unconscious processes the explicit policy instruments create in the system.

These scores clearly indicate the operation of a dual system that assures the continued success of some students, white and Asian American, and the continued failure of others, predominantly African American, Latino, and

Native American. How can we look at the recent results of the MCAS and other education policies and not draw the unshakable conclusion that as a society we do not want "these children" to succeed? As Darling-Hammond (1997) wrote, "some children are worth less in the eyes of society." If they were not, then we would not devise a school system that relies upon a high level of attrition in overcrowded schools, insufficient resources for some schools, and the continued failure of entire segments of our population.

Assessment results like the MCAS described above are consistent over time. The sheer persistence of this pattern begs us to question what unconscious purpose it might serve. Society is more comfortable with the disparity of access to educational resources and outcomes than it is with the risk of equalizing them. Perhaps there is a synergy and safety in this limited access?

As Kozol's (1991) description of a conversation with the students at New Trier (suburban Chicago) suggested, improving opportunities for "these children" poses a danger to the supremacy for "our" children. If we increase the per pupil allocation in East Harlem, we threaten the much higher allocation in Scarsdale (suburban New York City). And if we bring all students' performance up to acceptable, passing levels, then we perhaps threaten to reveal the hypocrisy rooted in the very foundation of our social system.

For all the sociopolitical and educational advances since the first standardized testing in the 1800s, how do we understand the continued debate about standardized "high-stakes" tests like the MCAS? Bowles and Gintis (1976) argued that schools reproduce the larger social system by preparing students for a capitalist system stratified by race and class. Carnoy and Levin (1985) identified this tension in the oppositional relationship between the capitalist production function and the unifying sense of democratic citizenship as an inherently contradictory aspect of American education. At the same time that the school system reinforces the opportunities of the American Dream that can be achieved by anyone possessing intelligence and a strong work ethic, it also conspires to ensure the continuing production of trained workers ready to feed the capitalist engine. The system requires many more low- and middle-level workers than it does CEOs, despite its protestations to the contrary, so it cannot afford for all children to learn. Some children must drop out of school in order to take up their positions in assigned bottom segments of the workforce. Yet, in order to maintain this production function, the stratification of students must remain covert. This has been done through the perpetuation of the myth of meritocracy that holds that success in American society is solely determined by effort and skill. If students do not succeed, then it is because they have less innate skill or potential rather than an organizational variable—"something in the air conditioning" (Fine, 1994b)—that assures inequity.

By maintaining this myth, we prevent many poorer students and students of color from discovering that their failure is largely predetermined, and we protect many more privileged students from confronting the possibility that their success may not be wholly earned.

Public Education: The Institution in the Mind

Our view of education reform has been especially influenced by Gutmann, Pierre, Ternier-David, and Verrier's (1997) description of a Group Relations conference conducted with Israeli and Arab members at the Arab University in Jerusalem. In this effort, Gutmann et al. made a clear distinction between institutional transformation stating that it differs from organization development because it has the explicit goal of taking into account the unconscious. Gutmann et al. argue that attending to expressions of the unconscious can provide a resource for opening and transforming situations that were previously experienced as blocked. The authors noted: "In the complex and moving context of the Middle East, questions like boundaries, identities and relationship are at the core.... Surely the conference would 'resonate' with its environment." This conference was not divorced from the explosive stalemate in the Middle East; it was designed to inquire into and make meaning of its social context. To have convened these two divergent groups without such multilayered inquiry would not have accurately represented the nature of either group alone, nor both together.

Gutmann et al. (1997) discovered that conference members acted from a specific mental state structured by a closed representation of one-self and one's society. They observed that each person confronted others from a "confined mood." For Palestinians, they called this "the prison in the mind," and for Israelis, "the ghetto in the mind."

Group Relations conferences held at schools of education have inadvertently served a similar function in unearthing the power of the "school in the mind." In the immediacy of Group Relations conferences, we discovered the unique institution we each have in our mind that reflects our own notions of power, privilege, race, gender, class, community, and opportunity. The conflict between these divergent internal "institutions" and the anxieties that attend them are shaped by and form the skeleton of American public schooling. In the here-and-now of Group Relations conferences, American primary and secondary education can be seen as an unexamined conflict among competing conceptions of learning, opportunity, democracy, and privilege.

In these conferences, we observed that schools and school systems are cultural symbols and enactments of our own experiences as children, our feelings about children as a group, and our feelings about the future. Schools carry a similar (although far less understood) charge, as does the institution "family." We have a symbolic, political, and psychological investment in schools, whether our children or we attend or attended them or not. Some of our school experiences asserted our value and potential. Other experiences threatened our sense of stability and competence. At best, we each experienced some ambivalence about the institution of school (Block, 1997). Most of us introject the positive school experiences into our inner world as good, stable, known objects, while we project the difficult, demanding aspects into the "school in the mind." Those of us who attended college and earned advanced degrees were, by definition, "successful" in school although we likely had a dizzying variety of complex experiences in school.

Over time, the authors believe that these representations become part of a complex self-system that says that we are good and deserving of our success academically, while the badness is projected into schools as ungovernable, teachers as incompetent, and public education as unsalvageable. This projection extends to our denigration of the work of creating good education and reforming schools. After all, "we all went to school: how hard can it be?" By diminishing the complexity and difficulty that characterize educational reform, we deny the systemic consequences of this split.

We carry the impact of our early experience into our work as teachers, administrators, and consultants. The connection to our adult lives is direct: Family is the first workplace, and school is the second for most of us (Shapiro and Carr, 1991; Style, 1998). We project our unworked authority issues from our childhood and schooling into education-oriented settings. We organize our perceptions and actions to protect ourselves from certain knowledge, rather than apprehend these complex systems more clearly. Our own unworked schooling experiences may prevent us from finding the issue of "school reform" compelling. Why do we leave these questions to the school board, a few foundations, the teachers' union, and the newspapers? What is the learned helplessness we often feel about this topic? What is our apathy or disconnection from this topic? Our inability to recognize our responsibility is a form of societal denial. It may be an overarching cultural repression; we collude to avoid investigating how we were damaged by our experiences in school and how we project those experiences into schools today.

The Intensification of Anxiety

The central role of anxiety is, in many ways, unique to the domain of dynamic psychology and social systems theory. When a feature of normal maturation—containing and mastering conflict—develops, the psyche's capacity to manage anxiety increases. The general role of anxiety in learning has been particularly noted by many sociologists and anthropologists of education and is considered a normal part of the process for learners.

Educators today face multiple sources of anxiety. The work itself, tending daily to the cognitive and emotional development of young people, is anxiety producing. Teaching children of poverty creates additional psychic demands on adults (Hilficker, 1994). As Kozol (1991) so poetically demonstrates, few adults are adequately prepared to confront the daily ravages of hunger, homelessness, family stress, and political powerlessness. Conflict and stimulation beyond school also influence its ability to educate young people. The changing nature of childhood brings new minds and bodies into the classroom: technology, the economy, and the media have affected family life as well as individual development. The perceived consensus of values between communities and schools has broken down. The authority of schools as organizations that speak for the children is eroding.

If we truly listen to children and adults in schools, we uncover the culture's almost psychotic anxiety over the future we are creating politically, culturally, and environmentally. Some educators describe an increasing sense of powerlessness. Many of the mechanisms we use to manage this anxiety are what Kozol would call "pathological denial." Despite the dangerous consequences, individuals and groups cultivate ways to "not know" and to "not learn." One mechanism is the hypnotic unregulated use of television, the Internet, video, and "violence as entertainment" (Minow and LeMay, 1995; Wolff, 1999; Mosley, 2000; Schlosser and Kanfer, 2000) by children and by adults. In a circular fashion, combined with the values of consumerism—competition, detachment, and individualism (Lasn, 2000)—popular culture undercuts school culture, preventing the critical development of a sense of mission and purpose.

It is important to differentiate, however, between an appropriate developmental anxiety that accompanies learning and school life from the anxiety that arises from internal conflict around incompatible ideas. Given the history of American education, there has always been a tension between an apparent task (teaching basic cognitive skills, "making" citizens) and an actual task (keeping students in a preassigned societal niche) of education.

These incompatible ideas only heighten the realistic individual, group, and intergroup anxiety. For these reasons, educational institutions today are sites of tremendous affect: strong feelings, deep values, and matters of the heart. Schools strenuously resist change efforts that do not attend to or honor these deep feelings of those who are within them. When we suppress this kind of exploration, important information about change is lost.

And that may be the highest price that we pay. The rising intensity of our anxiety prevents us from learning during the process of placing poor children at the center of their education. Genuine reform initiatives that have any chance at transforming education open up questions of equity and merit. We cannot pursue sophisticated change interventions without gathering new data about ourselves, about the children and families in those schools, about urban communities, and about the unspoken assumptions of American education. These questions cause us to reflect on our own schooling and our past practice. Any serious look at these issues threatens our internal images of ourselves as fair and deserving and makes us look at the foundations of all of our institutions.

Social Systems as a Defense against Anxiety

The manufactured inequalities Kozol (1991) described are a form of splitting, a way of managing intensifying anxiety about children, education, and the future. From this perspective, many of our difficulties creating vibrant schools are the symptom of a deeper problem, not the problem itself. The ways we fund, govern, and design schools are actually attempts to protect ourselves from the intensity of the conflict that surrounds the work of education. Almost fifty years ago, two social systems theorists in the psychoanalytic tradition articulated an approach to understanding the connection between the individual personality and the social structures that we create to allay those anxieties. In "Social Systems as a Defense against Persecutory and Depressive Anxiety," Jacques (1955) postulated an important parallel between the individual and the social system. He appropriated Bion's (1961) fundamental notion that group life is psychotic, that joining a social system is extremely powerful in a way that remains out of our immediate awareness. Every organization has a "personality" under-girded by an unconscious process that can support the primary task of the organization or distract from it. When the unconscious process "organizes" or binds up anxiety in a useful way, it frees energy and attention for the real work of the organization.

In exploring the parallel between the individual and the social system the individual helps to create, Jacques emphasized the critical importance of projective and introjective processes. Jacques studied a factory attempting to change the way in which wages are calculated. He explored the various uses of projection and introjection that workers and management used to carry the change task forward while protecting the primary task of the group. This is simply splitting off parts of the self that are complex or objectionable and putting them into others in the system. In this factory, for example, the workers projected their concerns about the new system onto their union leaders, who were negotiating the agreement. The leaders were suddenly seen as slightly untrustworthy and "suspect" but not in a disabling way. The managers of the factory projected their hope for the new system onto the workers, idealizing them as perfect and uniformly committed to them. By keeping these objectionable ideas out of the self, the workers and management were able to proceed with the daily work and the change intervention.

Menzies's (1975) classic study of nurses in a teaching hospital went more deeply into the specific dynamics of caregiving or dependency-oriented organizations (Shapiro and Carr, 1991; Kahn, 1993a, 1993b; Obholzer and Roberts, 1994). Invited in as a consultant at the point of breakdown, Menzies and her colleagues pursued this examination of the organizational anxiety in a teaching hospital and its impact on task. They reported two important findings relevant for those interested in school reform. One was that the work of nursing (like teaching) is psychologically demanding for the nursing staff. Caring for sick and dying patients stirs up primitive unconscious reactions that are separate from their conscious "professional discourse." They then determined that many of the hospital's "difficulties" were actually ill-directed attempts to manage these reactions. For example, various problems that seemed related to lack of resources and confusion over patient care were in actuality attempts by the nursing staff to avoid attachment to patients and their families. They were more likely to experience the intense anxiety in these attachments, and so unconsciously the system began to act to avoid attachment with rotation schedules, training courses, and so forth, while individual nurses simply took more time off.

Powell (1994) previously argued that urban schools, like that hospital, employ a particular set of maladaptive defenses aimed at reducing anxiety of the adults and children who attend them. Anonymity is used as a form of denial and avoidance of the intensity of affect that exists in urban schools generally and more intensely when they try to improve. Menzies's (1975) exploration of social defenses was particularly helpful, as so many of them could apply to individual urban schools. This is due to the similarity in the conflict in the primary task of these organizations and to the role of dependency in caregiving organizations.

In these three studies, the level of analysis was within a single institution—a factory, a hospital, a school—identifying the ways in which social systems serve to alleviate the persecutory and depressive anxiety that members bring to them. One could expand this reasoning to the system or even cultural level by looking at dynamics across education as a whole and within districts of urban schools as a way to understand the resistances to systemic reform where it is most needed. As we move beyond the individual school in educational bureaucracies, the audience for public education expands. The number and range of "stakeholders" increases to include businesses, government, social services, institutions of higher education, and faith communities. From a symbolic standpoint, this level of analysis includes those of us who never "consciously" think about public education while unconsciously colluding in its failures and "simply" footing the bill for public education.

Reframing the Crisis in Urban Education

One of our major working hypotheses is that public education is itself, in part, an attempt to manage the conflicts around "becoming/being an American," and that social systems defenses have always been employed in public education to manage the ensuing anxiety. Increasing levels of conflict in society and in our own psyches, however, are leading to higher levels of anxiety and the need for more dramatic social systems defenses in urban districts and schools. In actuality, what appear to be our "failures" in urban education are extreme and unconscious attempts to protect adults from fundamental questions about "merit" and "value" of various demographic groups.

History demonstrates that schools have always been laboratories for social change and control. Urban schools are currently being used as even more tightly bounded microcosms (Smith, Simmons, and Thames, 1989) where our country unconsciously tries to solve intractable social problems. School districts struggle with racism, poverty, the withdrawal of government from the public sphere, new developments in family life, the impact of technology, and the fast growing "digital divide" on a daily basis. Urban schools become the stand-ins in our coded conversation about the future, carrying the entirety of our concern about what to do about kids, what the future should look like, and what we can expect from education in a media-dominated world. Historic concerns about merit and achievement are projected into urban schools, freeing other schools to act "as if" they have no difficulties assessing merit or identifying quality. Urban schools are loaded up with fear, incompetence, and rage, leaving other systems freer to hold hope, competence, and stability. Burdened in this way, urban schools become even more intractable and difficult to change.

As urban schools take on these tasks, the ability of other schools to forward their articulated primary task of preparing the privileged is preserved. Private, independent, and the new "charter" schools become more defended in their own difficulties that arise from these traditional conflicts and less able to work with them effectively. These privileged schools often use traditional urban schools psychologically and politically to "feel better" about themselves.

The "institution in the mind" of school requires a denigrated "other," someone to do badly, someone to fail, and someone to be less capable. The unconscious sorting and ranking function of education leaves each of us needing a "home" for our incompetence, and urban education has taken that role. Urban schools become the receptacles of all of our unworked feelings about learning, our own experiences in schools and in the future. Projections of incompetence, disability, and inferiority flood urban schools from the entire educational world and beyond. Given the choice of resisting these projections or absorbing them, individuals inside the system behave in ways that appear erratic, unstable, and incompetent. These systems appear to be organized to reject help although this really reflects the urban schools' intuitive understanding that help is not empathically offered; they sense that they are being used. Scapegoated by the entire culture, then denied sufficient resources for this historic, high-stakes task, urban schools fall into the "politics of despair" (Cytrynbaum, 1999).

Any analysis of urban education that focuses only on the immediate players, however, blames the victims for their fate in a system designed to assure their failure. It simultaneously relieves us from examining how we psychically (and potentially materially) benefit and of our complicity in its operation. Revitalizing the primary task of providing authentic teaching and learning for urban children would have to include some opportunity for them to make sense of why they find themselves in their circumstances, and to make meaning out of their own lives. And any curriculum that systematically grapples with those larger questions such as race, poverty, homelessness, gender, and so forth, begins to indict the larger citizenry, our culture, and us. If we question why urban children are relegated to the weakest, poorest performing parts of the system, as Kozol (1991) so tellingly suggests, then we make ourselves vulnerable to the exploration of how we have "earned" our positions of privilege.

The response to and defense against anxiety in urban systems take on many forms: fear of innovation, workaholism, political paralysis, turf wars, etc. among them. Filled with unacknowledged conflict and unworked authority issues, these complex systems generate a palpable intensity. Unexamined projective and introjective processes heighten the genuine sense of urgency, creating unrealistic fantasies about "corporate" models and "rescue" by outsiders.

We primarily collude in a fantasy that all children need the same knowledge that can be imparted in a low-cost way and measured without need for interpretation. As a result, we blindly seek the "one best system" via standardized curricula or high-stakes testing programs or contracts to private management companies that unconsciously perpetuate the idea of the one best student, usually white, usually in the upper echelon of the socioeconomic strata. The "politics of despair" influence and shape the social defenses of related institutions, making foundations cautious, advocacy organizations strident, corporations aggressive, unions intractable, and schools of education impotent. This increased anxiety and more rigid social systems defense structure creates massive resistance to any systemic change that threatens the individuals with being overrun by anxiety.

When we look across the education industry as a whole, however, the adult anxiety is managed in the adult subsystems via these various social defenses. Like the administrators in Menzies's (1975) study, educational leaders in all sectors express concern about the failures of the system, but it is the students (like the patients in Menzies's study) who suffer the immediate consequences of the loss of the primary task. Adult "work" in education can, and does, grind forward for decades.

Simply put, the core of every successful effort for urban students replicates the way children of privilege are educated. Poor children succeed when they are placed at the center of their educational experience and treated as if they are valuable. Adults in these schools sufficiently manage their own anxiety about race, poverty, and merit to create environments that are less conflicted about the "ability" of poor children of color. The success of these students dramatically increases the anxiety of some adults, however, activating material from our own schooling experiences and unmasking fundamental inconsistencies in our lives and politics.[2]

The Leap to Transformation

As we imagine our world in fifty years, further and dramatic change appears certain. If current trends continue, we can anticipate advances in technology that dislocate employment in whole sectors of the economy such as farming and manufacturing (Rivkin, 1995). We can anticipate further expansion of the service- and Internet-driven economies and wonder which "consumers" in the "second" and "third" worlds will have the capacity to consume the "services" provided by the "first" world. Our demographics and social constructs grow increasingly diverse. Who knows what we can anticipate with confidence, except more change? If futurists such as Coates and Jarrett (1992), Davis (2001), and Lewis (2001) are believed, the next generation must be better at learning, at managing diversity, peacemaking, and at making tough decisions about resources. This prescription fulfills Newman's mid-1970s prophecy that adults are now responsible for teaching a set of skills that we do not yet have. This demand only increases the cultural anxiety about young people and their education.

These continued changes, affecting both the children to be educated and the society in which we all live, will complicate the tasks of educators and the role they play preparing tomorrow's generations to take up their responsibilities. The adaptive challenge (Heifetz, 1994) for our society is to anticipate the vast and pervasive changes in the economic, political, and social fabric of our society; to end a set of ingrained practices that create inequity; and to create approaches to teaching and learning that develop and disseminate an evolving set of skills for graduates of the classes of 2020 and those of 2050.

The hypothesis we offer about anxiety and schooling is easily tested, namely, by taking better advantage of the opportunities already available to explore and metabolize strong affect. Schools offer a disturbing wealth of moments that invite us to consider and confront the tensions and dynamics in our world. We must stop denying irrationality and unconscious material and start using it as information that can fuel and support change.

The recommendations that follow are not proposed policies or models, but rather ideas that invite participation in conversation, reflection, and action. These ideas operate at the individual, group, and systems levels, within and beyond schools and education systems. They operate simultaneously in the realm of psychology and in the domain of education. These suggestions have the potential to influence the source of anxiety, despite the fact that the experience may "feel bad" as the psychic numbing wears off (Lifton, 1974).

They also provide a benchmark to evaluate more technical school reform initiatives, such as standards, high-stakes testing, or small schools. We need to question whether the proposed idea actually helps the system cope with anxiety in the system (a strategy designed to deal with the source of conflict) or does it promote stronger defenses against anxiety (ignore sources while relieving the discomfort of some). In fact, as our Group Relations experiences suggest, a solution that feels good may indicate that critical underlying issues are being neglected. Seven recommendations follow.

1. Do our own internal work about education. It is critical that we understand the "institution of the mind," the story of school that we each carry from childhood and project onto schools today. To do this we must turn inward and grapple with our own experiences in school especially related to merit and equity. The tools of psychoanalytic mindfulness can help us confront our internalized constructs of learning and schooling. It is unthinkable that family

therapists could do their work without intense understanding of their own family dynamics, and yet thousands of policy workers, advocates, and educators go about their daily activities with no sense of the impact of their own childhood or schooling on their efforts. At the same time, many clinicians work intensely with individual and organizational clients without exploring their defensive strategies about schooling and "privilege" in their character structure. Personal narrative is an amazingly rich data source. People of all ages, socioeconomic, and racial/ethnic backgrounds must start telling their schooling experience to develop and deepen an accurate understanding of "education-as-a-whole."

2. Risk caring more about urban education. Other than Columbine, or sensationalized media coverage about the achievement gap, or the situation of our own child, many of us know very little about education. We may feel content to ignore public education or too overwhelmed to investigate. Others of us have many facts and yet know few students, teachers, or administrators. One might consider building a relationship with a local school, teacher network, or parent group. One could offer to facilitate team-building experiences, reflective practice groups, or support groups for new teachers. We could find ways to learn about the specific pulls and pressures in dependency-oriented organizations. As we relinquish our "expert status" or "privileged role" we experience firsthand the projective and introjective processes that surround these groups on a daily basis.

3. Create external holding environments for difficult conversations. The historic complex issues of education like race, change, varieties of school improvement, role of faith communities, and so forth, are often split into black or white, "as if" one right solution exists. A new cadre of "friends of education" could strive to resist the tremendous environmental pressures to join the process of splitting and projection. This new cadre could create opportunities to bring the fragmented parts together, assisting individuals and groups to hold complex ideas about issues of educational change such as the Public Conversations Project (2000). The goal is to help each community develop the capacity to hold multiple perspectives for the development of solutions. Schools of education, faith communities, and local education funds can offer valuable spaces for this kind of work.

4. Create internal structures for working through anxiety. Districts working toward systemic reform quickly discover that any action that brings genuine improvement will require working through

unconscious material. These districts must change policies and practices while simultaneously responding to the various strong community reactions in ways that metabolize, rather than collude with, the anxiety the changes bring. When we consult with superintendents, foundations, school boards, principals, or parent groups involved in these efforts, it is essential that we make apparent the power of interventions that confront rather than evade the realistic anxiety of our task (Schall, 1995). Most educators are more familiar with the compliant, non-confrontative culture that has characterized most of the field. In general, strategies include encouraging these groups to build dialogue and reflective processes into their daily work, even though it will seem foreign and initially disruptive; reminding them that the ability to work with conflict is a skill that systems can and must develop; consultants can support them in this over time; encouraging schools and districts to develop internal mechanisms like family groups for students (Powell, Barry, and Davis, 1997) and SEED seminars for faculty (McIntosh and Style, 1994).

5. Work "the evaded curriculum" (American Association of University Women, 1992) in public. The history of American public education has always been about whose children, whose values, and who pays. It has always been about power, and that is increasingly difficult to explore inside schools because of the defensive conversations around high-stakes testing and curriculum standards. We must, therefore, begin the conversation beyond the school walls and create ways to talk about the curriculum of power. Race, class, and gender are so closely woven into the education "institution in the mind" that they have been rendered unspeakable in public, especially around whiteness and privilege. Public policy efforts create opportunities for these conversations: Fiscal equity questions and disaggregated data around achievement are ripe issues that have internal, psychological referents as well as external realistic consequences. Educators holding formal authority may not be able to risk these explosive conversations, but those outside of the system might use our informal authority to open them.

6. Create and support clinical programs for educators. Groups are fundamental throughout education and its organizational processes. Even the primary context of learning, the classroom, is essentially a group fraught with matters of the unconscious, authority, and leadership. In addition, much of the work of school reform moves forward in groups: staff meetings, leadership teams, school site councils, parent advisory committees, and so forth. Thus, with groups

serving such an integral part of the educational process, it is critical that teacher preparation and leadership development programs prepare graduates with skills to understand and intervene in group dynamics. Teacher preparation and leadership development programs must have access to Group Relations experience to prepare future educators for the intensity of the unconscious. Students in our courses routinely say experiential learning should be required for those interested in school reform. Change agents must be inoculated against the force of the irrationality in our school systems. We can create opportunities for psychoanalytically informed Group Relations training and ongoing postconference application groups available to all stakeholders involved in education.[3]

7. Imagine alternatives. We need to join our families, psychotherapy patients, and corporate coaching clients in envisioning alternatives, both in our consultations and in our teaching. This starts first in ourselves, as we create internal images of public schools that serve all children well. If needed, we confront rather than avoid the anxiety that inevitably emerges: Fantasies of scarcity, and of new forms of competition, of an inevitable confrontation with the entertainment/violence complex, and so forth. We must examine the current dynamics of authority, learning, and innovation as they operate in the public sector. Render the idea of successful public schools visible and palpable.

An Unfortunately Predictable Future

From the earliest days of the westward expansion of the United States, the myth of the new frontier has been tied inextricably to our philosophical roots in Manifest Destiny (O'Sullivan, 1845). Just as we abandoned one homestead whose fields had grown fallow to move onto better, fertile land, we continue to quit our struggling schools in search of something better. While much of this philosophy accounts for our success as a nation, ever striving toward new opportunity, it also reflects our failure to face the implications of our actions.

Those with the resources and mobility to leave behind one life or home for another reap the best of choices, while those without are left behind to make the best of their circumstances, in fields (or schools) that have been drained of resources and hope (Stephanson, 1995). As long as those who hold the power and resources can move on to a new and better school, there will be no need to improve the failing school or to save the children we are failing. And yet, at the same time that we continue to split our children between successes and failures, do we not also perpetuate the American Dream of providing something better for our children?

The recent fascination with school choice and privatization schemes reflects the complexity of this dynamic. Dissatisfied with the test scores, dropout rates, and the reports of violence, educators and policymakers are seeking solutions to the woes of the public school by moving outside of the traditional public system. This has triggered a heated debate that has brought to the surface the questions of the fundamental inequity of the system (Coons and Sugarman, 1978). The proponents of vouchers and charter schools are drawn from opposite sides of traditional political alliances. At the same time that fundamentalist Christians seek the right to use public tuition dollars to send their children to private religious schools and African American parents demand vouchers and charter schools as a way of gaining enriching, quality schooling options for their children, conservative Republicans regard them as a vehicle to advance their free market ideas. We can understand this uneasy alliance as the intersection within a shared policy sphere of competing agendas (Barber, 1999) that pervades the larger schooling system as a whole.

Privatization can be understood as a dual mechanism supported by multiple communities with divergent agendas. While some leaders of the African American community tout vouchers and other forms of privatization as part of the ongoing civil rights movement (King, 1999; Holt, 2000), researchers are frequently discovering that the families who choose charter or private schools or vouchers and other forms of scholarship tend to be better educated, wealthier, and more involved in their children's lives than their peers (Fuller and Elmore, 1996). And is this any different from the phenomenon Kozol (1991) described in our most desperate schools? If we merely seek new reform models, changing only the terrain in which that policy is enacted, then the failings of our public education system, the splitting and manufacture of savage inequalities, will simply be imported into the new model. Until we face the unconscious system we are continually recreating, the pursuit of the new frontier on the backs of poor students and students of color, then our education reforms will continue to offer only technical solutions that function as the next social defense.

While we acknowledge that issues of politics and resources are crucial, the psychodynamics of change offer a means of understanding the paradigm in which these policies are resources and are created and deployed (Kuhn, 1962). Exploration of the irrational processes of social systems is not a panacea. History suggests, however, that no intervention will be effective in improving education for all children unless we become more competent in the management of these powerful dynamics. White (2001) recently noted that, in large measure, "the psychoanalytic enterprise" has been a success in this country. Ideas like covert process, the unconscious, interest in dreams, etc. are well established and often embraced within mainstream culture. We need to move this more deeply into the discourse of school change.

Change agents today require a complex set of interdisciplinary analytic, political, and interpersonal skills that will not be developed without substantial shifts in how we think about adult development, about learning, and about schools as organizations. The policies and programs we implement attempt to "fix" failing schools but ignore the fundamental split reality that characterizes our education system. This division exists within us, our schools, and our communities. We split our competencies and our failings, our hope and our despair, our opportunities and our disappointments. We project the good, the successful, the limitless potential onto the suburban and private schools populated by the middle and upper socio-economic groups. At the same time, we push away the damage, crime, violence, and hopelessness onto the urban schools of the poor and often of color students.

What we need is not just the half-hearted implementation of the next technical innovation for its own sake, but processes and opportunities that give children and adults new skills. We can be better prepared to work through the anxiety that accompanies any transformation in structure, process, or language at the systemic level. In order to change the system we have perpetuated since the early days of schooling in America, we must do more than acknowledge injustice; we must do the internal work to recognize our role in this injustice and to make meaning of how we can benefit from confronting it.[4]

Notes

1. For our education colleagues who would like a parallel single-volume introduction to psychological issues in groups and organizations, we recommend the 1987 Smith and Berg classic, "Paradoxes of Group Life: Understanding Conflict, Paralysis and Movement in Group Dynamics."

2. A most compelling example of resistance, from the point of group relations theory, is the issue of school size. The research is absolutely uncontroverted that poor children of color learn more, persist longer, and create safer schools than their counterparts in the (typically large) urban high school (most recently see Fine and Sommerville, 1998; Wasley et al., 2000). And yet, no district has made a realistic commitment to smaller schools as a driver of systemic reform. Our hypothesis is that these smaller units are more effective because they provide a sufficient container (Kahn, 1993a) to contain and work through the various organizational conflicts raised by academic

excellence and intellectual prowess in poor children of color (Powell, 2000). However, few systems are structured to manage the anxiety provoked by routine or predictable success of "these" children.

3. The University of San Diego and the School District of Del Paseo Heights, California, offer contrasting avenues for providing this kind of clinical training. Theresa Monroe, R.S.C.J., directs a group relations conference for graduate students in education leadership as well as aspiring principals. Carl Mack, Ph.D., directs an annual conference for school district employees, parents, and community members.

4. Many thanks to all of our group relations colleagues who commented on and contributed to this chapter.

References

Alderfer, C. (1980). Consulting to underbounded systems. In C. P. Alderfer & C. L. Cooper (Eds.), *Advances in experiential social processes* (pp. 267–278). New York: John Wiley & Sons.

American Association of University Women. (1992). *How schools shortchange girls: A study of major findings on girls and education.* Washington, DC: AAUW Educational Foundation, The Wellesley College Center for Research on Women.

Bailey, S. and Campbell, P. (1992–1993, Winter). Gender equity: The unexamined basic of school reform. *Stanford Law & Policy Review, 4*, 73–86.

Banet, A. G., Jr., & Hayden, C. (1977). The Tavistock primer. In J. E. Jones & J. W. Pfeiffer (Eds.), *The 1977 handbook for group facilitators* (pp. 155–167). La Jolla, CA: University Associates.

Banks, J. (1988). *Multi ethnic education theory and practice.* Boston: Allyn & Bacon.

Barber, M. E. (1999). Educational vouchers and democracy in education. Unpublished manuscript, Teachers College, Columbia University, New York.

Bion, W.R. (1961). *Experiences in groups.* New York: Basic Books.

Block, A. (1997). *I'm only bleeding: Education as the practice of social violence against children.* New York: Peter Lang.

Bowles, S., & Gintis, H. (1976). *Schooling in capitalist America.* New York: Basic Books.

Campaign for Fiscal Equity. (2001, January) Special report: The trial court's decision" In *Evidence: Policy reports from the CFE trial,* 3.

Carnoy, M., & Levin, H. M. (1985). *Schooling and work in the democratic state.* Stanford, CA: Stanford University Press.

CFE v. State of New York (1995), No. 117, Court of Appeals of New York, 2d 307.

Coates, J. F., & Jarrett, J. (Eds.). (1992). *The future: Trends into the twenty-first century.* Newbury Park, CA: Sage.

Cohen, M. (1999, September 19). Making a case for school equality: Sizer's new book asks tough questions about the education the poor in America are receiving. *Boston Globe,* p. H5.

Coles, R. (1994). *The call of service: A witness to idealism.* Boston: Houghton Mifflin.

Coons, J. E., & Sugarman, S. D. (1978). *Education by choice: The case for family control*. Berkeley, CA: University of California Press.

Cremin, L. A. (1951). *The American common school: An historic conception*. New York: Teachers College Press.

Cytrynbaum, S. (1999). Personal communication.

Darling-Hammond, L. (1997). *The right to learn*. San Francisco: Jossey-Bass.

Davis, S. (2001). *Lessons from the future: Making sense of a blurred world from the world's leading futurist*. Dover, NH: Capstone Publishing.

Delpit, L. (1995). *Other people's children*. New York: New Press.

Edelman, M. W. (2000). *Guide my feet: Prayers and meditations for our children*. New York: HarperCollins.

Eisold, K. (1997, Spring). The task of leadership: Leadership as an attribute of group life. *ADE Bulletin, 116*.

Elmore, R. (2000). Remarks at meeting of Public Education Network, Washington, DC.

Erikson, E. H. (1950). *Childhood and society*. New York: Norton.

Fine, M. (Ed.). (1994a). *Chartering urban school reform: Reflections on public high schools in the midst of change*. New York: Teachers College Press.

Fine, M. (1994b). Remarks at Winter Roundtable in Social Psychology, Teachers College, New York.

Fine, M. (1994c). *Framing dropouts: Notes on the politics of an urban public high school*. Albany, NY: State University of New York Press.

Fine, M., & Somerville, J. I. (Eds.). (1998). *Small schools, big imaginations: A creative look at urban public schools*. Chicago: Cross City Campaign for Urban School Reform.

Fuller, B., & Elmore, R. (Eds.). (1996). *Who chooses, who loses? Culture, institutions, and the unequal effects of school choice*. New York: Teachers College Press.

Giles, H. C. (2001). Transforming the deficit narrative: Race, class and social capital in parent-school relations. In C. Korn & A. Bursztyn (Eds.), *Re-thinking multi-cultural education: Case studies in cultural transition*: (pp. 130–159). Westport, CT: Greenwood Press.

Gutmann, D., Pierre, R., Ternier-David, J., & Verrier, C. (1997). The Paths of authority: From the unconscious to the transcendental. Intervention at the Arab University of Jerusalem. In F. Avallone, J. Arnold & K. de Witte (Eds.), *Feelings work in Europe* (pp. 172–181). Milan: Guerini Studio.

Hayden, C., & Molenkamp, R. (2004). Tavistock Primer II. In S. Cytrynbaum & D. A. Noumair (Eds.), *Group Relations reader 3*. Jupiter, FL: A. K. Rice Institute.

Heifetz, R. (1994). *Leadership without easy answers*. Cambridge, MA: Belknap Press of Harvard University Press.

Hess, G. A. (1995). *Restructuring urban schools: A Chicago experience*. New York: Teachers College Press.

Hilfiker, D. (1994). *Not all of us are saints: A doctor's journey with the poor*. New York: Hill & Wang.

Hochschild, J. L. (1984). *The new American dilemma: Liberal democracy and school desegregation*. New Haven, CT: Yale University Press.

Holt, M. (2000). *Not yet "free at last": The unfinished battle of the civil rights movement: Our battle for school choice.* Oakland, CA: ICS Press.

Jaques, E. (1955). Social systems as a defense against persecutory and depression anxiety. In M. Klein, P. Heimann, & R. E. Money-Kyrle (Eds.), *New directions in psychoanalysis* (pp. 277–299). London: Tavistock.

Kahn, W. A. (1993a). Facilitating and undermining organizational change: A case study. *Journal of Applied Behavioral Science, 29*(1), 32–35.

Kahn, W. A. (1993b). Caring for the caregivers: Patterns of organizational care giving. *Administrative Science Quarterly, 38,* 539–563.

Kegan, R. (1995). *In over our heads: The mental demands of modern life.* New York: W. W. Norton.

Kessler, R. (2000). *The soul of education: Helping students find connection, compassion and character at school.* Alexandria, VA: Association for Supervision and Curriculum Development.

King, M. L., III. (1999). Introductory remarks to Teachers College, Columbia University and Columbia University Law School students for Ted Forstmann Lecture. December 1, 1999.

Kozol, J. (1991). *Savage inequalities.* New York: Crown.

Kris, E. (1952). *Psychoanalytic explorations in art.* New York: International Universities Press.

Kuhn, T. (1962). *Structure of scientific revolutions.* Chicago: University of Chicago Press.

Lasn, K. (2000). *Culture jam: How to reverse America's suicidal consumer binge— And why we must.* New York: Quill.

Lewis, M. (2001). *Next: The future just happened.* New York: W. W. Norton.

Lifton, R. J. (1974). *Home from the war: Neither victims nor executioners.* New York: Simon & Schuster.

Loeb, P. R. (1999). *Soul of a citizen: Living with conviction in a cynical time.* New York: St. Martin's Press.

Mack, C. (1995). *Leadership and improving school performance in a multi-ethnic, cultural, and linguistic public school district: There's going to be bedlam if we get 'em.* Sacramento, CA: AKRI Scientific Meeting Proceedings.

Massachusetts Department of Education. (2001). Report of 2000 Massachusetts and local school district MCAS results by race/ethnicity. July 2001 [Online]. Available: http://www.doe.mass.edu/mcas/ 00results/rande.pdf.

McIntosh, P., & Style, E. (1994). Faculty-centered faculty development. In L. Crosier & P. Bassett (Eds.), *Looking ahead: Independent school issues and answers.* Gilsum, NH: Avocus.

Meier, D. (1995). *The power of their ideas: Lessons for America from a small school in Harlem.* Boston: Beacon Press.

Menzies, I. E. P. (1975). A case-study in the functioning of social systems as a defense against anxiety. In A. D. Colman & W. H. Bexton (Eds.), *Group relations reader I* (pp. 281–312). Washington, DC: A. K. Rice Institute.

Merrill Lynch. (1999, April 9). *The book of knowledge.* New York: Merrill Lynch.

Miller, E. J., & Rice, A. K. (1975). Selections from: "Systems of organization." In A. D. Colman & W. H. Bexton (Eds.), *Group Relations reader I* (pp. 43–68). Washington, DC: A. K. Rice Institute.

Minow, N. N., & LeMay, C. L. (1995). *Abandoned in the wasteland: Children, television, and the first amendment.* New York: Hill & Wang.

Monroe, T. (2001). Director's Conference Summary from Chaos, Courage, and Change; A group relations workshop in conjunction with the UCLA Center for the Study of Organizational Group Dynamics, January 12–14, 2001.

Mosley, W. (2000). *Workin' on the chain gang: Shaking off the dead hand of history.* New York: Ballantine.

Newman, R. G. (1974). *Groups in schools.* New York: Simon & Schuster.

Obholzer, A., & Roberts, V. Z. (Eds.). (1994). *The unconscious at work: Individual and organizational stress in the human services.* London; New York: Routledge.

O'Sullivan, J. (1845). Annexation. *United States Magazine and Democratic Review, 17*(85–86), 5–10.

Palmer, P. J. (1997). *The courage to teach: Exploring the inner landscape of a teacher's life.* San Francisco: Jossey-Bass, Inc.

Payne, C. P. (2000). *So much reform, so little change: Building-level obstacles to urban school reform.* Evanston, IL: Institute for Policy Research at Northwestern University.

Powell, L. C. (1994). Interpreting social defenses: Family groups in an urban setting. In M. Fine (Ed.), *Chartering urban school reform: Reflections on public high schools in the midst of change* (pp. 112–121). New York: Teachers College Press.

Powell, L. C. (2000). Small schools and the issue of race. *Bank Street College of Education Occasional Paper Series*, 3:4 (pp. 5–13). New York: Bank Street College.

Powell, L.C. (2002). Labouring in the counter story factory: Experiential teaching about authority. *International Journal of Critical Psychology*, 5 (pp. 141–157).

Powell, L. C., Barry, M., & Davis, G. (1997). Facing reality: Family group in urban schools. In C. E. Thompson & R. T. Carter (Eds.), *Racial identity theory: Applications to individual, group, and organizational interventions* (pp. 147–158). Mahwah, NJ: Lawrence Erlbaum Associates.

Public Conversations Project [On-line]. Available: http://www.publicconversations.org.

Rice, A. K. (1970). *The modern university: A model organization.* London: Tavistock.

Richardson, E. (1975). Selections from: "The environment of learning." In A. D. Colman & W. H. Bexton (Eds.), *Group Relations reader I* (pp. 215–224). Washington, DC: A. K. Rice Institute.

Rioch, M. J. (1975). "All we like sheep" [Isaiah 53:6]: Followers and leaders. In A. D. Colman & W. H. Bexton (Eds.), *Group Relations reader I* (pp. 159–178). Washington, DC: A. K. Rice Institute.

Rivkin, J., & Heilbroner, R. L. (1995). *The end of work: The decline of the global labor force and the dawn of the post-market era.* New York: G.P. Putnam's Sons.

Sarason, S. B. (1990). *The predictable failure of educational reform*. San Francisco: Jossey-Bass.

Schall, E. (1995). Learning to love the swamp: Reshaping education for public service. *Journal of Policy Analysis and Management, 14*(2), 202–220.

Schlosser, A., & Kanfer, A. (2000). Culture clash in Internet marketing. In M. J. Shaw, R. Blanning, T. Strader & A. Whinston (Eds.), *Handbook on electronic commerce* (pp. 195–211). New York: Springer Verlag.

Shapiro, E. R., & Carr, A. W. (1991). *Lost in familiar places: Creating new connections between the individual and society*. New Haven, CT: Yale University Press.

Sizer, T. R. (1985). *Horace's compromise: The dilemma of the American high school*. Boston: Houghton Mifflin.

Smith, K. K., & Berg, D. N. (1987). *Paradoxes of group life: Understanding conflict, paralysis, and movement in group dynamics*. San Francisco: Jossey Bass.

Smith, K. K., Simmons, V. M., & Thames, T. B. (1989). "Fix the women": An intervention into an organizational conflict based on parallel process thinking. *Journal of Applied Behavioral Science, 25*(1), 11–29.

Spence, H., & Powell, L. C. (2001). Group relations and education reform. Seminar presentation at Human Relations for Leaders: A Group Relations Working Conference, April 2001.

Stephanson, A. (1995). *Manifest destiny: American expansionism and the empire of right*. New York: Hill & Wang.

Style, E. (1998, April 7). Personal communication.

Style, E., & Powell, L. C. (1995, Fall). In our own hands: A diversity primer. In *Transformations, 2*, 65–84.

Tyack, D. B. (1974). *The one best system*. Cambridge, MA: Harvard University Press.

Tyack, D. B., & Cuban, L. (1995). *Tinkering toward utopia: A century of public school reform*. Cambridge, MA: Harvard University Press.

Ward, T. (1995). *Classroom containment of hostile gang irrationality can be transformed into student learning*. Sacramento, CA: AKRI Scientific Meeting Proceedings.

Wasley, P., Fine, M., Gladden, M., Holland, N. E., King, S. P., Mosak, E., & Powell, L. C. (2000). Executive summary: Small schools: Great strides: A study of new small schools in Chicago. New York: Bank Street College.

Wells, L., Jr. (1985). The group-as-a-whole perspective and its theoretical roots. In A. D. Colman & M. H. Geller (Eds.), *Group Relations reader 2* (pp. 109–126). Washington, DC: A. K. Rice Institute.

White, E. (1996). Finding voice: Gender, race, and authority in new school leaders. Paper presented at Tenth Annual Women in Educational Leadership Conference, Lincoln, NE, September 1996.

White, E. (2000). Not too hot to handle: Pushing issues of gender, race, and authority beyond consciousness-raising in faculty development. Paper presented at American Anthropology Association Annual Conference, San Francisco, CA, November 2000.

White, E., & Bernard, H. (1986, March–June). The relationship between person-role conflict and systemic dysfunction. *Group and Organizational Studies: An International Journal*, 1–31.

White, K. P. (2001, September 2). Personal communication.
Wolff, M. J. (1999). *The entertainment economy: How media forces are transforming our lives*. New York: Crown.

Scenes from the Black Couch

Film: *Dottie Gets Spanked*

Paired chapters: *On the Vicissitudes of Love and Hate: Anne Sexton's
Pedagogy of Loss and Reparation* by Paula M. Salvio
Mother Love's Education by Alice Pitt

Throughout the essays written by Alice Pitt and Paula Salvio maternal figures circulate, each of whom exceeds conventional expectations for being
nurturing. Salvio writes of poet Anne Sexton, who presents as a loving
and destructive force in her home. The mothers appearing in the essay by
Pitt are excluded from history and denied the debt owed to them for the
reproduction of the species, for human creativity and knowledge. Each of
these essays raises difficult questions about the anxieties provoked by the
maternal figure in the context of teaching and learning.

A troubling and troubled maternal figure likewise emerges in Todd
Haynes's 1993 semiautobiographical film, *Dottie Gets Spanked*. This film
combines Freud's 1919 essay, "A Child Is Being Beaten" with a Lucille
Ball-like character in a 1960s narrative about how a shy, sensitive six-year-
old boy named Steven Gale becomes privately fixated on spanking. The

prohibition on spanking in Steven's family—"We just don't believe in hitting"—is announced by his mother to a neighbor early in the film. This ban is in marked contrast to the life of Dottie, Steven's favorite television character. *The Dottie Show* closely recreates the 1960s television hit *The Lucille Ball Show*, and like Lucy, Dottie is spanked for her transgressions. The collision of these scenes with the family prohibition provokes a tireless tug at Steven's imagination, and begins to figure prominently in his dreams and drawings. Each evening, Steven sits dutifully in front of the television screen, lovingly drawing his idol, Dottie, in crayon, much to his mother's naïve delight and the growing concern of his athletic-minded father. In fact, Steven's father becomes more and more anxious as his son becomes more and more obsessed with "everything Dottie": hairstyles, wigs, makeup, and spanking. Eventually, Steven wins a magazine competition to visit *The Dottie Show* during an episode taping. His mother is delighted, while his father begins to express stronger feelings of disgust.

In the commentary track that accompanies the DVD release of this film, Todd Haynes describes how during his own 1960s childhood, he met his idol, Lucille Ball, under similar circumstances. Whatever drawings Haynes did not give Lucy at the time were used as primary source material for Steven's drawings of Dottie. Like Steven, little Haynes lived in a world dominated by his obsessions with female stars, and was even questioned about his gender palette by friends: "Why do you only draw pictures of women?" Asked one child, "Are you bad at men?"

Once in the studio, Steven witnesses a different side of Dottie. She is not simply the passive woman of *The Dottie Show*; she is at times active, domineering, and even playfully bossy. Above all else, she is a shrewd businesswoman, and she is not timid about stepping into the role of director to improve a scene. In a review of this film, Daniel Mudie Cunningham aptly notes that Dottie is invested with a "bottom" that holds all the power on the set. Afterwards, Dottie begins to figure in Steven's dreams as "a terrifying masculine force, one that arouses a sexual awakening he doesn't fully comprehend."

At first, the figure of Steven's mother in *Dottie Gets Spanked* takes on the status of the Winnicottian "good enough mother." She is responsive to her son's interests, and she protects him from his father's aggression. But there is a turning point in the film, a moment when the mother turns away from her son, and absorbs her husband's anxieties entirely. Steven knows she has abandoned him. At this moment, Steven decides to bury his drawings and his obsessions under the tree in the backyard. This burial is both literal and symbolic, and in our estimation, it speaks, not only to the demand that children bury what is culturally perceived as their transgressive desires but also to the demand that maternal authority must be tamed as well. Steven's mother establishes her recognizable domesticated status when she takes her place alongside her husband.

As you place this film alongside the essays written by Alice Pitt and Paula Salvio, we recommend returning to an issue raised by Freud's essay, "A Child Is Being Beaten," and portrayed in varied degrees by our authors: the issue of our imagining of Others, and violence to others; what we might perhaps identify as the element of pleasure in Freud's fantasy-structure. What forms of pleasure are felt upon destruction of the mother or in the child's transgressive desires? Like our authors, Haynes seems to suggest that to imagine violence against anyone is to register an actual violence against oneself, and the shame of that violence is carried across the generations as a perversion of love. Several questions surface when placing these essays alongside this film: What perversions of love are we most attached to as educators? What harm do we do in the name of education, and at what points in our pedagogical practices do we bury the authority associated with maternal desire?

CHAPTER 3

On the Vicissitudes of Love and Hate

Anne Sexton's Pedagogy of Loss and Reparation

PAULA M. SALVIO

Prologue

Anne Sexton is most often remembered as a Pulitzer Prize–winning poet who, in her poetry, "confessed" the anguish of depression, addiction, and a suicidal mother's love for her daughters. She filled the most tightly wrought of poetic forms—the lyric—with characters and plots about adultery, death, and the myths encrypted in what she referred to as the Gothic New England family romance, spinning haunting tales out of ordinary life in the suburbs. In her low, husky smoker's voice, standing at the podium in her elegant red reading dress, shoes off, drink in hand, Sexton would lodge her complaint at the misery of American middle-class women, ironically making use of middle-class style.

Her poetry foregrounds the female body, particularly the female medical body, by making a spectacle of the culture of beauty, domesticity, psychiatry, and medicine. The bodies in Sexton's poetry are plagued with disease, feelings of abandonment, madness, and the anguish of losing family, lovers, and ideals. Sexton's bodies are broken; they endure the pain of starving, bloated stomachs (1981, p. 370), sagging midriffs and splintered hips; they are "strung out" by the poet, "as if they were still reaching for each other" (1981, p. 23).

It is possible, as her biographer, Diane Wood Middlebrook suggests, to read Sexton's complete work of poetry as a narrative—an autobiography if you will—about a character named Anne who was born to privilege in the New England suburb of Newton, Massachusetts, on November 9, 1928. She married, had a child in 1953, and struggled with the physical and psychological demands of an infant. Sexton gave birth to another daughter in 1955, only to slide into what she described as "terrible spells of depression." She felt agitated, disoriented, and subject to feeling "unreal" (see Middlebrook, 1991, p. 31). Diagnosed with postpartum depression, she took medications and pursued therapy with the psychoanalyst Dr. Martha Brunner-Orne and, still, her condition continued to worsen. Sexton began to seize her daughter Linda, to choke and slap her, and she feared that she was incapable of controlling such destructive outbursts. In November, one day before her twenty-eighth birthday, alone at home, Sexton made the first of many suicide attempts; she was eventually to end her life at her own hand 19 years later.

Despite this serious mental illness that defied diagnosis and cure, Sexton managed to summon up enough resilience and strength to win almost all the prestigious awards available to American poets, including the Pulitzer and Shelley prizes. She was published in major popular literary magazines and newspapers such as *Esquire* and the *New York Times*, and became a regular contributor to the *New Yorker*. She became one of the highest-paid poetry performers in America and, as Middlebrook points out, she cleverly brought poetry to public audiences who ordinarily found it dull. Sexton also secured teaching positions for herself at a time when it was unusual to find women teaching in higher education. What often goes unnoticed about Sexton is that in the face of her continual struggles with mental illness, addictions, and an education that she has described as anemic—her formal education ended at Garland Junior College—Sexton developed a reputation as a dedicated teacher, eventually rising to the rank of professor at Boston University. In addition to teaching at Boston University, Sexton taught poetry at McLean Psychiatric Hospital, Colgate University, and Wayland High School in Wayland, Massachusetts. Her collaboration with Herbert Kohl and the Teachers and Writers Collaborative in the 1960s made significant contributions to revitalizing English education, in part by initiating teaching partnerships among writers, artists, and teachers.

Despite the substantial collection of lecture notes, correspondences with students, and journals that Sexton left behind, the remains of her teaching life are rarely addressed, nor have their implications for classroom pedagogy and curriculum been explored. This chapter, which is part of a larger, book-length project on the life and pedagogy of Anne Sexton, does not offer a biographical portrait of Anne Sexton. Rather, it literally performs a method of writing auto/biographically in which Sexton functions as an interlocutor, indirectly illuminating the gender, sexual, and cultural struggles that influence our conscious and unconscious interests, and therefore inevitably are expressed in our scholarship, and our teaching. Throughout this chapter, I analyze Sexton's teaching life and her confessional writings in light of her attempts to resist the normalizing effects of the "cures" that are prescribed for Sexton, whether these cures take the form of the culture of domesticity and motherhood, criticism of the content and style of her poetry, or questions about her comportment as a teacher and a writer.

In the following pages, I analyze how the psychic dilemmas that Anne Sexton faced as a mother influenced her teaching life. I argue that Sexton suffered in part from middle-class demands put on women in post–World War II America to be what psychoanalyst D. W. Winnicott (1987) described as "the good enough mother." Despite the intentions of Winnicott to lower the bar on the demands placed on women when faced with ideals of "good mothering," I argue that the position of the good enough mother requires women to overwrite their own desires with those of their children, and to deny the rage, pain, fear, and ambivalence that is an inevitable part of mothering. My analysis builds on the scholarship of Wendy Atwell-Vasey (1998), Valerie Walkerdine (1991), and Madeleine Grumet (1988), who elaborate on the specific ways in which the ideals of motherhood have affected educators' notions of what it means to be a good teacher, and how such goodness is assessed.

Moving from Sexton's life as a mother to her life as a teacher, I consider how the idea of the good enough mother structures the work of teaching. I turn to Sexton's teaching to suggest that her pedagogy critiques and exceeds the categories of both "good enough mother" and "good enough teacher," offering possibilities for recognizing alterity (Alain-Miller, 1988) and making reparation for both the teacher and the students.

This is not a romantic story; I will not ignore the difficult story of the pain that Sexton experienced or that she inflicted on those who loved her. In exploring the possibility of reparation in writing and teaching, I consider the project of cultivating a "true self," for women who, like Sexton, have experienced what I will refer to as subtle, "as yet unnamed" traumas. Because language fails in the presence of trauma, but is simultaneously recognized as the very medium through which a survivor can heal, trauma poses difficult rhetorical challenges to self-representation. How can a person represent a self in writing and teaching when that self longs for a place to hide so as to avoid shame, scrutiny, dismissal, or humiliation? How can anyone who has experienced the intolerable pain of trauma represent a "true" self? Can trauma be spoken about in any mode other than the literal?

To address these questions, I read the lecture notes that Sexton wrote while teaching at Boston and Colgate Universities as exemplary of a pedagogy of reparation that works to make good the injuries she experienced and to repair the injuries she inflicted upon her family. The work of reparation unfolds on the other side of hate and loss. It calls upon us to live within the tension of opposites: love and hate, anxiety and composure, desire and responsibility, the will to hide and be known, to create and destroy. The lecture notes of Anne Sexton present us with meditations on how personal modes of address—in teaching and in writing—can give coherent form to despair and the sense of disorganization inflicted by trauma by working at a distance from the normative conventions of the autobiographical *I*. Sexton's refrain, "I am often being personal, but I'm not being personal about myself," indeed refers to the stipulation that autobiography pertain to the unique and the conventionally representative. But Sexton does not offer her readers or her students a rational representative *I*; rather, she crafts a range of masks and personae to articulate what the normative narratives in postwar America could not contain. Her personae displace the notion of an autobiographical *I* that is far too limiting to tell the story of a life tied to family secrets, violence, and shame. In interviews and in conversations with her students and colleagues, Sexton suggests that she used the act of composing poetry to resist a merger with death, and to work toward restoring profound psychological injuries. She openly spoke of how she turned to teaching to offer relief for others who suffered with acute depression and suicidal ideations. "Poetry led me by the hand out of madness," Sexton wrote to Eugenia Plunkett, a student with whom she worked while teaching a poetry course at McLean Psychiatric Hospital. "I am hoping that I can show others that route" (HRHRC).

I

Anne Sexton has a particular purchase on the image of the suicidal female poet who failed as a mother and wife. Consider these accounts from *Searching for Mercy Street: A Journey Back to My Mother*, written by Sexton's daughter Linda Grey Sexton. It is an autumn weeknight and Linda is eight years old. A dinner of calves' liver and baked potatoes is over. Sexton is sitting at the table, smoking, twirling her hair, and, as Linda recalls, "stirring the melting ice in her martini with her finger" (1994). This evening, there will be a violent fight that begins because Sexton wants Linda to do the dishes. Sexton's husband, Kayo, becomes angry. He accuses Sexton of "just not wanting to do them herself." Their "discussion," which is the family euphemism for "fight," deteriorates. And in the midst of their arguing, Sexton screams at Kayo, "Go ahead and hit me. It'd be a relief to have you kill me" (1994, p. 45). This evening, Sexton accuses her husband of babying their children, dishes clatter, noises rise and fall as the rage between Anne and Kayo finally subsides amid their daughters' pleas for them to leave one another alone. The traces from evenings like this are evident in Linda's memoirs—but in order to locate the fear and anxiety that accrues there, one has to look beyond what is available to ordinary perception. One has to sustain an engagement with the image and what lies beyond it. One has to be willing to complicate what appears evident or straightforward.

What other narratives are housed in Linda's account? Throughout the texts there are the times when Sexton offered her children love and comfort in what Linda describes as the "proper proportion." In the following memory scene, it is late afternoon, and dusk settles in on this Thanksgiving day:

> Mother and I nestle beneath a thick wool afghan on top of the bed in Nana's bedroom. We are meant to be taking a nap, but, as usual, we are talking, sharing what we see and feel. Without knowing it, in this exchange of ideas and emotions Mother passes on to me her powers of observation; she shows me how to watch, how to see, how to record what transpires in the world around me. This is how I inherit her greatest gift..... The tree I have named the broccoli tree stands like a sentinel, silent and upright. It is not large, but it is sturdy and distinct. Mother's body curls around me in warm shelter. I am utterly cocooned. I am happy. Her fingers, long and lovely, trace a dance of tenderness across my face. Feelings become memories; this memory becomes emblematic, the truth of that particular day. (1994, p. 61)

Here, Sexton presents us with an emblem of the Winnicottian notion of the "good enough" mother who offers her child a "holding environment" that keeps the body of the child and parent distinct, but close. In stark contrast to the violent episodes between Sexton and Kayo that brought their daughters to tears, this scene portrays Linda nested in an intimate milieu. Sexton passes the time with Linda talking, actively observing, and recording the subtle details outside the bedroom window. Snuggling beneath a thick wool afghan, this mother and daughter feel fully alive in the presence of one another.

The closeness that Linda remembers is not an isolated incident. Linda's junior and high school years were decidedly different from earlier years, when her mother was overwhelmed with the demands of her infants. As a teenager, Linda would come home from school, and often find Sexton on the phone, "her legs propped high against the bookshelf in her writing room, tilted backward in her desk chair, smoking" (1994, p. 98). Sexton would hang up and together, they would review the day. Linda recalls discussing poetry over tea as she and her mother read Linda's drafts of poems. Linda knew full well that the sound of her mother's voice—its low throatiness combined with her fine sense of timing—could easily "make a bad line sound like a good line." "She was gentle—kind, really, with the lines that did not work, and never embarrassed me, even when I had written something truly terrible..." (1994, p. 97). Given the testimony offered by Sexton's daughters, it appears that she had the capacity to provide them with a secure, playful environment free from the weight of her depression and demands. As her daughter Joy notes what Sexton could not provide for her children, she made sure they obtained from others.

Nonetheless, as I review the materials documenting Sexton's relationship with her daughters—letters exchanged, Linda's memoir, transcripts from Sexton's psychiatric sessions with Dr. Orne—I find recurring narratives that raise concern about Sexton's place in the classroom. Anne Sexton did not solely suffer with alcoholism and depression. In the early years of her daughters' infancies, she feared that she would kill her children, and during Linda's adolescence, she made sexual use of her daughter's body. Linda recalls these early mornings with terror and disgust:

> I remember seventh grade, my first year of junior high, when I had to get up earlier than either Joy or Daddy to catch my bus. That spring, Mother was not sleeping well, and she often crept into my room just as the sun came around the corner of my window. Sliding between the covers, she pressed her long body against mine and I would wake to find her curled around me. Under the warm heap of covers, her naked belly and thighs pressed against my back and bare buttocks, my nightgown having bunched up around my waist during the night. As she rocked herself back and forth against me, her flesh damp and sticky, I closed my eyes and lay still, choking with disgust, my throat clenched against a scream I tamped down inside. I wanted to shove her away, but instead I waited for her to finish. The sound of that unvoiced scream echoes still inside my body. (1994, p. 107)

Linda can barely experience this trauma as it occurs, "I tamped down inside …" and later, during an interview with Middlebrook, she recalls "waiting for something to be over. I don't think I wanted to know what it was" (1991, p. 223). Sexton's act of violence against her daughter is in fact a repetition of an earlier violent act Sexton's father, Ralph Harvey, committed against her when she was a child. Years later, Sexton reported this abuse to Martin Orne in therapy.

Was Anne Sexton's compulsion to repeat this event a perverse confrontation with a trauma that had imposed itself again and again? In *Beyond the Pleasure Principle*, Freud reminds us of the Greek meaning of the word trauma—wound, originally referring to an injury on the body. But in his text, he uses this word to refer to a wound inflicted on the mind—a breach in the mind's experience of time, self, and the world. Thus trauma is not like a wound on the body, a physical and healable event. It is, as we learn from accounts of incestuous intrusions, a wound experienced too soon, too unexpectedly to be fully known. Trauma is therefore not available to consciousness until it imposes itself again, repeatedly, in the nightmares, flashbacks, and repetitive actions of the survivor (cf. Daly, 1998).

The double meaning of the word trauma—a wound to the mind or the body—raises difficult questions about the ways in which trauma affects memory, forgetting, and the capacity to narrate traumatic experience. In her study of the emotional and rhetorical challenges writers of autobiographical narratives face when they attempt to remember and organize traumatic experience, Lee Gilmore turns to the work of psychologist Jennifer Freyd to consider the logic and function of an apparent forgetting. How does memory influence the narrative accounts of trauma? Freyd argues that the logic driving a child's pull to forget a traumatic event involving a parent is an adaptive response to the anguish and betrayal of losing a parent or caregiver (1996). The parent kills himself or herself as a parent through the act of incest; the act of incest works, in fact, to create for the parent a place to hide from the child, leaving the child in the throes of a terrible, heartbreaking abandonment that is often resented more acutely than the abuse itself (see Judith Herman, 1993, p. 101). The experience of trauma endured by the child is often accompanied by a loss or disruption of memory that Freyd refers to as a "motivated forgetting." The child is not only motivated to forget the event, but once the parent is lost through incest, a part of the child disappears as well. The loss of a secure and reliable holding environment coupled with the sexual intrusion of a parental figure generates a stigmatized identity in the child, blatantly provoking her to hide her "true self," for, in the words of psychoanalyst D. W. Winnicott, "the true self has been traumatized and it must never be found and wounded again" (1987,

p. 33). To secure a sense of attachment with the abusive parent, the child persistently attempts to forget and be "good," becoming, as Judith Herman notes, "a superb performer.... She may become an empathic caretaker for her parents, an efficient housekeeper, an academic achiever, a model of social conformity" (1993, p. 105). Or, as with Anne Sexton, the daughter may take on the role of the father's interlocutor with whom she addresses questions of identity, death, destruction, and creativity. In such cases, the daughter both identifies with the abusive parent, and defies the parent. Whether the child becomes a superb performer, or the parent's interlocutor, what remains difficult is the capacity to "feel real."

In fact, the actions I describe above combine to form a "false self front" to cope with a painful and unpredictable world and to protect the "true self" that Winnicott associates with health and ingenuity. Thus, from the perspective of Winnicott, the true and false self exists within a field of concerns that must be negotiated within and against difficult emotions that include aggression, love, anxiety, loss, and fear. The use of a "false self front" to cope with the often inarticulate concerns provoked by incest offers the child a means through which to endure the loss of bodily integrity and the rupture in ordinary life, a rupture that defies the social conventions of bereavement, for cultural rituals provide little consolation for persons who have endured the trauma of incest and sexual abuse.[1]

I want to consider Anne Sexton's psychic predicament—her failure to be, in Winnicott's terms, a *good-enough mother*—as a failure brought about by an inherited melancholic strain, a loss that was attached to shameful acts of incest and intensified by the demands that post–World War II America placed on middle-class women to be "good enough" mothers, demands that often thrust women into states described by Michael Eigen as the "lost-I feeling."[2] The lost-I feeling that Eigen strives to capture feels so intruded upon and unable to breathe, so lost to the desires of others, that it hardens and contracts to the point of insensibility. Left with an impoverished sense of being, this sense of loss sabotages the trusted boundaries between self and other and poses specific threats to the project of "self-representation." How can a writer or a teacher represent a self, if that self is vulnerable to feeling shamed, impoverished, or threatened?

II

To what extent do the demands placed on the maternal figure to be good enough ironically leave her vulnerable to sliding into a false self in order to provide her child with the proper holding environment. Winnicott's postwar writings are fraught with a subtle ambivalence about how active the subjectivity of the mother should be with respect to her child's ruthless love—the child's need to make repeated and absolute claims upon her. While the good enough mother must be available and "identified" with her child, she must not be too satiating, otherwise the "developing self" that must struggle in order to gain strength by wrestling with frustration and loss is obstructed (Kavaler-Adler 2000, p. 62). In the event that she is incapable of providing the child with what she needs, the mother must learn to "act as if ..." she is good enough, masquerading, if you will, so as to provide her child with what is necessary for her development. Thus we bump up against a paradox in the work of Winnicott. While on the one hand, a mother must be genuine, personal, confident, and spontaneous, on the other hand, if she is depressed, anxious, or preoccupied, she must "act" in the presence of the child who is too anxious or fearful to bear the presence of the mother's difficult subjectivities (see Phillips 1988, p. 67).

Winnicott is steady in his belief that if the maternal figure fails to withstand her child's "imperial claims" and impinges her will upon her child, then the child is inclined to adapt by resorting to compliance, which in turn creates a lost sense of "aliveness" and "feeling real" (Winnicott 1969, p. 20). These terms exceed the idea of simply existing. They call for a particular capacity to exist as "oneself," and to have a self to, as Phillips explains, "retreat to for relaxation" (1989, p. 128). The absolute patience, sense of attunement, and sustained resilience necessary to be good enough, so as to provide the child with the strength to pursue her curiosities stands as quite remarkable, ideal really. And while Winnicott's concept of good enough mothering is compelling, I fear that it demands from the maternal figure a set of serious compromises that affects her capacity for cultivating her own curiosities and interests. Before turning to Sexton's early years as a mother, I want to take some time to discuss my concerns about Winnicott's claims, particularly because the question of what it means to be a subject, especially a subject of desire, has important implications for understanding the impact that authority and agency has for female teachers and the teaching life of Anne Sexton. I turn to Anne Sexton's struggles as a mother and teacher in order to consider the implications of what it means when "maternal work" is so essential, not only to the constitution of the developing mind of the child, but to the psychic strength of a nation. These implications are particularly important to attend to given that female subjectivity is so rarely represented in maternal and educational discourses as active and desirous. Moreover, the theory Winnicott develops with respect to cultivating a "true self" in the presence of a social field that barely tolerates the sexual and intellectual appetites of women raise important questions about what it means to represent a self, in writing and in the classroom, when that self is inclined to hide so as not to be vulnerable to shame, scrutiny, or humiliation.

Winnicott shows little regard for the difficult subjectivities of the mother. In fact, Winnicott insists that in instances when the mother must disillusion her child by turning to her own work and interests, the good enough mother must do so in the name of the infant, not in the name of her own curiosities or needs. The mother who is inattentive, particularly at the beginning of an infant's life, was, in Winnicott's view, a "saboteur" of the child's developmental process—moving dangerously close to imping-ing on the continuity of care that was so crucial in creating a sense of well-being for the baby. Adam Phillips confirms this assessment of Winnicott's disregard for the subjectivity of the mother in the following passage:

> Though not blaming mothers for their "failures," he was implic-itly demanding everything of them at the very beginning. "Only if a mother is sensitized in the way I am describing," he writes with unusually dogmatic conviction, "can she feel herself into her infant's place and so meet the infant's needs." (1989, p. 122)

The sensitized position required of the good enough mother can-not account for the ruptures and sorrow that emerge in the life of the mother—nor do these theories offer places for transgression or renewal outside of platitudes of exercising compassion for Others or attuning to the child's needs. The concerns I raise here resonate with the recent scholarship of Alice Pitt (this volume). In her analysis of the place of the mother in psychoanalytic studies, literary and educational theory, Pitt also turns to Winnicott's concept of the good enough mother, to ask why "the mother must be destroyed and what remains after such a terrifying act." Pitt addresses not only the lack of regard that Winnicott shows for the subjectivities of the mother, but the contingency he establishes in his work between becoming a "speaking subject," of our own histories and destroying the mother—body, breast, and subjectivity. Pitt's close reading of Winnicott advances the argument that while he placed the maternal figure at the center of his psychoanalytic theory, he did so solely for the purpose of raising good enough children. Paradoxically, he made it neces-sary for the child to aggressively devour the mother so that the child can in turn claim the status of a speaking subject who has the capacity to engage her interests and curiosities—to *use* the world rather than solely *relate* to it. Again, keeping our attention on the mother, in order for the child to achieve symbolization, the child must symbolize the fantasy of the loss of the mother. Hence, symbol formation is contingent upon a fantasy of the mother's destruction. What is less often attended to is the psychic and exis-tential impact this destruction brings about for women and their children (see Pitt, this volume).

We can hear the anxiety of mothers forsaking their appetites in the personae who circulate throughout Sexton's poetry. In her poem, "Two Sons," the persona of the mother has grown "old on her bitterness," abandoned by her sons who have married.

> Both of you monopolized
> with no real forwarding address
> except for two silly postcards you bothered to send home,
> one of them written in grease
> as you undid her dress. (*Complete Poems*, 1981)

What emerges from these lines are disturbing images of an abandoned, intrusive, and bitter mother. But there is more. One has to wonder if Sexton was mimicking the maternal ideal here—offering her readers a "double vision" that disrupts the selfless, ever-gracious portrait of the good enough mother, warning her readers of the bitterness that festers when appetites are harnessed and one is asked to live alienated from desire. While her boys are, as the narrator suggests "made of my cooking, those suppers of starch and beef, and with my library, my medicine, my bath water," ... they grow as they should and move on. The discourse of mimicry expresses not only what is known and permitted, but also what is known but must be kept concealed; it is in this sense that mimicry is a discourse that is uttered between the lines, both against the rules and within them (see Bhaba, 1994, p. 88). Lacan describes mimicry as camouflage that refuses to harmonize the repression of difference. While the figure in this poem appears as mother—her status as a "jilted nurturer," produces a menacing taste that raises questions about what aspects of herself the maternal figure must abandon, and what aspects of the maternal her children are required to destroy in order to *use* the world. These questions are not addressed explicitly by Winnicott, but they can be explored between the lines of Sexton's poetry, and within the narratives that shape her life as a mother and a teacher.

III

In an interview with Barbara Kevles in 1971, Sexton describes the first attempt to end her life as a departure from the middle-class conventions of the time:

> Until I was twenty-eight I had a kind of buried self who didn't know she could do anything but make white sauce and diaper babies. I didn't know I had any creative depths. I was a victim of

the American Dream, the bourgeois, middle-class dream. All I wanted was a little piece of life, to be married, to have children. I thought the nightmares, the visions, the demons would go away if there were enough love to put them down. I was trying my damnedest to lead a conventional life, for that was how I was brought up, and it was what my husband wanted of me. But one can't build little white picket fences to keep nightmares out. The surface cracked when I was about twenty-eight. I had a psychotic break and tried to kill myself. (1971, p. 84)

What do these nightmares contain? This retrospective account of her first suicide attempt invokes one of her signature images—the cracked surface of a conventional, bourgeois dream shattered by the emergence of a self that had been submerged in a belief in love. What kind of love was Sexton referring to in this statement? Idealized maternal love comes to mind— embedded in the stifling social situation that existed for women at the time. "All I wanted was … to be married, to have children.… I thought the … demons would go away if there were enough love to put them down." In her description of struggle, Sexton introduces us to a bourgeois domestic space, a site, if you will, for demonic invasions that crack and displace her from home and family. The unhomely moments portrayed by Sexton in her poetry relate her traumatic personal, psychic history to a wider political existence. Sexton, molested by her own father, relays a belated repetition of the violent history of women who became objects of their fathers' power, fear, and desire to kill themselves off as fathers. Sexton does not hide from sight her father's sexual use of her body. By making this moment visible as one among many of the demonic visions that are rendered in her poetry, in therapy and more subtly in her teaching, she specifies the patriarchal, gendered nature of civil society. Sexton provokes us to consider the ways in which we might direct our pedagogy toward what we cannot bear to know, asking us to create an inconsolable memory in the face of the violence of incest. We would then conceptualize incest as a profound form of domestic colonization that begins at home and naturalizes the invasions of psyche, consciousness, body, and nation. The father is oppressor; just and unjust, moderate and rapacious, vigorous and despotic; these instances of contradictory belief raise questions about the act of incest, an act of violence that happens between the lines and borders of identity itself, between parent and child, siblings, intermingling and contaminating blood lines and genealogical lines, erasing difference, and in the extreme, erupting into the degeneration of family and narrative.

Among the few places that Sexton confessed to "feeling real," was in the world of poets—and in the classroom. These feelings are recorded in the teaching journals she kept for Herbert Kohl while working with the Teachers & Writers Collaborative in 1967. "When I give a reading, I feel that I'm faking it, and when I'm in class, I'm not faking it. No ... not any more." The self that emerges after Sexton's "psychotic break" would be what Winnicott would call her "true self," for it offered her the opportunity to feel alive, to experience spontaneity, and to begin to be free from the demands of authoritative figures. Sexton often described writing poetry as a movement through death to a new life, "Inherent in the process is a rebirth of a sense of self, each time stripping away a dead self" (Kevles, 1971, p. 86).

Between having children, writing, and teaching, however, Sexton broke. Despite stretches of confidence and remarkable achievements, her psyche became more and more fragile. As Sexton notes in her retrospective account to Barbara Kevles, motherhood and marriage provoked her to feel torn up, anxious, and lonely. In 1955, she began to feel the intensifying pain of her deepening breakdown, as she no longer was able to care for her children, to cook, or to feel any sense of direction. In a handwritten note to Dr. Orne, after more than a year of treatment, she writes:

> I am so alone—nothing seems worth while—I walk from room to room trying to think of something to do—for a while I will do something, make cookies or clean the bathroom—make beds— answer the telephone—but all along I have this almost terrible energy in me and nothing seems to help.... I sit in a chair and try to read a magazine and I twirl my hair until it is a mass [of] snarls—then as I pass a mirror I see myself and comb it again. Then I walk up and down the room—back and forth—and I feel like a caged tiger.[...]

> I had Joy for the weekend and she has gone back today—I love her, she is adorable and winning—but seems to take so much patience and energy and I was glad to see her go. I guess I don't love anyone—that is a terrible statement and now I am crying[....] My heart pounds and it's all I can hear—my feeling for my children does not surpass my desire to be free of their demands upon my emotions. What have I got? Who would want to live feeling that way? (Middlebrook, 1991, pp. 36–37)

"My feeling for my children does not surpass my desire to be free of their demands upon my emotions. What have I got?" Sexton's daughters were young at this time, and she had barely been capable of caring for them. Soon after giving birth to Joy in August of 1955, she began to experience serious episodes of depression and developed a fear of being alone with her babies. She could not withstand the acute demands of her infants. Sexton began to feel intense rage at Linda, she would grab her and begin slapping and choking her. Fearful that she would kill her children, she turned to her extended family, who offered practical help—housekeeping, payment of medical bills, and company while her husband was away on business trips.

Only in her poetry did she display understanding of the infant's needs. In one of her most well-known poems, "Unknown Girl in the Maternity Ward," she wrote:

> Child, the current of your breath is six days long.
> You lie, a small knuckle on my white bed;
> lie, fisted like a snail, so small and strong
> at my breast. Your lips are animals; you are fed
> with love. At first hunger is not wrong.

Unlike the poet who wrote this poem, the narrator understands the early hungers of the infant, their ruthless love and desire for constant susten- ance. This poem is in fact part of a larger recurring pattern in which Sexton performs a precarious inversion of a psychic anguish that she can no longer contain after the birth of her daughters. One year after giving birth to Joyce, Sexton began her therapeutic sessions with Dr. Martin Orne. Their work together led to Sexton's ushering into the writing work- shops with poet John Holmes. It was in the workshop that Sexton found a "potential space" that cultivated within her the stunning sensation of "feeling real."

IV

The year 1960 marked the fourth anniversary of Sexton's first hospital- ization. She continued to grow as a writer, forging important and lasting relationships with fellow poets, and attending bimonthly workshops with her colleagues in the living room of John Holmes. Holmes had established the signature method through which poets critiqued one another's work, and sought out from one another, as Robert Creeley once noted, "water to drink." The tradition of the workshop was long, and is eloquently docu- mented by Holmes in a chapter entitled "Biographies of Five Poems" in his book, *Writing Poetry*. In this collection, Holmes praised the workshop as a form of artistic collaboration and openly discussed with his readers how his poems evolved through multiple drafts, from first notes to finished form. For Sexton, who never attended college or formally studied litera- ture, the workshops she participated in with John Holmes were akin to a prestigious tutorial. Poets gathered to present works-in-progress, to work out lines, to listen for the half-spoken image, and to engage in wordplay.

Sexton gravitated toward generating images, exploring their emotional life, and working toward releasing conventional response. She often described how the creative impulse contributed, in significant ways, to challenging her desire for oblivion. Even when Sexton fell into the deepest of depressions, she remained grateful to the power of poetry to "exorcise her death wishes," a phrase given to her by Maxine Kumin and from which she derived comfort. In a letter to Anne Clarke, a psychiatrist, close friend, and one-time lover, Sexton discusses the plans she has for her collection of poems, *The Death Notebooks*. She speculates that she may call one section "The Wood of the Suicides," after Dante's *Inferno*—"I am fascinated with the whole thing and as I work on it I create it (instead of doing it) … a fine substitute!" (Sexton, Linda Gray, 1994, p. 232).

The structure of the writing workshops Sexton attended offered her access to a collaborative and social milieu that enabled her to repair some of the profound sense of loss, anxiety, isolation, and displacement she felt as a mother, daughter, and wife in post–World War II America. However, I want to underscore that the workshops Sexton conducted with her students *did not* create a congenial milieu in which she could perform as a "good enough teacher." The workshops she led at Boston and Colgate Universities can be read as exemplary of how Sexton used pedagogical and narrative tactics to represent female experiences that *exceeded* the limits of the good enough mother or the good enough teacher. The writing exercises that Sexton used in her workshops illuminate the constraints inherent in the ideal of the good enough mother and the good enough teacher as well as the "tricks" or "pedagogical tactics" available for comprehensively transgressing the limits of these images. This work exceeds the role of good enough mothering and teaching because it actively engages the difficult-to-articulate aspects of female subjectivity. Sexton believed, recalls Maxine Kumin, "that the hardest truths would come to light if they were made to fit a stanzaic pattern, a rhyme scheme, a prevailing meter" ("How It Was," 1988, p. xxv). Indeed, Sexton was fearless in her study of the vicissitudes between love and hate and her inquiry into the love that both hurts and comforts us.

The work of understanding reparation as both a reflective and an imaginative act has been described by Rinaldo Wolcott (2001) and Ursula A. Kelly (2004) as a radical form of pedagogical consciousness. Neither Wolcott nor Kelly romanticizes such a project. They fully understand that much harm has been taken up by educators in the name of "good intentions." What urges each of them on is the possibility of using a pedagogy that productively addresses defeat and trauma as more than loss. A pedagogy of reparation calls upon educators to study our problematic attachments, as well as to consider how the loves in our lives have both helped and hindered us, cared for and hurt us (Kelly, 2004, pp. 165–166; Walcott, 2005). One place such work might begin is to address the simultaneous presence of irreconcilables—the daughter's love for the mother who cannot care for her; the daughter's attachment to a rapacious, cruel father. Sexton combines self-representation, fiction, fairytales, poetry, and plays to create a means through which to love her shameful and shamed family, for throughout the story of Anne Sexton and her daughter Linda, love persists, even in the midst of rage, even as it allows for harm, even as it opens the front door of the house on 12 Clearwater Drive, where violence enters over cocktails and calls it "home" (see Gilmore, 2001, p. 66).

In the following section, I present two exercises that Sexton devised for the workshops she taught at Boston and Colgate Universities. In each instance, she speaks to her students about the emotions that lie beneath grief—sorrow, feelings of guilt and forgiveness—as she refrains from preoccupations with injury and victimization. As Sexton speaks about her composing process to her students, she contemplates the objects of her displacement, clearly scrutinizing what she refers to as the "left-overs of a life…" searching among the inheritance of objects—"the suites, the cars, the scrapbook …" (Sexton, 1981) for what they can tell her of how love both taught and hurt her (Gilmore, 2001). Her pedagogical tactics, like many of the lines in her writing, offer a kind of serious playfulness where studies of *our* Otherness can unfold.

V

In 1969, when Sexton began teaching at Boston University, she had accrued some important experiences in the seminar room. Prior to this appointment at Boston University, she had taught a seminar at Radcliffe College, enjoyed the numerous postreading visits at college campuses, and through her affiliation with *Teachers and Writers*, Sexton taught English at Wayland High School in Wayland, Massachusetts. In her work at Boston University, Sexton drew a good deal on the pedagogical approach taken by John Holmes in her writing workshops, often informing her students on the first day of class that they will learn, "how badly a poem can begin," and then, through revision, and a series of what she referred to as her "tricks," how her drafts evolved into a complete poem. In a 1972 workshop she gave at Colgate University, Sexton presents her students with a set of her manuscripts for her poem, "All My Pretty Ones."

> I have on my desk 6 pages of what is called beginning worksheets
> of *All My Pretty Ones*. I thought I'd kind of read you parts from
> each page so you might see, line by line, how very badly it began,
> how it almost never got written. We will play detective. We're
> going to see how a poem is made and remade and remade. I pur-
> posefully have not re-read these. What they will show you of my
> personal life I have no idea. It is a very vulnerable position to show
> your worksheets, but I felt it would greatly enhance your knowl-
> edge of me as well as show you how badly a poem can begin and
> then how it can be rescued. We will play detective together. We
> will look at the beginnings, the early fumblings, the jottings and
> find clues. I want you to look as hard as I will look.... I began
> badly, with raw emotion and bitterness, with no good lines, no
> form nothing but the need to give reality to feelings.... I'll give it
> to you rough as it was.

Apparently, a poem, like a life, can start out badly. But there are rhetorical tactics a person can draw on to "rescue" bitterness and bad lines from
demise—to repair it, so to speak, to make it "good." Sexton moves her narrative forward by filling her students in on the significance of the list of the
objects she includes.

> *All My Pretty Ones* tells the story of an inheritance of objects, the
> suits, the cars, the pictures, the scrapbook, my mother's diary ...
> We have the leftovers of a life, the gifts I did not choose, a gold
> key, half of a woolen mill, twenty suits, an English Ford, boxes of
> pictures, and my mother's diary in which she wrote of my father
> (HRHRC). I'm not sure of the time lapses, probably these five
> pages took me over a week of attempts.

There are traces of ambivalence threaded through this pedagogical
scene, for Sexton's inheritance is both contained and exceeded by the limits of this list. Embodied in each object are memories of hate, guilt, and
love. What Sexton does not include in this workshop discussion, but renders in her poem are a series of facts. The golden key refers to the residence
her father could no longer afford, many of the pictures were of people "I do
not know. I touched their cardboard faces. They must go." The diary contains all that her mother "does not say" of her father's "alcoholic tendency."
Perhaps one reason I find this poem compelling is because "All My Pretty
Ones" works to redirect the guilt, destruction, and sense of abandonment
felt in this family, to the question of forgiveness and of love. The final lines
of the published poem read like this:

Only in this hoarded span will love persevere.
Whether you are pretty or not, I outlive you,
bend down my strange face to yours and forgive you.

Not only does Sexton speak to her students of what and whom have been destroyed, but she moves through an arch of emotion, thereby displacing her anger with forgiveness, and making it possible to love again. This love takes hold in the face of difference, separation, and the fear that one's lineage can seep into one's psyche uninvited. "My God, father, each Christmas Day with your blood, will I drink down your glass of wine" (*Collected Poems*, 1982).

Here, the analogy between Anne Sexton's performance as a teacher and the psychic dilemmas she struggled with as a daughter and a mother become especially vivid. The exercises to which she introduced her students in writing workshops engaged them in claiming or giving voice to alterity. In other words, Sexton asserted her difference from the assigned role of the good enough mother, by drawing upon her concerns rather than displacing them, and by disrupting and interfering in her students' taken-for-granted notions about what forms of personae offer educative possibilities. Included among Sexton's central concerns is a study of problematic attachments to family, lovers, and addictions. Her teaching and her poetry call forth the encrypted presence of kernels of traumatic knowledge housed in the symbolic register where repressed material returns. Sexton hoped her workshops would revive a sense of the uncanny, and self-estrangement, as made evident in the following questions she poses to her students at Colgate University:

> Now, if I'm not a cripple, how can I write a poem about being one? In what ways am I a cripple still? How did I come to writing about myself? How did I come to be a confessional poet who vomits up her past every ugly detail onto the page? I started to write about myself because it was something I knew well. Beyond this is the need to confess and admit one's guilt and be forgiven. With every poem it is as if I were on trial, pleading my case before the court of angels and hoping for a pardon. And now, I'm going to give you an in-class assignment: Write a short poem or character sketch using a persona. Suggestions: the wife beater from the point of view of the man who beats his wife telling something of his psyche or the wife who is beaten telling something of her psyche. Why in each case do they stay together? What imagery is called up by their different attitudes? Become that person. Put on that mask. Or … find a persona poem and explain what techniques are used to convince

you that this is authentic. Verify with examples from the poem. Write out in prose the story being told. Examples of persona poems are Keats "Crazy Jane"; Browning's "My Last Duchess," in books by Randal Jarrell you ought to find a female persona. John Crow Ransom's *Piazza Piece*, or to get a little more contemporary, and perhaps interesting, Ted Hughes … lots of persona." (HRHRC)

When Melanie Klein writes that "a good relation to ourselves is a condition for tolerance and wisdom toward others" (1961, p. 342) and that this ability to love has developed from those who meant much to us in the past, even if they have betrayed us, she is calling upon us to learn to live within the tension of opposites—within the tension of love and hate—innocence and guilt. Sexton's question, "In what ways am I a cripple still?" opens up the possibility to imagine a tangle of belonging and not belonging, vulnerability and strength, losing and finding again the lost object of love. The poem this question refers to, "Cripples and Other Stories" (1981), presents a traumatized daughter. Her mother, "brilliant," her father, "fat on scotch, rich and clean," her doctor, a "comedian," each assembled to portray the history of a woman who remains "in her father's crib," afflicted with a wound she fears will show, shamed by her wasted life, and diminished by the disapproval of her family. This poem is not one of Sexton's best, but her question, "In what ways am I a cripple still?" does perform differently from the way yet another trauma story might. This poem can be read as an example of a different kind of cultural work that reports family trauma without having to be accountable to the limited criteria for representing the "truth" of abuse and the implications for being taught of "love too late."

At the beginning of this chapter, I indicated my intention to question the demands Winnicott placed upon the good enough mother. As a woman who experienced the unnamable trauma of incest, Anne Sexton inherited a melancholic strain that was intensified by the demands that post–World War II America placed on middle-class women to be good enough mothers, paradoxically leaving her vulnerable to the "lost-I" feeling. The teaching life of Anne Sexton offers us a case of a pedagogy of reparation, in part because it presents a teacher engaging in the study of problematic attachments. Her pedagogy is overlaid with emotions that underlie grief—sorrow and feelings of guilt, rage, and horror. Finally, Sexton also offers us a way to think differently about what is at stake in discussions about education that hold fast to regressive images of good enough mothers who care for and nurture their students at the expense of their own subjectivities. The lectures in which she discusses her composing process are a generative site for reading the tensions involved in thinking about maternal metaphors in educational discourse and the lingering thematics of anxiety about maternal desire.

I would like to end this chapter by emphasizing that the metaphor of the good enough mother is inadequate for educators because neither the mother nor the teacher can remain continually attuned, placid, contained, or unflappable. In addition, a student cannot become immersed in educative inquiry without experiencing conflict, and a loss of equilibrium. Anne Sexton's use of personae building, as a rhetorical tactic, offers educators and students a process through which to shift from the Winnicottian metaphor of the good enough mother, to images of "being" and "doing." At various moments during the composing process, the teacher may work like an actor rather than a container. As an actor, the teacher may provide stimulation—probing, elaborating, interpreting, or questioning the students' experiences and actively setting boundaries that structure the work of composing, and of responding to one another's work. By creating a place for students to struggle with the teacher's subjectivities as well as their own, writing can be used as a process of inquiry through which to achieve a deeper level of interchange between them.

The implications that writing has for making reparation—for revising a life—is quite crucial to how I imagine Sexton's pedagogy. I am suggesting that Sexton's pedagogical narratives about her composing process combine to form a narrative of reparation that is used to recognize and work through ambivalent relationships with the lost object, in this case, "a safe and secure home." It is in this sense that the pedagogy of Anne Sexton constitutes a limit-case in self-representation; for she presents her students with a series of inquiries into making reparation with a traumatized self through the "playful" act of writing and teaching. This work suggests that the notions of good enough set forth by Winnicott does not account for the difficult to engage subjectivities that are in fact necessary for reparative work. Thus, if we rely on the Winnicottian image of the good enough maternal figure as teachers, we will unwittingly undermine the possibility for reparative work to take place in teaching and learning.

Notes

1. In my book-length exploration of the life, writing, and pedagogy of Anne Sexton, I analyze in some detail the controversy that surrounds the question of whether Sexton was in fact subjected to physical sexual assault at the hands of her father and aunt. I draw on Leigh Gilmore's (2001) work in particular to consider the politics of belief and disbelief. I draw from Freyd's (1996; also see Edgerton, 2002; Haaken, 1998; Skorczewski, 1996) important insight that trauma incest narratives are the culturally available narrative

terms made available to women through which they can capture a range of very real psychic traumas and physical abuse, and I argue that at the very least Sexton suffered from genuine trauma that was delivered and received in gendered and sexualized terms.

2. Again in the book-length version of this chapter, I offer a discussion of the intolerable abuse that Sexton inflicted upon her daughter Linda. In speaking of Sexton with compassion, I am in no way downplaying the trauma to her daughter.

References

Alain-Miller, Jacques. (1988). "Extimite." *Prose Studies* 11 (December): 121–30.

Atwell-Vasey, Wendy. (1998). *Nourishing Words: Bridging Private Reading with Public Teaching.* Albany: State University of New York Press.

Bhaba, Homi. (1994). *The Location of Culture.* New York: Routledge.

Daly, Brenda. (1998). *Authoring a Life: Women's Survival in and through Literary Studies.* Albany: State University of New York Press.

Edgerton, Susan. (2002). "Learning to Listen and Listening to Learn: The Significance of Listening to Histories of Trauma." Paper presented at the Philosophy of Education Society.

Eigen, Michael. (1993). *The Electrified Tightrope.* Northvale, NJ: Jason Aronson.

Freud, Sigmund. (1959). *Beyond the Pleasure Principle.* New York: Liveright Publishers.

Freyd, J. Jennifer. (1996). *Betrayal Trauma: The Logic of Forgetting Childhood Abuse.* Cambridge, MA: Harvard University Press.

Gilmore, Leigh. (2001). *The Limits of Autobiography: Trauma and Testimony.* Ithaca, NY: Cornell University Press.

Grumet, M. (1988). *Bitter Milk: Women and Teaching.* Amherst: University of Massachusetts Press.

Haaken, Janice. (1998). *The Pillar of Salt: Gender, Memory and the Politics of Looking Back.* New Brunswick, NJ: Rutgers University Press.

Herman, Judith. (1993). *Trauma and Recovery: The Aftermath of Violence—From Domestic Abuse to Political Terror.* New York: Basic Books.

Holmes, John. (1960). *Writing Poetry.* Boston: Writer, Inc.

HRHRC (Harry Ransome Humanities Research Center) at the University of Texas, Austin.

Kavaler-Adler, Susan. (2000). *The Compulsion to Create: Women Writers and Their Demon Lovers.* New York: Other Press.

Kelly, Ursula. (2004). "The Place of Reparation: Love, Loss, Ambivalence and Teaching." In *Teaching, Learning and Loving: Reclaiming Passion in Educational Practice,* edited by Daniel Liston and Jim Garrison. New York, London: Routledge Falmer.

Kevles, Barbara. (1971). "The Art of Poetry: Anne Sexton." *Paris Review* 13 (Summer): 158–91.

Klein, Melanie. (1961). *Narrative of a Child Analysis: The Conduct of the Psycho-Analysis of Children of a Ten-Year-Old Boy.* London: Hogarth Press.

Kumin, Maxine. (1982). "Preface." In Anne Sexton, *Complete Poems*. Boston: Houghton Mifflin.

Middlebrook, Diane Wood. (1991). *Anne Sexton: A Biography*. New York: Houghton Mifflin.

Orne, Martin. (1991). Interview with Samuel M. Hughes. *Pennsylvania Gazette*, pp. 12–91.

Phillips, Adam. (1988). *Winnicott*. Cambridge, MA: Harvard University Press.

Sexton, Anne. (1962). *All My Pretty Ones*. New York: Houghton Mifflin.

———. (1981). *The Complete Poems*. Boston: Houghton Mifflin.

———. (1974). *The Death Notebooks*. Boston: Houghton Mifflin.

Sexton, Linda Gray. (1994). *Searching for Mercy Street: The Journey back to My Mother*. Boston: Little Brown.

Sexton, Linda Gray, and Lois Ames (Eds.). (1977). *Anne Sexton: A Self-Portrait in Letters*. New York: Teachers and Writers Collaborative Archive.

Skorczewski, Dawn. (1996). "What Prison Is This?: Literary Critics Cover Incest in Anne Sexton's 'Briar Rose.'" *Signs: Journal of Women, Culture and Society* 21 (Winter): 309–342.

Walcott, R. (2005). "Land to Light On?: Making Reparation in a Time of Transnationality." Paper presented at Wilfried Laurier University, Waterloo Ontario, Canada, conference entitled *Beyond Autoethnography: Writing, Race and Ethnicity in Canada*.

Walkerdine, Valerie. (1991). *Schoolgirl Fictions*. London: Verso Press.

Winnicott, Donald. (1987). *Babies and Their Mothers*: London: Free Association Press.

———. (1958). *Collected Papers: Through Paediatrics to Psycho-Analysis*. London: Tavistock.

———. (1969). "The Uses of an Object." *Introduction to Journal of Psychoanalysis* 50: 711–716.

CHAPTER 4

Mother Love's Education

ALICE PITT

The figure of the mother is a vexatious one in education, psychoanalysis, and feminism, the trio of intellectual, practical, and political projects that preoccupy me. She is represented as scorned and celebrated, excluded yet responsible, as bearing the promise of salvation but also as threatening engulfment. She both suffers from male dominance and plays the dominant role in reproducing male and female gender identities. She embodies eroticism and flees sexuality. While much second-wave feminist scholarship has focused on recuperating, for women, the figure of the mother as a prototype of feminist subjectivity, recent discussions on the theme of matricide in mythology, psychoanalytic theory, literary studies, and popular culture waiver between familiar and less familiar ways of thinking about the uses of the maternal figure within feminist debates. I will explore several of these discussions here but not with a view to settle or even contribute to debates within feminism. Instead, I explore a different sense of mother destruction to ask: Why must the mother be destroyed and what remains after such a terrifying act?

Matricide is, admittedly, a harsh term, and my use of it may startle readers. Taken literally, it refers to the killing of one's mother. I will be using matricide in the psychoanalytic sense to convey an act that belongs to fantasy but is no less violently felt than if an actual murder had taken place. Patricide, the killing of one's father, is more easily recognized as a fantasy because Freud's postulation of the Oedipal complex has moved it into common parlance as a necessary rite of passage for male children. We come across jokes in education that the student must kill the teacher in order to become an educated subject capable of thinking for himself. Such an act, although usually confined to fantasy, is violently felt because the father and the teacher, if they are effective in their roles, are necessarily both beloved and feared objects whose authority and approval are desired at the same time as they are experienced as obstacles to creativity and autonomy.

Just as Freud turned to myth to represent psychical reality, the theorists of matricide discussed here also draw upon myths. Myths are powerful narratives in this regard, and part of their enduring quality has to do with their capacity to represent something to us that is compelling to our present, but we can apprehend their horrifying content only because of their distance and difference from our ordinary lives. Myths are not the news. Myths allow us to consider notions of truth as symbolic, and, in turn, symbolic truth allows us to consider the work of symbolization. Symbolization, a process that traverses psychical and external reality as well as thought and fantasy, takes the act of naming the world to a deeper level where one is able to reflect upon one's representations. To put it another way, we use language to represent, to ourselves and to others, objects, concepts, and affects. Symbolization is the capacity to know our representational acts as such (Pitt and Britzman, 2003; Britzman and Pitt, 2004), and its presence and absence marks both learning and the failure or refusal to learn.

In psychoanalysis, the symbolic act of patricide, whether one partakes or is cast in the role of onlooker, structures time in a forward flow; "When I grow up," "When I am the real teacher," "When I am in charge"—these are some of its calling cards. It marks the assumption of and the wish to take one's place, an arrival made possible by the removal of the hated, though also beloved, rival.

Matricide, which also affects both sexes, tells a very different story and is characterized by the pull of time back through one's lived and prehistoric biography. In this story, the unbearable loss of a beloved object causes suffering but also allows for the creation of an internal psychical reality. What the discussions of matricide that I will consider here have in common, I believe, is that they bring to the fore, albeit in very different ways, the thorny question that occupies this chapter, that of what it means to bring the mother into representation. The chapter culminates in some observations about my own reading of a significant contribution to feminist educational philosophy, Madeleine Grumet's (1988) *Bitter Milk: Women and Teaching*. I explore the ways in which the problem of representing the mother is repeated in reading and also plays a role in the dynamics of teaching and learning.

In this chapter, I discuss three orientations to the question of matricide. The first orientation has to do with feminist discussions of women's exclusion from history and culture. Here matricide is represented as a trauma of history that inaugurates women's social status as inferior and subject to laws and knowledge made for and by men. This orientation will be viewed through the lenses of feminist literary critic, Miglena Nikolchina (2004) and cultural theorist Amber Jacobs (2004). The problem of representation of the mother is her absence from representation, and matricide is the means by which her absence is assured.

The second orientation concerns object relations psychoanalysis and the role of the mother in infancy and early childhood. On this view, matricide is represented as a trauma of subjectivity that is both inevitable and painful. I discuss aspects of the work of Melanie Klein and D. W. Winnicott for whom the need of the infant to become a speaking, symbolizing being is tied up with the fantasy of the loss of the mother. Here, the problem of representation turns less on the absence of the mother than on the impossibility of representing what came before the infant's ability to encounter and create representation. The suffering this generates also brings the search for objects that substitute for the mother and so the possibility of living a life. In this orientation, representation of the mother always falls short because it is the loss of the early fantasized mother that inaugurates representation as mode of communicating to and with the self and others.

Here, matricide names the gap between the time of language and representation and the time of infancy (literally, without speech), a gap that can be traversed only in one direction even though it remains marked by the body's passionate memory. As Adam Phillips notes,

> Learning to talk is difficult, and it doesn't get any easier. The child at nursery school is at that age when he or she is making for the first, but not the last time, that fateful transition—that can never be complete, that can never be wholehearted because the renunciation, the loss of the unspoken self—to joining the language group, to participating in the community of competent speakers. "Why are words the thing?" the child might wonder, if it could. "What is learning to speak learning to do?" Or, to ask a more obviously psychoanalytic question, what exactly must be given up in order to speak? (1998, p. 43)

For the infant, the mother lives on both sides of the fateful transition into language, but with difference and indifference. On one side, the infant knows the mother who babbles, coos, and cuddles; on the other side, the infant is suddenly faced with the knowledge that the mother's play is more purposeful, instructive even, and, most of all, her speech is carried on the wings of her desire for a world and objects beyond the baby. Matricide, in this orientation, is the name of that loss. Our day and night dreaming and fantasizing life recalls this time of wordlessness, nourishes our curiosity, and provokes the singularity of our creativity. We do not, Phillips insists, simply progress from wordlessness, when "passionate life … was articulated without words" (p. 51), to the word-filled world with its world-filled words. Nor does one translate into the other; they mix, frustrate, and transform each other endlessly.

The third orientation represented in this chapter is made from the first two, at the point where the history of culture and the history of the speaking subject intermingle in the autobiographical account of my reading, repeated over a number of years, of Grumet's (1988) text. Only now am I able to see this text as a philosophical encounter with the impossibility yet necessity of representing the mother we once had (or believed or wished we had) and have lost. On their own, neither of my first two orientations will suffice to explain my autobiography of reading and learning Grumet. I believe that both orientations to matricide—that of matricide as the deliberate erasure of the mother from history and that of the infant's annihilation of the mother in the transition into language are implicated (or, I am implicated in both). It was only when I began to organize my feelings about reading Grumet as a narrative of not learning and learning, that I sought out (or discovered) the theoretical elaboration made possible by the first two orientations. Still more puzzling, at least to me, is what I have made of the movements between the two orientations and thinking about reading Grumet. My third orientation presents the mother as paradox: our mothers create the grounds for our eventual understanding that we cannot represent them; they both hold the illusion of unmediated understanding and allow for its disillusion through a fantasy of matricide.

I began working with the notion of matricide in a recent essay about women's autobiography and the problems my female students had with the mothers populating these autobiographies (Pitt, 2004). This essay provided me with the opportunity to work with an aspect of Shoshana Felman's writing about women and autobiography that had been eluding me. Returning to Freud's question, what does a woman want? Felman "discovers the problem of self-resistance and the attendant difficulty of 'assuming one's own sexual difference in the very act of reading; of assuming, that is, not the false security of an 'identity' or a substantial definition (however nonconformist or divergent) but the very insecurity of a differential movement, which no ideology can fix…" (1993, p. 10). In other words, Felman cautions the reader against settling into identities that owe allegiance to ideology. In response to this observation, I wrote the following: "I can observe one aspect of my own self-resistance in the fact that I have never set out to write about the maternal figure, and yet, when I look over conference papers as well as published essays, I am astonished to see that I have never ceased to write about her" (p. 277). The difficulty my students had with women's representations of their mothers became the grounds for their belief that they had little to learn from these women. This conclusion astonished me, but it also resonated with my own history of learning and with my perception that women's contributions to theory, art, and culture continue to be less valued and less actively worked with than those of men.

In what follows, I will explore in greater depth the underlying reasons for this strange play between, on the one hand, my profound mistrust of much feminist educational and psychoanalytic writing about the maternal figure and, on the other hand, the persistence of her compelling power for me as well as my concern for her intellectual well-being. To do this, I turn first to the writing about our relationships to the mother in the writing of psychoanalysts D. W. Winnicott and Melanie Klein. I then look to the work of Miglena Nikolchina and Amber Jacobs who explore the annihilation of the mother in the stories of Diotema and Orestes.

The Erasure of the Mother from the History of Thought

I begin to discern the oppositional pull in the ambivalence that my students felt toward the maternal figure through the work of D. W. Winnicott, who has provided me with much pleasure and many rich occasions for thinking about the problems of learning. Winnicott considered the maternal figure so important to human development and mental health that he used her as a model for much of his psychoanalytic technique in his practice with both child and adult patients. However, he also argues that our fear of our early absolute dependence on the mother and the debt to her that cannot be paid have cultural consequences for all women and for all of our relations to women:

> If there is no true recognition of the mother's part, then there must remain a vague fear of dependence. This fear will sometimes take the form of a fear of women in general or fear of a particular women, and at other times will take on less recognized forms, always including the fear of domination. (1991a, p. 10)

Freud did not emphasize the role of the mother though he did acknowledge the significance of the infant's helplessness. Fear of the mother's omnipotence features more significantly in Melanie Klein's work on object relations psychoanalytic theory and its feminist appropriations. This plays a role in both orientations: The matricide that occurs in the erasure of the maternal figure from history, and in the matricide that occurs in the infant's fantasy.

In the first orientation, matricide is experienced as the mother's absence from representation. Her absence is the consequence of her removal, and her removal is tantamount to a takeover. Julia Kristeva associates fear of the mother with her power: "Fear of the archaic mother turns out to be essentially fear of generative power. It is this power, a dreaded one, that patrilineal filiation has the burden of subduing" (1982, p. 77). Sons and daughters are both implicated in this burden, if differently. The question remains, why is generative power of the mother so feared? My first orientation to matricide does not answer this question, but it does frame the problem of patrilineal filiation as particularly problematic for women.

The Erasure of the Mother from Philosophy

Nikolchina (2004) sets out to "address the enigma of the persistent depletion of women's contributions to culture" (p. 1). She argues that, "in spite of the huge efforts of feminist theory and history to turn the tide, this process is with us still" (p. 1). She takes as emblematic the repeated removal of Diotema, "the wise priestess who offers the crucial speech in Plato's dialogue *The Symposium*, from the site of the birth of Western Philosophy" (p. 1). Socrates reports what he learned from Diotema about Love and his works. Diotema, whose identity is uncertain, is a controversial figure in traditional classical studies, but she turns out to be just as slippery for feminist scholars. The questions revolve around whether or not she is an historical figure, a foil for Plato, or perhaps even the representative of his own unclaimed point of view. Nikolchina studies the various efforts, some authored by women, to sort through these questions and comes to this bleak conclusion:

> At the extreme end, outlining the logical limits of the enigma, all questions pertaining to Diotema's presence in Plato's dialogue receive a negative answer. It does not matter whether Diotema existed, and if it does, well, she did not exist, and if she did, well, she does not stand for Plato's truth, and if she does, well, she is not a woman, and if she is, Plato's truth is passé anyway. (p. 100)

With all the bases covered, the mysteries of love and beauty remain safely within the purview of men, or at least of the inventive philosophical masculine mind. Nikolchina, who explores the literary and theoretical qualities and texts of Julia Kristeva and Virginia Woolf, finds matricide as the cause of the persistent erasure of Diotema from our intellectual heritage and forgetfulness as its permission slip:

> The intertextual approach to Kristeva and Woolf will bring to light "matricide" as the silent engine behind this vanishing, which is not a given but which is constantly resumed. The reason we do not heed sufficiently this constantly resuming vanishing process, the reason we can even afford to assert the redundancy of theory for addressing the problems of women, problems, presumably, that are always reducible to the mundane and the everyday, is the specific cunning of the depletion. The maleness of all wisdom with its entrancing speeches is a retroactive phenomenon: it produces the illusion that the present, any present, is always far more generous than the past in terms of its recognition of women's names. The past was unfair, the present is full of promise, and the future will set things right. The driving force behind this perennial optimism is the work of forgetfulness. (pp. 1–2)

Forgetfulness, another name for erasure, is recorded in the laments of women writers, from Wollstonecraft to Woolf to Cixous, who insist on their lonely uniqueness. Their laments are symptomatic of the violence of erasure, but they also expose a matricidal impulse. Nikolchina does not exempt contemporary feminists from contributing to the production of the "strange spaces of silence" that "separate the solitary female utterances throughout history" (p. 2). She cites the antiintellectualism of activism, the marginalization of French feminists in North America, and " attacks on 'difficult' writing" (p. 2) as forces against female theoretical and artistic creativity. She illustrates her accusations in her substantive discussions of Diotema and in Elaine Showalter's reading of Virginia Woolf's writing as emblematic of madness, not artistic creativity. I imagine Nikolchina's claims are a matter of much debate within feminist literary circles, but they resonate with me on two levels. As I have suggested, and will discuss in greater depth below, my own personal history of learning/reading is implicated in matricidal erasure. More generally, within educational studies and teacher education research and practice, the air is stultifying with demands for "clear language" and repressive insistences on standards, achievement, outcomes, competencies, and so on.

These signs of patriarchal education, renewed under the sweep of conservatism and having coopted critical investments in diversity, safety, and the responsibility for the education of all children and adolescents, bear allegiance to patrilineal filiation. And yet, as Nikolchina observes, there is "no symmetry between patricide and matricide. Patricide produces lineage; matricide is perpetuated as the erasure of the 'name of the mother'" (p. 3). While Nikolchina finds the violence of matricide behind the repetitive vanishing of women's creativity, it is Julia Kristeva's psychoanalytic semiosis of matricide that offers her a way to understand the problem and respond to it. I return to Kristeva and her reading of Melanie Klein below, but I now turn to a second example of the orientation to matricide as a response to her generative power that is represented as historical trauma. In this instance, the trauma repeats in psychoanalytic theory where the wound of matricide is concealed but cannot be overcome. Where Nikolchina takes the birth of Western philosophy as having arrived at the cost of matricide, Amber Jacobs (2004) turns to the origins of Western politics and the question of democratic justice.

The Erasure of the Mother from the History of Politics and Justice

Man-made justice, Jacobs (2004) tells us, has at its origins a distinction, and this distinction had to do with differentiating between the crimes of matricide and patricide. She argues that the lack of symmetry between these two intimate crimes is embedded in cultural history and repeated in psychoanalysis:

> If patricide in the Oedipal myth has been interpreted as the Name-of-the-Father, allowing for filiation, symbolic loss and genealogy, matricide in the Oresteian myth has not been translated into such clear conceptual terms.... The lack of attention to the mother's place within the structural laws of the human order means that psychoanalysis remains complicit with a model that relegates the mother to the realm of the imaginary. Such a model denies the mother a subject position and renders her an object of fantasy that is only ever described in terms of the infant's needs or desires. (p. 19)

Patricide, in other words, is named in the psychoanalytic account as the crisis that impels us to turn from the family to society and therefore is credited as an important structuring moment in the maintenance of culture. Matricide, on the other hand, while a real trauma, is given no place, remaining largely unacknowledged and unmourned. The loss of the mother is accorded no significance as a psychical or cultural event, and the mother plays no role beyond the object of infantile fantasy. To demonstrate this observation, Jacobs turns to the Aeschylus dramatization of the Oresteian myth and the role played by the goddess Athena who ushers in democratic justice with a judgment that allows Orestes's murder of his mother Clytemnestra to go unpunished. Athena gives as the reason for her decision the fact that "No mother gave me birth ... with all my heart I am my Father's child" (Aeschylus, cited in Jacobs, p. 24). The myth of Athena's birth is that she sprang fully formed and armored from Zeus's forehead. Jacobs challenges this familiar narrative and turns to another myth that is documented by Hesiod but goes unmentioned by Aeschylus, Sophocles, and Euripides. This is the myth of Metis the Titaness who was a priestess of knowledge and wisdom. Metis rebuffed Zeus's advances but was raped by the god. She became pregnant with Athena, and Zeus swallowed her whole. Zeus acquired the indomitable Athena who became known as a motherless daughter. He acquired something else as well: "From inside his belly Metis spoke to him, giving him all her knowledge and wisdom" (Hesiod, cited in Jacobs, p. 25). Nikolchina, who also recalls the story of Metis, relates Hesiod's descriptions this way: "Zeus had Metis' counsel always at hand and could use it without having to recur to an Other" (p. 94). In her reading, it was this nonrelational pretense to knowledge that was the cause of Zeus's great headache. Nikolchina describes this powerful myth as inaugurating "a cannibalistic culture forever trying to vomit the mother whom it has swallowed in the first place" (p. 94).

Metis disappears, and Athena is never to learn of her existence. In Oresteia, the installation of the father as the "prime author of identity" (p. 25) is convincingly established. Jacob notes that Freud either never knew of Metis or did not let on that he did. He did have in his large collection of antiquities a statue of Athena that he once described as his favorite and as perfect (p. 27). And, like Diotema, subsequent psychoanalytic treatments of the Oresteia repeat the omission. However, Diotema's name does appear in Plato's dialogue, and it is her body that must be repeatedly erased from interpretations. Here it is the *absence* of Metis's name that is repeated.

Jacobs identifies several psychoanalytic contributions to the exploration of the Oresteia, but notes that these focus on "the wrong matricide," that is, the murder of Clytemnestra. Jacobs finds what she takes to be a trace of Metis's exclusion in Melanie Klein's reading of the drama. Klein writes, "... she is also the daughter without a mother and in this way *avoids* the Oedipal complex. But she also has another and very fundamental function; she makes for peace and balance ... symbolically representing the *avoidance* of hostility within the family" (cited in Jacobs, p. 29, her emphasis). The use of "avoid" and "avoidance" signals to Jacobs a departure from Klein's usual vocabulary; she finds it vague and out of place. She argues that "*in avoiding something one is actively involved in the process of making something absent*" (p. 31, emphasis in original). What Klein makes absent and Athena represents is "the process of voiding Metis" (p. 31). Jacobs concludes this section of her text with a statement that reverses the process of making Diotema absent:

> We will never know if Klein was aware of the story of Metis and, in a sense, it makes no difference. The point is that Klein will not refer to Metis directly; yet Metis will nevertheless surface in the text. (p. 31)

Klein, according to Jacobs, cannot admit to Metis's existence because such an admission would require the recognition of "the mother's law," which "prohibits the fantasy that the child and the father can give birth and that subjects the child and the father to a limit, a distinction, a loss" (p. 32). This parallel law is proposed by Juliet Mitchell (2000). According to Jacobs, the consequence of Zeus's incorporation of Metis is that the mother's law cannot be "symbolized, theorized or represented." At the same time, however, the father's fantasy of being the author of identity is unrestrained. I would add that the father's fantasy that he is the sole guarantor of knowledge also goes unchecked.

If the mother's law prohibits the fantasy that the child and the father can give birth, its status as structural law remains difficult to conceptualize. Jacobs raises important questions about the missing theorization of matricide. She wonders if it is possible to "theorize a matricidal structure that organizes a different kind of loss, one that may not necessarily involve the particular loss (murder, castration) outlined in the Oedipal paradigm" (p. 21). By addressing the matricidal law that prohibits the male fantasy of parthenogenesis and by including "the maternal as an active element in the symbolic network" (p. 23), along with a different fantasy, a different kind of loss, and thus "different kinds of mourning, of remembering, of symbolizing" (p. 23) she tests the hypothesis that "the dominant symbolic order is *not* inevitable" (p. 23, emphasis in original). Her call for a structural theory may reveal its own fantasy and thus also belong to an orientation to matricide that would perpetuate the wish that structural laws do in fact do what they are supposed to do, that is, tell the truth about our archaic history and our future.[1] On this view, the myth sets the course, and an interpretation of the myth that points to its exclusion holds the potential for retroactively generating new myths of origin and, thus, new possibilities for representation and social arrangements. Of the two perspectives on matricide with an emphasis on cultural origins and repetitions, this wish is more clearly stated in Jacobs than in Nikolchina.

I think this is so for two reasons that have to do with the different ways these theorists answer the question, posed at the beginning of the chapter, of what remains after the act of matricide. What remains for Jacobs is the task of generating new (theoretical) stories that acknowledge the crime of matricide and the law of the maternal that might exist as "a structural constellation alongside Oedipus, signifying another field of desire producing alternative systems of meaning" (p. 20). The prohibition of the maternal law sets this in motion.

It may, however, not be so straightforward. What Juliet Mitchell (2000) proposes as "the Law of the Mother" distinguishes between a pre-Oedipal mother and an Oedipalized mother, that is, a mother whose speech exists within an already existing system of meaning. She writes:

> Most psychoanalytical theory added the importance of the pre-Oedipal mother to that of the father. It is this mother that feminism has explored in order to understand femininity. But there is no pre-Oedipal mother—or rather, she is the caregiver, for better or for worse, before she is Oedipalized by the displaced child regressing to demand that he will be her only lover. The Oedipalized mother then prohibits the child's fantasy of parthenogenetic procreation: You cannot make babies. If this prohibition is accepted and the possibility abandoned and mourned, then the girl will grow up to be in the position of the mother (in whatever way—actual or symbolic—she may use it), but the boy will not. (p. 344)

In other words, the Mother continues to function only within the Oedipal economy; the mother who is the object of the infant's fantasy of complete ownership is replaced by the mother who is the vehicle for delivering the Law of the Father. While the child's fantasy of giving birth is not gender specific, the Oedipal crisis anticipates the outcome of the prohibition as experienced from two gendered positions. Girls and boys, men and women all share the fantasy of giving birth—to our mothers, to ourselves, to ideas, but what is not accounted for is that the maternal is excluded from history. This suggests that the acknowledgment of matricidal fantasy, however important to our understanding of psychical and social life, may allow us to participate in new ways in the systems of meaning we inherit while stopping short of creating the new systems for which Jacobs hopes.

For Nikolchina, it is already possible, if we can bear it, to come face to face with matricidal destruction and the mourning of the loss. Her exploration of language is oriented toward efforts, using Kristeva and Woolf, to consider that one aspect of human fate is to be troubled and driven by problems of making present that which is absent, of representing the gaps in meaning, and of speaking a suffering that is unspeakable. The removal of women's contributions to culture and to generation reverberates throughout history *and* requires constant and vigilant renewal. On this both Nikolchina and Jacobs are clear.

For Jacobs, however, psychoanalysis is a cultural narrative that repeats symptomatically the anxious necessity of eliminating women's contributions both to the reproduction of the species and to human creativity and knowledge. In her view, the absence of a maternal law is an effect of and produces the asymmetry between patricide and matricide. Or to put it somewhat differently, the installation of a structural law featuring the mother's prohibition would permit a working through rather than the repetition of matricide.

Nikolchina's resentment toward women's exclusion is of a different order in that women's search for a conventional history and genealogy interferes with their capacity to comment upon the limits and impossibilities of stabilizing such a history. From this vantage, the fact that we are psychical beings who cannot fully bring under our control either our biological or our social histories presents us with the interminable problem of interpreting our experience at the limits of, rather than from within the laws of, language and the social contract.

My first orientation to matricide begins with its status as non-representable, as excluded, and, therefore, as fully in the service of denying our debt to the mother. The repetition of this status in literature, for Nikolchina, and in psychoanalysis, for Jacobs, draws our attention to the cultural consequences of "forgetting" to record matricide in our myths of origin. I now turn to my second orientation, which takes us to another mythical time of origins, that is, the time of infancy. This time before knowledge about the difference between the sexes can be apprehended orients us very differently to the problem of matricide.

The Psychical Consequences of the Loss of the Mother

Nikolchina and Jacobs center the consequences of forgetting the name of the mother, a forgetting that is either tantamount to murder or that renders the murder inconsequential. My second orientation operates from the other direction to consider the loss of the mother as a feature of human development and as a condition for becoming a speaking subject. Klein, as is well known, was the founder of object relations theory, which emphasizes the role of the mother in early childhood. While there may not be a structural law propping up this role, there is an original structuring object—the breast. This breast meets an infant who, for Klein, "is consumed with anxiety and racked by destructive drives that put him in danger of being disintegrated" (Kristeva, 2001, p. 61). These destructive drives are turned against the object, which is split into good and bad, and it is this distinction that becomes elaborated as the child develops and becomes less dependent on the presence or thrown into terror by the absence of the mother's body. The splitting of the breast into good and bad and the fragile ego's early experience of love and hate are the preconditions for the "child's subsequent acquisition of the symbol" (p. 64).

Klein's matricide is the fantasy that one's destructiveness has effected a murder, and that this agony can be mitigated by representing the loss. Winnicott provides us with a theoretical distinction that allows us to explain how representation changes over time as the baby's relationship to the mother develops from complete to less dependence. He makes a distinction between object relating and object usage that hints at the possibility of the mother's restoration as gratified and gratifying. Object relating, for Winnicott, is akin to rudimentary symbol formation. An object becomes meaningful for the infant, her desire is ignited in her interaction with the object. However, in object relating, the infant retains the fantasy of having created the object, a fantasy that must not be interfered with. Object relating becomes object usage when the infant can tolerate the reality of the object's existence as outside of her control; it has its own qualities and a separate existence. Here is how Winnicott describes the movement between relating and usage:

> The thing that there is in between relating and use is the subject's placing of the object outside the area of the subject's omnipotent control; that is, the subject's perception of the object as an external phenomenon, not as a projective entity, in fact recognition of it as an entity in its own right. (1971, p. 89)

When the subject places an object outside her control, it is, from the vantage of having been created by the subject, destroyed. No longer is the object perceived as a projective entity. It is now on its way to being reborn as an entity in its own right. Winnicott is very interested in the mother's response to the infant's encounter with reality and insists that the mother's part in this move from object relating to object usage is to survive the destruction. If the object (read now as the mother) survives the destruction and does not retaliate, the subject forms a relation with her. The subject too begins to tolerate and even enjoy living in a world where words do not mean what you want them to and where people exist whose desires oppose your own. What becomes possible for the infant is the coexistence of two contradictory feeling states: "I destroyed you. I love you." Winnicott finds the infant's aggression at work in all early forms of representation. The passages of Winnicott that I have cited gesture toward three "degrees" of symbol formation. The first two, incorporation, where the object is greedily taken inside, and substitution, where one thing stands for another, are acts of object destruction but also rudimentary acts of representation. In object relating, there is a mixture between the object that is created by the infant and the object located outside the infant's sphere of control. Finally, in object usage, a relation with the object is formed, where the object's qualities are not exhausted by its significance for the subject. In this final move, if the object is in fact another person—such as the mother—her subjectivity can be acknowledged and enjoyed.

More than this, her destruction in fantasy can be mourned. The fantasy of matricide is conceptualized here as a defense against the loss of the mother, a loss that is experienced as catastrophic. In Kristeva's reading of Klein, mourning the loss allows for the formation of "an internal psychic reality ... as something separated from the lost object and different from it" (p. 177). Kristeva refers to the dynamic proper to this formation as *significance* and, while it must be distinguished from the equation between the symbol and the object, it also relies upon these earlier forms of symbol formation: "Only then do we see the symbol, a product of a psyche that evokes a *lost reality* that for that reason alone is recognized as being truly real" (p. 177).

The two orientations to matricide that I have discussed here gesture toward two realms of lost reality that are both eerily marked by the fantasy of matricide. In the first, the mother's destruction founds a social order while in the second her destruction founds the human subject.[2] That is, we face, in these accounts of matricide, the radical impossibility of ever fully accounting for either cultural or personal history or of subsuming the narratives of one to those of the other. It may be more profitable to try to hold onto both orientations and their promise of testing, again and again, what we think we know, how we have come to know it, and what we use our knowledge to do.

Matricide as Paradox

My encounters with Grumet's *Bitter Milk* illustrate modes of reading that are implicated in the matricidal impulse both in the sense that Nikolchina describes it and in relation to the question of symbolization as a difficult process involving destruction and mourning or object relating and object usage. I first read *Bitter Milk* soon after it was published in 1988. I was a doctoral student, and the book was recommended by my supervisor. Several women read and discussed it. At the time we were struggling to gain a purchase on theoretical discussions that were new, exciting, and frightening, and I quickly dismissed Grumet's ideas as being too mired in the personal, too insistent upon forging a bridge between the messy intimacies of the home and the cool rationality of the school, and definitely too celebra-tory of mother love, to be of use in my efforts to pin down the ideological in subjectivity and the subjective (and subjected) in ideology. Like many of Grumet's male colleagues, I was excited by very sociological theories of reproduction that Grumet problematizes:

> This critique of reproduction planted procreation on the very assembly line it was trying to dismantle. The experience of family life was understood as a set of relations that had evolved to sup-port the relations and values of the workplace. Manipulated and duped by the "system," parents apparently relinquished their chil-dren to schools that denied them knowledge, self-understanding, social mobility, economic security, and training for participation in democracy. (1988, p. xiv)

Overlooked in my first reading was the way that Grumet's project flowed from her observation that critical theories of reproduction, while powerful in so many ways, could not explain why parents, including those authoring the critiques, continued to send their children to school. When I read the book again several years later, I was quickened by Grumet's study of the contradiction between our willingness to send our children off to these horrible schools and, indeed, our own willingness to use these places to launch and elaborate our own subjectivities. Her perspective seemed somehow to have been lurking all along in the margins of my own work, unrecognized and unclaimed. As I mentioned above, I have written and spoken, endlessly it now seems, about the mother in relation to education and pedagogy without ever having identified this as my project. Moreover, where the celebration of mother love and what I thought was an unprob-lematized notion of nurturance had dominated my early reading of Gru-met's text, I now discovered, to my great astonishment, ambivalence and caution about teachers administering great doses of love in the mother's absence. And how had I failed to be won over by the humor and beautifully wrought arguments about so many things I cared about?

More than a dozen years after that first encounter, I am now familiar with many of the texts and authors to which Grumet refers. I am no longer learning the history of women in education or exploring the contours of curriculum theory for the first time. I am able to attend to some of the "notes" that were not previously audible. And, most importantly, I have become accustomed to paying attention not only to what I am learning, but how I am learning. Some of the most original work in Grumet illus-trates and theorizes this practice, and I have taken up her ideas in rela-tion to pedagogy and the question of the personal in another essay (in

Pitt, 2003). Indeed, working with her essay, "Scholae Personae: Masks for Meaning" (1995) in relation to my own misgivings about the pedagogical uses of the personal in education became my impetus to return to *Bitter Milk*. I laughed out loud when I read a section describing the distaste for hermeneutics and phenomenology that Grumet met in progressive education circles. I am reminded of the raised eyebrows that the very mention of these philosophical traditions provoked where I studied and how, completely lacking in knowledge about them, I took the hint and read without even trying to understand and without believing that following Grumet's ideas back to the sources she identified would be useful or exciting to me.

My refusal to be affected by Grumet signaled a moment in my own learning where I could theorize the problem of binary thinking but could not bring two different discourses into conversation with each other. Early on, my reading was trapped within the confines of object relating masquerading as critical thought. Later, when I had begun to form my own ideas about the limits of thinking sociologically about education, I *forgot* that Grumet was responsible for introducing me to more psychoanalytic orientations and the value of paying close attention to stories about learning and not learning in order to catch the drift of what needed to be theorized or what sparked my interest. Here matricide appears first as a problem of thinking that begins in rudimentary processes of symbol formation, with all of the hallmarks of aggression, and culminates in symbolization, where the affective experience of reading can be brought to bear on the conceptual experience. To return to Winnicott's distinction, this is the place where object relating gives way to object usage, and another subject appears whose interests and investments have not taken me as their point of departure.

It is not a coincidence that, for this reader, the text that gave so much trouble and turns out to have such a powerful influence on me was about women and teaching. Even though Grumet does not talk about matricide, she offers a great deal to my discussion here to think about the mother as paradox, my third orientation to the problem of matricide. She concludes her collection of essays with a discussion of Virginia Woolf's famous observation "We think back through our mothers, if we are women" (cited in Grumet, p. 183). What follows is an extended theoretical meditation on thinking itself, on the process of assuming a gender identity, and on what it might means to teach as a woman:

> … we women who would teach as women find ourselves in a bare room that is not empty. We can clean out the male curriculum, banking education, the process/product paradigm, the myth of

objectivity.... We can make it a demilitarized zone. But still we are
not in an empty space. (p. 186)

What we cannot clear from the space is what Woolf referred to as the
Angel in the House, the spirit of her mother. Woolf creates a character,
Mrs. Ramsey, in order to think back through her mother, and Grumet
uses Woolf to think back though her own mother. This thinking back,
according to Grumet, resists either trying to become our mothers or
repudiating them. It is a mediation between daughters and mothers that
requires a third. Is this not also a way of saying that we cannot represent
our mothers? Here is how I described the mother as paradox: Our mothers
create the grounds for our eventual understanding that we cannot represent them; they both hold the illusion of unmediated understanding and
allow for its disillusion through a fantasy of matricide. When we think
back through those who will become our intellectual mothers, we may
remain for some time in a state of wordlessness. Claiming their influence
on us is an act of symbolization that is belated in arriving. In "Scholae
Personae," Grumet describes getting lost in her students' autobiographical
writing:

> Green-robed, I could crawl through their leaves, feel the rhythm
> of their sentences. Move to the places they skipped over. A semi-
> otic reading if you will. I hated entering those texts, giving up
> my world for theirs, but once I had migrated, I started speaking
> in their tongue, I became a citizen, started taking notes, started
> speaking back, asking questions. (1995, p. 39)

Grumet's students provoke her to think about her own childhood,
but bringing the teacher and the student into a more intimate relation is
not the purpose of the autobiographical writing. What Grumet wants to
elaborate with her students is their shared world of cultural experience.
Autobiographical narratives serve not to reveal the world but to launch
the possibility of finding things that matter and to sustain an appetite for
the difficult work of teaching and learning with others and alone (see Pitt,
2000). My history of reading Grumet speaks to the difficulty of learning
as you crawl, so to speak, through the rich intellectual landscapes of those
who inspire you to dream, borrow, and even steal on the way to becoming articulate. Our intellectual mothers may be those artists and philosophers who provoke such flagrant behavior. As teachers, we learn to survive
matricidal impulses as we seek to bring our students into the shared world
of cultural experience. As students, we atone for our matricidal acts by
attending to traces of influence that take us by surprise and shatter our
illusions of originality. This is the work of thinking back *to* our mothers.

By doing so we learn a great deal about learning, and we may also be able to stem the tide of forgetting.

Notes

1. Jacobs's suggestion that a parallel law would produce theoretical symmetry while also acknowledging the specificity of the mother may be what Elizabeth Young Breuhl (2001) describes as a theory of what women want, rather than what women need. What would be symbolized by the story of Metis as a story of the presence of an absence that repeats—the mother's generative power and wisdom or her erasure from representation? In Freud, the fantasy of the dead father functions as both structure and a developmental phase. In *Totem and Taboo* (1913), Freud describes the murder of the father as the moment of origin of the primal horde setting in motion an acknowledgment of guilt and remorse as well as the capacity for collectivity. Can the myth of Metis, with its insistence upon "generative loss," function as the equivalent to the structuring narrative of the primal horde—a myth Freud invented? Or, can it serve as the equivalent to Freud's use of the tragedies of Euripides which we inherit, not as myth but rather as a work of literature? I think this is unlikely. It is still possible to read fresh interpretations of the Oedipus trilogy and, with each, be reminded that Freud's psychoanalysis is a theory about human nature not, in fact, a history of human subjects.

2. Christina Wieland (2002) disagrees with Kristeva's interpretation of matricide as necessary for the separation of the child from the mother, arguing that this is "the way Western culture has followed—a way which leads to an individual becoming fatally divided against himself and perpetually in terror of the powerful 'murdered object'" (p. 11). For Wieland, the murder cannot, in fact, lead to separation because "murder ties the murderer irrevocably to his victim" (p. 11) and "creates a persecutory present object, rather than an absent one" (p. 12). Wieland reminds us just how difficult it is to contemplate the matricide as fantasy, and she alerts us to the risks of celebrating or idealizing matricide. Wieland seems reluctant to consider, in ways that the orientations to matricide I have been considering are not, that the mothers who populate our lost reality cannot be known to us, and we cannot be known to them.

References

Britzman, D., & Pitt, A. (2004). Pedagogy and clinical knowledge: Some psychoanalytic observations on losing and refinding significance." *jac, 24*(2), 354–374.

Felman, S. (1993). *What does a woman want: Reading and sexual difference.* Baltimore: Johns Hopkins University Press.

Freud, Sigmund. (1913). In *The Standard Edition of the Complete Psychological Works of Sigmund Freud.* Edited and translated by James Strachey, in collaboration with Anna Freud, assisted by Alix Strachey and Alan Tyson. 1953–1974., 24 vols. London: Hogarth Press and Institute for Psychoanalysis.

Grumet, M. (1988). *Bitter milk: Women and teaching.* Amherst: University of Massachusetts Press.

Grumet, M. (1995). Scholae personae: Masks for meaning. In J. Gallop (Ed.), *Pedagogy: The question of impersonation* (pp. 36–45). Bloomington: Indiana University Press.

Jacobs, A. (2004). Towards a structural theory of matricide: Psychoanalysis, the *Oresteia* and the maternal prohibition. *Women: A Cultural Review, 15*(1), 19–34.

Kristeva, J. (1982). *Powers of horror: An essay on abjection.* L. S. Roudiez (Trans.). New York: Columbia University Press.

Kristeva, J. (2001). *Melanie Klein.* R. Guberman (Trans.). New York: Columbia University Press.

Mitchell, J. (2000). *Mad men and Medusas: Reclaiming hysteria.* New York: Basic Books.

Nikolchina, M. (2004). *Matricide in language: Kristeva and Woolf.* New York: Other Press.

Phillips, A. (1998). *The beast in the nursery: On curiosity and other appetites.* New York: Pantheon Books.

Pitt, A. (2000). Hide and seek: The play of the personal in education. *Changing English: Studies in Reading and Culture, 7*(1), 65–74.

Pitt, A. (2003). *The play of the personal: Psychoanalytic narratives of feminist education.* New York: Peter Lang.

Pitt, A. (2004). Reading women's autobiography: On losing and refinding the mother. *Changing English: Studies in Reading and Culture, 11*(2), 267–278.

Pitt, A., & Britzman, D. (2003). Speculations on difficult knowledge: An experiment in psychoanalytic research. *International Journal of Qualitative Research in Education, 16*(6), 1–22.

Wieland, C. (2000). *The undead mother: Psychoanalytic explorations of masculinity, femininity and matricide.* London: Karnac.

Winnicott, D. W. (1964/1991a). Introduction. In *The child, the family and the outside world.* London: Penguin Books.

Winnicott, D. W. (1964/1991b). The roots of aggression. In *The child the family and the outside world* (pp. 232–239). London: Penguin Books.

Winnicott, D. W. (1971). *Playing and reality.* New York: Routledge.

Young Bruehl, E. (2001). *Subject to biography: Psychoanalysis, feminism, and writing women's lives.* Cambridge, MA: Harvard University Press.

INTERLUDE **III**

The Painful Politics of Love and History

Film: *Rabbit Proof Fence*

Paired chapters: *Transnational Adoption and Queer Diasporas* by
David L. Eng
Parenting and the Narcissistic Demands of Whiteness
by Gail M. Boldt

The problems posed by home, exile, and dispossession and the ways that place as a geographic location and psychic state plays out as a problem are eloquently theorized by David Eng and Gail Boldt in their chapters on the racial politics that structure transnational adoption and biracial parenting. Eng addresses the psychic investments that come into play through the adoption by North American parents of Asian children. Eng argues that for both heterosexual and homosexual parents, these adoptees perform a kind of labor that allows parents to seek reparation and social belonging through participation in the romance of the nuclear family. The Asian child performs this labor in an historical and psychic context that denies the child full identification with either the family or the nation. To illustrate his argument, Eng works from a documentary film about the life of

Deann Borshay Liem, brought to the United States at eight years old, after being given up for adoption by her Korean birth parents who did not have the financial resources to care for her. In her American family's insistence that her true life began when she came to them, we see American attachments to imperialism and troubling constructions of race and history that are so intimate that they remain opaque to the family. In spite of the love that exists between Borshay Liem and her families, racial and psychic politics mean that she is forever claimed and denied by both families, both cultures. Eng documents Borshay Liem's failed attempt to find relief from the depression, longing, and alienation that plague her through bringing her birth mother and her adoptive mother together in a return trip to her motherland, Korea. The psychic construction of the good mother/bad mother is central in Eng's analysis of this story. It is to her mothers, Eng notes, that Borshay Liem assigns responsibility for her struggles, it is her adoptive mother who struggles with this guilt, and it is finally to becoming a wife and a mother that Borshay Liem turns in the attempt to find belonging and peace in the romance of the nuclear family.

Eng's account begins with the story of the child who turns to the mother for reparation and ends with the suggestion that she will seek reparation in her relationship with her child. Gail Boldt tells this story from the other direction, from the perspective of the mother who seeks reparation from psychic injuries through needs and demands projected onto her son. Drawing from autobiography, Boldt offers a consideration of the politics of race and belonging as she reflects on the desires she feels as a white mother toward her son's performance of a biracial identity. Describing the childhood trauma of her failed efforts at belonging in her rural, working-class, white community, Boldt's story is a firsthand account of the attempt to comprise "family" as a place wherein she might find comfort and safety. However, Boldt finds that insofar as she denies that racial politics continue to play a troubled role in this fantasy, she is forced to construct categories of good and bad identities, good and bad locales, and good and bad love. The conclusions to the chapters by Boldt and Eng take us where Borshay Liem could not go; these chapters invite us to consider how interracial families and adoptive families, entering a new territory, have the potential to provoke questions and ponder love and ethics in way that are critically important to our entire nation.

The anguish of broken attachments and imperialist impulses are also portrayed in *Rabbit Proof Fence*, the film we have chosen to pair with these chapters. Directed by Phillip Noyce and based on Doris Pilkington's novel, *Follow the Rabbit Proof Fence*, the narrative structuring this film belongs to the "Stolen Generations" of Aboriginal children in Australia.

Pilkington is the daughter and the granddaughter of Aboriginal women who lost their children to the 1931 Australian policy of removing all "half-caste" Aboriginal children (the offspring of a white parent and an Aboriginal parent) from their Aboriginal families to be raised in orphanages where they could be "civilized" with the intention of marrying them to a white person or grooming them to become domestic servants. In the film, the responsibility of European Australians for this policy is portrayed largely through the character of Chief Aboriginal Protector, A. O. Neville, to whom this policy of separating a child from his or her mother and home culture does not appear cruel or inhuman. Neville rather states one of the central propositions used to justify colonialism—that the colonizers were benefactors and that "in spite of himself, the native must be helped."

The story of *Rabbit Proof Fence* follows three young "half-caste" girls, Molly (Pilkington's mother), Daisy, and Gracey, who are taken from their Aboriginal mothers and placed in a settlement camp 2000 kilometers from home. The three girls make their escape and travel for many weeks, always pursued by the forces of Protector Neville, across the often-harsh Australian landscape. The girls are able to find their way home by following a series of fences that run for thousands of kilometers through Australia, fences that had been erected to keep rabbits out of the farmlands. Although two of the girls do find their ways back to their mothers and community, we learn at the end of the film that not only are the girls kidnapped from their families again, but that later their own children, including Doris Pilkington, are kidnapped from them.

The dramatic arcs structured through imperialism and shaping this film—the politics of race and mothering, the introduction of competing worlds, projected hopes and aspirations, and a haunting notion of homecoming—resonate in the chapters by Eng and Boldt, and challenges the psychoanalytic structure of the conventional family. Perhaps even more telling than the themes emerging in the film—themes that are, after all, safely placed in Australia's past—is the half-spoken story of the making of this film, a story that repeats some of the same demands and denials of race and love, that tells us that history is never safely contained. This is a story that breaks through in the thirty-minute documentary on the making of *Rabbit Proof Fence* that accompanied the DVD release. In this documentary, we can see the emotional demands made by the director, Phillip Noyce, on the young actresses who played the Aboriginal girls. In one scene, in an eerie repetition of the film itself, we see Everlyn Sampi, the Aboriginal actress who played Molly, so traumatized by demand that she cut her hair for the filming that she considers running away from the set. In other sections, scenes of Noyce cajoling the girls that they must not allow their fame to go to their heads are interspersed with scenes of the girls being used in publicity shoots to generate greater sales of the film. In perhaps the most haunting image, we see the Aboriginal actors and crew members break down with grief after shooting the horrific scene of the girls' first kidnapping, while the white Australian cast and crew can only stand and watch. The documentary's only response to visceral testimony of this very real and present trauma of white racist policies toward Aboriginals is to show scenes that give testimony to the claim that the three girls love Noyce. This attempt to appeal to love to overwrite the pain of history and the present reality of racial and imperialist policies resonate with, but lack the reflexivity of Boldt's attempts to use the race of her loved ones to overwrite her own troubled and racist past. It bears an uncanny likeness to Eng's image of Borshay Liem's family insisting that all questions are erased because they love her and "she is one of us." These haunting repetitions remind us that the exclusions, loses, and denial that we do not come to terms with or seek to repair, return, in this case, in the form of a terrible repetition of exilic consciousness. Noyce sets out to give dignified voice to the experiences and perspectives of Aboriginal Australians under colonial rule and in some ways he succeeds; in other ways, however, we might argue that finally and on his own set he fails to excavate the buried logic of the policies of containment and oppression that he sought to make visible.

As you read the chapters by Eng and Boldt alongside this film, we suggest that you consider whether the problematics articulated in these narratives open up the possibility for an inviting pluralism rather than solely announcing histories wrought with unbearable violence and loss. Both chapters demonstrate the potential for engaging two or more cultural contexts simultaneously, of inhabiting two or more homes. This work is an extension of what Gomez-Pena (1993) describes as "border aesthetics" and it is, as he says, an ongoing project, far from complete: "By coming to *El Norte* I paid a high price for my curiosity. I unknowingly became part of a lost tribe. As citizens of nowhere, or better said, of everywhere, we were condemned to roam around the foggy unspecific territory known as border culture. Today ... we still haven't been able to 'return' completely" (p. 21). Perhaps what Eng and Boldt suggest to us, and what is portrayed by the history rendered by Pilkington, is that for citizens of nowhere and everywhere—there is a vision beyond homecoming, of return, but a return that includes a consciousness of the past, and a commitment on the part of those of us who have inherited the imperialist impulse, to make reparation. To address these inheritances is among the most profound challenges we can take up as educators.

Reference

Gomez-Pena, G. (1993). *Warrior for Gringostroika*. St. Paul, MN: Graywolf Press.

CHAPTER **5**

Transnational Adoption and Queer Diasporas

DAVID L. ENG

Deann Borshay Liem's 2000 documentary on transnational adoption, *First Person Plural,* recounts the filmmaker's 1966 adoption from a Korean orphanage by Alveen and Donald Borshay, a white American couple in Fremont, California, as well as Borshay Liem's eventual discovery some twenty years later of her birth mother in Kunsan, Korea.[1] With the hopes of alleviating the clinical depression from which she has suffered since college, Borshay Liem decides that she must see her two families together, in one room, in the same physical space. And so she orchestrates what can be described only as an excruciating "reunion" between her American parents and her Korean family, a journey of recuperation and return to origins compelled as much by fantasy as by fact. Midway through *First Person Plural,* however, Borshay Liem halts her narrative of reunion to offer this painful disclosure. Looking straight into the camera lens, she bluntly admits: "There wasn't room in my mind for two mothers."

I begin with this statement of a *psychic* predicament—the dearth of space in Borshay Liem's psyche for two mothers—because I am struck by the complicated ways by which female subjectivity and maternal blame become the site for working out a host of material and psychic contradictions associated with the practice of transnational adoption. This practice, in which infants are entangled in transnational flows of human capital, is a post–World War

II phenomenon closely associated with American liberalism, postwar prosperity, and Cold War politics. In the late twentieth century, transnational adoption has proliferated alongside global consumer markets, becoming a popular and viable option not only for heterosexual but also—and increasingly—for homosexual couples and singles seeking to (re)consolidate and (re)occupy conventional structures of family and kinship.

Through this contemporary emergence of new family and kinship relations, we come to recognize transnational adoption as one of the most privileged forms of diaspora and immigration in the late twentieth century. In turn, we are confronted with an interlocking set of gender, racial, national, political, economic, and cultural questions. Is the transnational adoptee an immigrant? Is she, as in those cases such as Borshay Liem's, an Asian American? Even more, is her adoptive family Asian American? How is the "otherness" of the transnational adoptee absorbed into the intimate space of the familial? And how are international and group histories of gender, race, poverty, and nation managed or erased within the "privatized" sphere of the domestic?

Attempts to answer these questions often result in significant confusion, and this difficulty suggests that transnational adoption must be analyzed not only in terms of "private" family and kinship dynamics but also in relation to larger "public" imperialist histories of race, gender, capitalism, and nation. Amy Kaplan, in the context of new Americanist studies of U.S. imperialism, argues that "imperialism as a political or economic process abroad is inseparable from the social relations and cultural discourses of race, gender, ethnicity, and class at home."[2] The vexing issues invoked by transnational adoption suggest that this practice might be usefully considered in relation to Kaplan's formulation. What would it mean to think about transnational adoption as a paradigmatic late-twentieth-century phenomenon situated at the intersection of imperialist processes "over there" and social relations "over here?" How might transnational adoption help us understand contemporary contradictions between processes of globalization and discourses of nationalism? For instance, how might late capitalist modes of flexible production and accumulation (in which the practice of transnational adoption must be situated) relate to the scaling back of civil rights and liberties in the U.S. nation–state, including access to the public sphere and participation in civil society, as well as claims to privacy, parenthood, and family?

It is crucial to investigate the material histories and implications of transnational adoption. However, it is equally important, as Borshay Liem's maternal predicament insists, to explore the psychic dimensions of the practice. And while we have a growing body of scholarship analyzing the political economy of transnational adoption, we lack a sustained analysis of its psychic range and limits. This essay explores both the political and the psychic economies of transnational adoption. It brings historical, anthropological, and legal scholarship on transnational adoption together with psychoanalysis—a rather unorthodox but, I would contend, necessary theoretical combination.

The chapter begins with a description of the evolving politics of family and kinship relations in the late twentieth century. It examines, through an analysis of a recent John Hancock commercial depicting American lesbians adopting a Chinese baby, the historical conditions and contradictions of transnational adoption that make new social formations of family and kinship thinkable. In the second part of this chapter, I elaborate upon the psychic structures that support these new social formations—that make them inhabitable and reproducible or, perhaps more accurately in Borshay Liem's recounting, unlivable and barren. Offering a theory of racial melancholia as well as a reading of Freud's essays on femininity and the negative Oedipus complex, I explore questions of origin and the psychic genealogy of Borshay Liem's maternal dilemma.

I recognize that Borshay Liem's documentary represents a singular set of experiences that may at first seem remote from the heterogeneous experiences of different transnational adoptees and their families. Nevertheless, I hope that my particular analyses of *First Person Plural* will not only resonate with the social and psychological issues of many of these various groups but also provide some new critical approaches to reframe and to broaden current discussions about this phenomenon.[3] Ever since the National Association of Black Social Workers (NABSW) issued a position paper in 1972 advocating the adoption of black children only by black families, there has been a contentious and long-standing debate concerning the politics of race in black/white transracial adoption and foster care. In comparison, little critical attention has been paid to the politics of race (not to mention the psychic issues) regarding transnational adoption of Asian children by white families. While transnational adoption practices implicate some of our most deeply held beliefs about family and identity and some of our most deeply held values about community and nation, there remains a dearth of available vocabularies to investigate this critical juncture of private and public.

The adoption of a child, domestically or from abroad, is a material and an affective enterprise of great magnitude. In unpacking its implications and effects, I do not want to be construed as either an advocate or an adversary of transnational adoption. Instead, the relentless moralizing that characterizes much of our contemporary debate on the erosion of "family values"—of traditional white, middle-class parenthood and the nuclear family—must give way to a sustained discussion of the ethics of multiculturalism in relation to the current emergence of what I call the "new global family." It is in this spirit that I offer a sustained analysis of transnational adoption's material contours and affective crossings. For without such examination, we will have few theoretical ways to understand and few therapeutic resources to alleviate the psychic pain associated with Borshay Liem's striking—indeed, heartbreaking—confession. How might the transnational adoptee come to have psychic space for two mothers? And what, in turn, would such an expansion of the psyche mean for the sociopolitical domain of contemporary family and kinship relations and the politics of diaspora?

Queer Diasporas

This chapter is part of a book-length project, "Queer Diasporas/Psychic Diasporas," exploring structures of family and kinship in the late twentieth century. "Queer Diasporas/Psychic Diasporas" investigates what might be gained politically by reconceptualizing diaspora not in conventional terms of ethnic dispersion, filiation, and biological traceability, but rather in terms of queerness, affiliation, and social contingency. By doing so, "queer diaspora" emerges as a concept providing new methods of contesting traditional family and kinship structures—of reorganizing national and transnational communities based not on origin, filiation, and genetics but on destination, affiliation, and the assumption of a common set of social practices or political commitments.[4]

"Queer Diasporas/Psychic Diasporas" focuses on this theoretical question: Why do we have numerous poststructuralist accounts of language but few poststructuralist accounts of kinship? In the 1970s, feminist anthropologists such as Gayle Rubin turned to structuralist accounts of kinship, most notably those of Claude Lévi-Strauss, to compare the exchange of women to the exchange of words.[5] Judith Butler observes that, when the study of kinship was combined with the study of structural linguistics, the exchange of women was likened to the trafficking of a sign, the linguistic currency facilitating a symbolic and communicative bond among men. "To recast particular structures of kinship as 'symbolic,'" Butler warns, "is precisely to posit them as preconditions of linguistic intelligibility and to suggest that these 'positions' bear an intractability that does not apply to contingent social norms."[6] In this manner, these structuralist accounts burdened us with traditional kinship relations underwritten by the Oedipal—a structuralist legacy establishing "certain forms of kinship as the only intelligible and livable ones."[7]

We have moved beyond structuralist accounts of language, but have we moved beyond structuralist accounts of kinship? Collectively, feminists have done much to challenge the idea of kinship as the exchange of women *tout court*. But insofar as there continues to be a privileged relationship between the exchange of women and the exchange of words, it would be difficult to imagine a poststructuralist accounting of kinship not predicated on the subordination of women and normative forms of Oedipalization. What would such a poststructuralist project look like?

"Queer Diasporas/Psychic Diasporas" explores these questions through an investigation of Asian transnational as well as gay and lesbian/queer social movements. The late twentieth century has witnessed the emergence of a spectrum of new social formations and identities. While idealized notions of family and kinship have been under duress throughout history, at this contemporary moment two of the most notable challenges to traditional orderings of family and kinship have come in the form of Asian transnational movements as well as queer reorganization of familial norms.

This crossing can be seen in the contemporary context of the transnational adoption of Chinese baby girls by Western couples and singles. A John Hancock commercial that aired nationally during the 2000 Olympics and World Series illustrates this crossing of queerness and diaspora—of contemporary sexual and racial formation, as well as exploitation and privilege—in the global system and domestic sphere of the nation–state. First broadcast during the U.S. women's gymnastics championships, the commercial depicts a white American lesbian couple at a major U.S. metropolitan airport with their newly arrived Chinese baby girl.[8] Interspersed between shots of busy white immigration officers, a close-up of the U.S. flag, and throngs of anonymous Asian faces restlessly waiting to gain entry into the country, we spy the couple with their nameless infant waiting patiently in line. The commercial then moves to a close-up of the trio.

"This is your new home," coos the dark-haired lesbian as she rocks the sleeping infant. "Don't tell her that; she's going to want to go back," jokes the other, a gangly blonde. "Hi, baby," the blonde whispers, as her partner asks, "Do you have her papers?" "Yeah, they're in the diaper bag," she responds. As the scene cuts away to a black screen, on which appears the list "Mutual Funds, Annuities, Life Insurance, Long Term Care Insurance," the dark-haired lesbian is heard in a voice-over stating wondrously, "Can you believe this? We're a family." The commercial cuts to her placing a tender kiss on the baby girl's head, as a second black screen appears with the words, "Insurance for the unexpected / Investments for the opportunities." A third black screen with the John Hancock logo comes into view as we hear a final off-screen exchange between the couple: "You're going to make a great mom." "So are you."

Given the long U.S. history of Chinese immigration exclusion and bars to naturalization and citizenship, and given the recent public outcry and legal repudiation of gay and lesbian parenting, we must pause to wonder exactly what John Hancock, one of the world's largest financial services companies, is seeking to insure. How does this depiction of transnational adoption and circuits of (human) exchange not only resignify past and present histories of exploited Asian immigrant labor but also situate the adoption of Chinese baby girls by an emerging consumer niche group—white lesbians with capital—as one of the late twentieth century's most privileged forms of immigration?

The commercial implies that, in crossing an invisible national boundary, a needy "object" left to wither in the dark corners of a Chinese orphanage is miraculously transformed into a treasured U.S. "subject" worthy of investment—economic protection (capital accumulation), political rights (citizenship), and social recognition (family). In this regard, we should note that, in the face of immediate right-wing outrage at the commercial, a John Hancock spokesman, waxing liberal-poetic about the company's advertisement, announced, "However a child comes into a family, that child is entitled to financial protection, and John Hancock can help."[9] How is the rhetoric of "financial protection" functioning here as moral justification for the ever greater accumulation and conflation of (economic) property and (legal) rights, including at this juncture child and family as property and rights for (white) lesbians and gays?[10] How is this respectable lesbian couple with money being positioned as the idealized inhabitants of an increasingly acceptable (and racialized) gay version of the nuclear family? How, in other words, is "financial protection" inextricably bound together with political citizenship and social belonging as the prerequisite for queer kinship?

Anthropologist Ann Anagnost suggests that, for white middle-class subjects in the era of late capitalism, the position of parent has become increasingly a measure of value, self-worth, and "completion."[11] Indeed, I would suggest that the possession of a child, whether biological or adopted, has today become the sign of guarantee not only for family but also full and robust citizenship—for being a fully realized political, economic, and social subject in American life. The demand for parenthood as economic entitlement and legal right not only by heterosexuals but also—and increasingly—by homosexuals seems to stem in large part from an unexamined belief in the traditional ideals of the nuclear family as the primary and contemporary measure of social respectability and value. Legally, U.S.

citizenship is granted on the basis of either birthplace (*jus solis*) or descent (*jus sanguinis*), deriving from parent to child. What does it mean that, in our present age, full and robust citizenship is *socially* effected from child to parent and, in many cases, through the position of the adoptee, its visible possession and spectacular display?

From the perspective of Asian American studies and history, we might consider how transnational adoption from Asia fits not only within a gendered postwar pattern of privileged immigration (war brides, mail-order brides, transnational adoptees) but also within nineteenth-century histories of anti-Asian immigration and bars to naturalization and citizenship. The period from 1882 to 1943 is often cited as the "official" years of Asian exclusion. However, legal scholar Leti Volpp has suggested that the Page Law of 1875, largely banning Chinese female immigration to the United States, might be a more appropriate historical date to mark the *gendered* form in which racialized exclusion of Asian immigrants from the U.S. nation–state took place.[12]

In this regard, the privileged migration of Chinese baby girls in our contemporary moment marks not only a striking gendered reversal of this history of racialized exclusion but also an emergent form of Asian American subjectivity of considerable consequence to Asian American politics, history, and community. Indeed, this reversal suggests not only that the transnational adoptee must be considered a "proper" subject of Asian American studies but also that the field has evolved to a point where a "subjectless" critique—a critique that does not rely upon an assumed or naturalized set of Asian American bodies—is indispensable.

What, we might ask, accounts for this gendered reversal of the Page Law? Further, how might we rethink time-honored paradigms relating to racial formation, gender subordination, and labor exploitation in Asian American studies in regard to the practice of transnational adoption? The historical period from the late nineteenth century to World War II—the era of the "Asian Alien" and "Yellow Peril"—is one during which a rapidly industrializing U.S. nation–state produced cheap and flexible labor through Asian exclusion laws and the creation of the "illegal (Asian) immigrant" outside the rights and privileges of citizenship.[13] If the transnational adoptee is, in fact, an Asian American immigrant, what kind of labor is she performing for the family, and for the nation?

Here, we need to broaden yet again our historical perspective to consider the intersection of transnational and domestic histories of race and racial formation. Due to declining birth rates in the post–World War II West, greater access to abortion and reliable methods of contraception, and an easing of the stigma against women bearing children outside of marriage, fewer white children are now available for domestic adoption.[14] As a result, white parents reluctant or unwilling to adopt black children in the United States (and/or fearful of domestic child custody battles with birth parents) have turned increasingly to transnational adoption as an alternative.[15] In this way, the Asian transnational adoptee serves to triangulate the domestic landscape of black–white race relations. Indeed, she might be described as performing a type of crucial ideological labor: the shoring up of an idealized notion of kinship, the making good of the white heterosexual nuclear family.

Hence, transnational adoption need not be understood as historically disparate from the prewar period of Asian exclusion, with its bars to naturalization and citizenship. In the postwar period of the Asian American *citizen* the practice of transnational adoption expands wage labor into arenas of consumer capitalism meant to effect a different type of labor power. We might describe this form not as "productive labor," in the traditional Marxian sense, but as "consumptive labor." Miranda Joseph argues that "consumptive labor is productive, but it is organized very differently from productive labor: it is not organized, procured, or exploited as wage labor."[16] Instead, as Joseph observes, in the shift to globalization and modes of flexible production and accumulation, consumptive labor serves to produce and to organize social community as a supplement to capital.

In the context of transnational adoption, consumptive labor produces and shores up the social and psychic boundaries of the white heterosexual nuclear family, guaranteeing its integrity and the sanctity of its ideals. Under the shadows of this imperative, then, we need to consider how transnational parenting might underwrite powerful regimes of racial, sexual, and economic containment. In constructing a cultural "identity" for their adoptee, for instance, how do parents utilize discourses of multiculturalism to absorb difference into the intimate space of the familial? How are discourses of multiculturalism being invoked to manage, to aestheticize, to reinscribe, and finally to deracinate culture of all meaningful difference?

In the context of this analysis, the practice of transnational adoption suggests that Asian baby girls *are* more easily folded into the imagined community of the white, heterosexual, middle-class nuclear family than are black children. All the more, then, we need to consider the multiple ways in which economic agency, political power, and social recognition are becoming increasingly privatized as a function of capital, while civil society continues to shrink and priorities are shifted from social services to capital maximization. Moreover, we need to explore how the racial management of gender and the gendered management of race assimilate the Asian adoptee into the intimate public sphere of the white nuclear family—into traditional, recognizable, and idealized family and kinship structures. How does the model minority myth help to facilitate this fit? How does the stereotype of the hard-working, agreeable, and passive Asian girl, ever eager to please, work to smooth over political problems, economic disparities, and cultural differences?[17]

These questions demand a deconstructive rereading of the Asian American model minority myth, whose genealogy is said to date from the Cold War necessity to produce "good" (anti-Communist) Asian subjects, as well as to the reformation of the 1965 Immigration and Nationality Act and its subsequent initiation of a professional "brain drain" from Asia in the form of a capitalist managerial class. How do war brides, mail-order brides, and transnational adoptees collectively challenge, broaden, and reorient traditional accountings of the transformation of "Asian alien" into "Asian American citizen?"

Relating this gendered history of Asian immigration, as well as white/black/yellow race relations, to the model minority discourse suggests that global histories of gendered commodification do, in fact, effect and affect domestic genealogies of race, racialization, and citizenship. Indeed, the practice of transnational adoption marks a contemporary crossing of global processes of flexible specialization and the production of new racialized communities—new global families—that must be considered against a politics of weak multiculturalism. This is a politics focused not on issues of social justice, material redistribution, and substantive equality, but on economic entitlement and the rights and privileges of family for an emergent class of multicultural elites. In this current state of emergency, to paraphrase Walter Benjamin, what are the psychic costs and burdens that underwrite transnational adoption's political, economic, and social contradictions? What is the psychic scaffolding that makes transnational adoption an inhabitable and livable, or an uninhabitable and barren, condition of existence? Let us return to the psychic dilemma of "two mothers."

Psychic Diasporas

For the transnational adoptee, where does history begin?

In the opening minutes of *First Person Plural*, we are given several conflicting answers to this question. The filmmaker presents a complex montage sequence that combines family photographs, her adoptive father's home movies, including scenes of Borshay Liem's arrival at the San Francisco airport on 3 March 1966, and her own interview footage of her American parents and siblings some thirty years later as they watch these home movies and recall their memories and feelings of that fateful day. The sequence begins with Denise, Borshay Liem's sister, explaining the excitement of "getting" a sister, "someone to play with," as she puts it. "I remember getting my hair done to go pick you up at the airport, and I was really jazzed about that," Denise tells us. But despite her "excitement" about picking up Cha Jung Hee, her new little sister from Korea, Denise's investment in (feminine) self-display belies a narcissistic logic that as a whole underwrites the entirety of the Borshay family's initial encounter with the eight-year-old adoptee. "I think mother went up to the wrong person," Denise admits. "Yeah. I think we didn't know until we checked your name tag or something who told us who you were. It did not matter. I mean, one of them was ours."

Here, the language of ownership, as well as the assumed interchange-ability of the variously "tagged" adoptees, constitutes a clear violation of the exclusive bond thought to exist between mother and child. This violation opens immediately upon the terrain of commodification—one of exchangeability and substitutability. Significantly, Borshay Liem's "acquisition" is accompanied by the simultaneous erasure of Cha Jung Hee's Korean identity through the dismissal of her prior history and family. "You know, to us an orphanage meant that you had no family," Alveen Borshay explains. "This way you were going to have a family." Suggesting that Borshay Liem's history begins only with her entry into their particular family unit, Denise concludes: "From the moment you came here, you were my sister and we were your family and that was it. And even though we look different—different nationality or whatever—we were your family."

Echoing Alveen's and Denise's sentiments, Donald Borshay's account is notably similar. And although the father recalls a momentary wrinkle in Borshay Liem's initial arrival, this problem is quickly smoothed out through its concerted willing away: "I remember very clearly your first meal," Donald recalls. "Mother prepared something that was very nice. And we were sitting at the table and you just kind of dropped your head and the tears started to come down. No words were spoken. Mother could see what was happening, and she simply took you away from the table and you were excused and from then on it was perfect."

"From then on it was perfect." I have spent some time detailing the various recollections of the "from then on" moment of Borshay Liem's arrival in the United States. I do so because these comments collectively illustrate the ways in which the transnational adoptee is commodified as an object to be enjoyed, while at the same time the particular histories of her past are denied, repressed, and effaced. In Denise's, Alveen's, and Donald's recollections, history "proper" begins only at the moment of Borshay Liem's arrival "over here," the privatized language of family working to overwrite histories of Korea as well as the particularities of Cha Jung Hee's Korean past.

Alveen admits quite forthrightly that her initial desire to adopt stemmed from watching Gary Moore commercials on NBC television advertising Foster Parents Plan through the plight of Korean War orphans. However, this history cannot be easily reconciled with Borshay Liem's past. Public histories of war, imperialism, domestic conflict, and poverty in Korea cannot be easily connected to the private sphere of the prosperous and upbeat American family.

Moreover, while there is no such thing as a motherless child, the opening sequence of *First Person Plural* highlights the management of Borshay Liem's past history through the valence of the "proper" name. Sent to the United States at eight, Borshay Liem has a series of identities and proper names that are erased through her transnational exchange. "My Name is Kang Ok Jin," Borshay Liem begins in the opening lines of *First Person Plural*. As her face flashes onto the screen and fades into an eerie solarized silhouette, she continues: "I was born on 14 June 1957. I feel like I've been several different people in one life. My name is Cha Jung Hee. I was born on 5 November 1956. I've had three names, three different sets of histories. My name is Deann Borshay. I was born 3 March 1966, the moment I stepped off the airplane in San Francisco. I've spoken different languages and I've had different families." First "Kang Ok Jin" and then deliberately substituted for another child, "Cha Jung Hee," by the Korean adoption agency, "Deann Borshay" is finally "born" on 3 March 1966, not by her Korean birth mother but by her arrival on the San Francisco jet way. Ultimately, through the animating desires and projections of her American family, she enters what they consider to be her "proper" history.

It is important to note that the repression of Borshay Liem's past is carried out not only as a collective family project but also, and more importantly, through the *strict management of the adoptee's affect*. That is, the contraction of Korean history into the privatized boundaries of the white American family is finessed through the repression and erasure of Borshay Liem's emotions. The silent tears that mark Borshay Liem's arrival as well as the negation of her past cannot have linguistic expression and thus have no symbolic life. These tears must necessarily be refused, as Donald Borshay does indeed refuse and then "excuse" them, such that Borshay Liem has little psychic recourse to work through her considerable losses. (Attitudes toward open adoption have shifted considerably from thirty years ago. However, given the ways in which difference is often appropriated and reinscribed by a politics of weak multiculturalism, the current acknowledgment of the adoptee's past may not have shifted this management of affect in any significant manner.)

How might we begin to analyze Borshay Liem's affective losses? Several years ago, in response to a series of Asian American student suicides at a university where I had been teaching, I cowrote with Shinhee Han, a clinical psychotherapist, an essay entitled "A Dialogue on Racial Melancholia."[18] In this article, we analyze Freud's theories of mourning and melancholia as presenting a compelling framework to conceptualize registers of loss and depression attendant to the conflicts and struggles associated with immigration, assimilation, and racialization for Asian Americans. In contrast to "normal" mourning, where libido is eventually withdrawn from a lost object to be invested elsewhere, melancholia as described by Freud is a "pathological" mourning without end. As Freud's privileged theory of unresolved grief, melancholia delineates a psychic condition whereby certain losses can never be avowed and, hence, can never be properly mourned. In our argument, racial melancholia describes both social and psychic structures of loss emerging from Asian immigrant experiences that can be worked through only with the greatest of considerable pain and difficulty.

Here it is important to emphasize that the experience of immigration is based on a structure of loss. In "Mourning and Melancholia," Freud describes the lost object as embodying a person, place, or ideal. When one leaves a country of origin, voluntarily or involuntarily (as in the case of transnational adoptees), a host of losses both concrete and abstract must be mourned. To the extent lost ideals of Asianness (including homeland, family, language, property, identity, custom, status) are irrecoverable, immigration, assimilation, and racialization are placed within a melancholic framework—a state of suspension between "over there" and "over here." In Freud's theory of mourning, one works through and finds closure to these losses by investing in new objects and ideals—in the American dream, for example.

To the extent, however, that Asian Americans are perpetually consigned to foreigner status and considered eccentric to the nation (as the recent Wen Ho Lee case yet again illustrates), and to the extent that ideals of whiteness remain unattainable and thus lost for Asian Americans, it might be said that they are denied the capacity to invest in new people, places, and ideals. This inability to invest in new objects is a crucial part of Freud's definition of melancholia. Racial melancholia thus describes a psychic process by which vexed identification and affiliations with lost objects, places, and ideals of both Asianness *and* whiteness remain estranged and unresolved.

In *First Person Plural*, we witness the numerous ways in which Borshay Liem's past is repressed, the continuous ways in which her racial difference and past history are managed and denied, so that she cannot mourn what she has lost in Korea. Furthermore, the documentary portrays Borshay Liem's frustrating and impossible identifications with ideals of whiteness that remain perpetually elusive. Speaking about her vain attempts to mimic the "American ways" of her siblings, Duncan and Denise, Borshay Liem presents us with numerous home movies documenting her torturous adolescent development: Deann sitting amid her white dolls; Deann dressed up like a Korean doll; Deann the prom queen; Deann with her towering white high school boyfriend; Deann as a perky college cheerleader.

Throughout the documentary, we witness in everyday acts, gestures, and offhand comments by her entire family the active production of Borshay Liem's Korean difference, accompanied by a simultaneous reinscription—an effacing and a whitewashing—of this difference. In the very opening minutes of Borshay Liem's documentary, her brother Duncan, in what can be described only as a smug tone of self-congratulation, tells her: "You didn't come from my mommy's womb. You don't have the family eyes, but you've got the family smile. Color and look doesn't make any difference. It's who you are. You're my sister." Duncan's statement underwrites a philosophy of weak multiculturalism, what Homi Bhabha describes as the irreducible failure of mimicry: "*Almost the same, but not quite.... Almost the same but not white.*"[19]

In an especially disturbing episode recounted by her mother, a young Borshay Liem is shown in a home movie combing the very blond hair of a doll. In a voice-over commentary that could easily be described as an Asian version of *The Bluest Eye*, Alveen tells Borshay Liem, "You said, 'Mother, my ears always stick out. I hate that.' I said, 'Honey, that can be fixed if you want,' and you wanted." At this point, Donald Borshay chimes in, "So we went to the plastic surgeon in San Jose ... and when they went to take the bandages off, then you began to cry." Again, the family is faced with tears, an overflow of affect that is met with bafflement, without real understanding.

Freud maintains in "Mourning and Melancholia" that melancholia emerges from a "pathological" disposition and can be distinguished from regular mourning by its inability to end.[20] In "A Dialogue on Racial Melancholia," Han and I contest Freud's distinction between mourning and melancholia. If experiences of immigration, assimilation, and racialization in the United States are fundamentally determined through both the forced relinquishing of lost but unspeakable Asian ideals and foreclosed investments in whiteness, then we might justifiably describe racial melancholia as a "normal" everyday group experience for Asian Americans. This insight places Asian American subjectivity and racial melancholia on the terrain of conflict, not damage. In this respect, racial melancholia might be better described as a depathologized "structure of feeling," to cite

Raymond Williams's term for those unidentified affects marking emergent group formations and identities.[21] Operating less as an individual than a group dynamic, racial melancholia for Asian Americans, we conclude, involves not just mourning or melancholia but a continual negotiation between mourning *and* melancholia.

Significantly, this negotiation is often and even exclusively configured within Asian American cultural politics as an *intergenerational* and *intersubjective* negotiation. That is, problems and contradictions arising from Asian American immigration are often interpreted in terms of master narratives of intergenerational conflict between parents and children, between the older and younger generation. The tendency to reduce all social issues, including those resulting from institutional racism and economic exploitation, to first-generation versus second-generation struggles threatens to displace them within the privatized space of the family. At the same time, it denies what are necessarily public problems and absolves the state and mainstream community from proper address or redress.

While I flag this palpable danger, what I would like to emphasize in this analysis of transnational adoption is the elimination of this intergenerational and intersubjective process, the loss of the communal nature of racial melancholia. As a collective unit, the family cannot recognize Borshay Liem's racial melancholia. Borshay Liem's losses remain unaffirmed and unacknowledged by those closest to her, by her own family, by those most affectively immediate to her. This is the striking difference between the ways in which racial melancholia is negotiated within Asian American immigrant families and the ways loss is negotiated by the Asian transnational adoptee. Earlier, I asked whether the transnational adoptee, as well as her adoptive family, was Asian American. To the extent that Borshay Liem's adoptive family recognizes her as a racialized subject, while not recognizing themselves as such, we witness an emotional gap of significant consequence in the intimate space of the family. That is, this failure of recognition serves to redouble racial melancholia's consequences, effectively severing Borshay Liem from the family unit, affectively segregating her, and ultimately forcing her to negotiate her losses in isolation. What should necessarily be an intergenerational and intersubjective negotiation of loss is thus reduced to intrasubjective isolation and silence.

"There was an unspoken contract between us, which we had all agreed upon—that I was an orphan with no family ties to Korea," Borshay Liem explains, using the "public" language of contracts and exchange to pierce the "private" bubble of the nuclear family.

> I belonged only to my American parents. It meant I didn't have a
> Korean history or Korean identity.... I think being adopted into

my family in some ways brought a lot of happiness for both me and for my parents, my American family. But there was also something that was—there was also a lot of sadness that we couldn't deal with as a family. And a lot of that sadness had to do with loss.

"I was never able to mourn what I had lost [in Korea] with my American parents," Borshay Liem adds, explaining the years of clinical depression that she suffered after leaving Fremont and her family to attend college at Berkeley.

What is especially disturbing here is not just the fact that the family cannot recognize Borshay Liem's racial melancholia, cannot easily conceive of her adoption as involving loss, cannot easily imagine her arrival in the United States as anything but a gain. Equally distressing is the fact that Borshay Liem's continual melancholy is a sadness that is read by many involved as ingratitude, serving to exacerbate Borshay Liem's enduring feelings of disloyalty and shame. What, after all, could be less "grateful" on the part of an adoptee than depression?

Hence, what is justifiably felt to be a happy event from the point of view of the parents and siblings comes to overdetermine the adoptee's affect. Deann's melancholia is countered by an overpowering joy on the part of the other family members, such that their collective will comes to overwrite her emotional states and experiences. In the end, Borshay Liem tells us, "I forgot everything. I forgot how to speak Korean. I forgot any memory of ever having had a family. And I even forgot my real name.... The only memories I have of my childhood are the images my father filmed while growing up. I relegated my real memories into the category of dreams."[22]

For Borshay Liem, racial melancholia involves the effacing and overwriting of her childhood memories and affective commitments. In this regard, transnational adoption's psychic predicament radically reduces any sense of the adoptee's agency. Indeed, though I earlier described the practice of transnational adoption as one of the most privileged forms of contemporary immigration, it is one largely devoid of emotional agency for the adoptee. In her attempts to mourn the unspeakable losses initiated by her (involuntary) exchange, the transnational adoptee might also be said to experience an affective curtailment that prevents her from transforming melancholy ever gradually into mourning. Here, I am delineating a profound form of racial melancholia, one that reduces memories to dreams, and agency to fantasy.

Importantly, it is only the mother who ultimately recognizes Borshay Liem's affective discrepancy. Reviewing the family movie of Borshay Liem's arrival, Alveen finally notices some thirty years later Borshay Liem's stricken facial expression. In a voice-over, she admits to her daughter, "When you arrived—little stoic face and bundled up in all those clothes.

We couldn't talk to you. You couldn't talk to us. I realize now that you were terrified. Because we were so happy, we just didn't think about that." As we witness in *First Person Plural,* the emotional clash between the Borshay family's affective joy and the young adoptee's obvious terror eventually becomes a "return of the repressed," a repetition compulsion that is psychically displaced and negotiated between mother and daughter.

Here, let us remember that adoption is often bound up with questions of faltering maternity—of failed reproduction and proper mothering. To the extent that adoption (rather than having no children) is often viewed as the last alternative to biological reproduction, the maternal bond with the adoptee is already overdetermined. In the case of transnational adoption, these issues become especially problematic because of the child's tenuous place within the biologized ideal of the nuclear family. Because the racialized link between the white mother and the Asian daughter elicits comment, because it becomes something that must be continually and repeatedly explained, the maternal bond appears as something not only unnatural but also in need of continual support.[23] "Some people would ask and others would kind of look," Alveen tells Borshay Liem, "and you knew they were wondering, but we didn't care." Given the challenge to negotiate radical alterity and racism within the intimate public sphere of the white family, Alveen's reaction is unfortunately less rather than more ideal, less rather than more caring, a missed opportunity. In the final analysis, the mother is not just responsible for removing Borshay Liem from the dinner table—literally burdened with handling her daughter's disjunctive affect. Indeed, the mother is ultimately blamed for the daughter's psychic condition. "Emotionally," Borshay Liem concludes, "there wasn't room in my mind for two mothers." Let us try to explore this mother/daughter predicament more carefully.

In psychoanalysis, of course, origin and history begin with the mother. It is important to recall that, in Freud's traditional narrative of the little girl's separation from the maternal, there is not only an account of two mothers, the phallic and the lacking, but also a genealogy of unrelenting recrimination and blame. Summarizing his views on the "riddle" of female subjectivity, Freud writes in "Femininity":

> A woman's identification with her mother allows us to distinguish two strata: the pre-Oedipus one which rests on her affectionate attachment to her mother and takes her as a model, and the latter one from the Oedipus complex which seeks to get rid of her mother and take her place with her father. We are no doubt justified in saying that much of both of them is left over for the future and that neither of them is adequately surmounted in the course

of development. But the phase of the affectionate pre-Oedipus attachment is the decisive one for a woman's future: during it preparations are made for the acquisition of the characteristics with which she will later fulfill her role in the sexual function and perform her invaluable social tasks. It is in this identification too that she acquires her attractiveness to a man, whose Oedipus attachment to his mother it kindles into passion. How often it happens, however, that it is only his son who obtains what he himself aspired to! One gets the impression that a man's love and a woman's are a phase apart psychologically.[24]

Commentators typically gloss Freud's famous lament—"that a man's love and a woman's are a phase apart psychologically"—as the notion that "women direct toward their children the love which their husbands desire for themselves."[25] What accounts for this cleaving and generational displacement of affect? What psychic mechanism forces the little girl to shift her desire for and pleasurable identifications with the pre-Oedipal mother to invest, ever so reluctantly, in the unforgiving figure and the name of the father?

According to Freud, the castration crisis and the subsequent penis envy it activates in the little girl work to alienate her from an affectionate attachment to the pre-Oedipal mother, or what Freud elsewhere labels the "negative Oedipus complex." In surrendering the negative-Oedipal mother to identify with the symbolic mother of lack, the little girl is not just exiled from activity into passivity, but also forced into an impossible psychic trajectory of contempt. "The suppression of women's aggressiveness which is prescribed for them constitutionally and imposed on them socially," Freud observes, "favors the development of powerful masochistic impulses, which succeed … in binding erotically the destructive trends which have been diverted inward."[26] Here, Freud delineates the emergence of the normative female subject as not just profoundly masochistic but melancholic. She is a subject not only estranged from the loved phallic mother and the pleasurable passion she represents but also narcissistically wounded and, finally, alienated from her own self, the psychic life of her original erotic investments.

The legacy of the little girl's severed history with the negative-Oedipal mother is one in which the affective bonds to the phallic nonlacking mother are melancholically transformed from intense love to magnified hate, such that it becomes, Freud observes, "very striking and [may] last all through life."[27] In covering up the passionate bonds of attachment between the little girl and her loved mother, the castration crisis inaugurates and makes way for the symbolic mother of lack, the positive-Oedipal mother, whom the little girl blames for her "mutilated" condition. This is an endless cycle of vilification. For every daughter who comes to blame her mother for her subordinated position is also liable to censure should she become a mother and thus be forced to relive this psychic rejection from the receiving end. This process of maternal melancholy explains how it is that the little girl comes to have no psychic room in her mind for two mothers. That is, it explains how the little girl comes to have no psychic room for the nonlacking negative-Oedipal mother but only psychic space for the castrated positive-Oedipal mother and the diminished world she comes to signify.

How might this paradigm of the negative and positive Oedipus complex play out specifically in terms of Borshay Liem's psychic predicament? How are the negative and positive Oedipus complex negotiated between the bodies of two mothers—Korean and white? What should be immediately clear in Borshay Liem's psychic predicament is that the negative and positive Oedipus complexes necessarily map not only a sexual but also a racial divide. This racial divide creates distinctions between Asianness and whiteness that must also be traced back to a kind of castration crisis where whiteness emerges as a symbolic and governing trope. For the Asian transnational adoptee, whose racialization might be said to be produced and denied by her family at once, issues of blame and recrimination are remarkably complicated.

Melanie Klein's notion of reinstatement of the mother to a world of loved internal objects is critical to understanding Borshay Liem's psychic dilemma. Klein tells us that psychic stability and health depend upon a subject's ability to align and to test continually the "real" mother against her phantasmatic images—both good and bad. In "The Psychogenesis of Manic-Depressive States," Klein writes:

> In some patients who had turned away from their mother in dislike or hate, or used other mechanisms to get away from her, I have found that there existed in their minds nevertheless a beautiful picture of the mother, but one which was felt to be a *picture* of her only, not her real self. The real object was felt to be unattractive—really an injured, incurable, and therefore dreaded person. The beautiful picture had been dissociated from the real object but had never been given up, and played a great part in the specific ways of their sublimations.[28]

What must be shorn away from the mother in order for reinstatement to occur, in order for Borshay Liem to create a beautiful picture of the mother? In "A Dialogue on Racial Melancholia," Han and I found that, in the case of biological Asian American immigrant children, race and sexuality must often cleave—that racial difference must often be dissociated from the figure of the "real" mother—for reinstatement to occur. But, for the transnational adoptee, who is the "real" mother? And what might her beautiful picture look like?

In the case of Borshay Liem, the negotiation of the good and the bad mother must be brokered across two maternal bodies, Korean and white. "I had a particular difficulty talking to my American mother about my Korean mother.... I didn't know how to talk about my mother with my mother because she was my mother," Borshay Liem states confusedly. For her, the question of who is the "real" mother oscillates wildly, so that recrimination and blame abound to the point that any creation of a beautiful picture is inevitably constrained. Borshay Liem admits that, even though "it was as if I had been born to them somehow," she cannot, as an adult, accept Alveen and Donald Borshay as her parents (even though, as we must remember, it is Alveen who largely lives through and negotiates Borshay Liem's recriminations and blame). Ultimately, Deann feels as if she must choose one family over the other, one mother over the other. Hoping to alleviate these feelings of "disloyalty," Borshay Liem confesses, "I felt if I could actually see them come together in real life that somehow both families could then live within myself. So I asked my parents to go to Korea with me."

However, Borshay Liem's attempt to merge her two mothers through her long-anticipated "reunion" with both women illustrates the difficulty of her psychic dilemma of the maternal and the racial. Her attempts to achieve psychic integration are met on the part of her two families with confusion and resistance, as well as a dearth of understanding about the absolute need to move beyond the singularity of the "real" mother. In fact, much of Borshay Liem's reunion in Korea is spent trying to determine who the "real" mother really is. As such, the initial trauma of Borshay Liem's transnational adoption is not just reenacted but redoubled through her initial rejection of the (white) mother and, in turn, her own repeated rejection by *both* mothers.

"You look like your mother," Alveen tells Borshay Liem upon their arrival at the birth mother's residence in Kunsan, Korea. However, Alveen's "gracious" relinquishing of Borshay Liem to her biological mother is met with equally "gracious" ambivalence and resistance. "She [the birth mother] says it's natural because she's her daughter," the translator first relates. "Yes," Alveen responds. But then the translator adds, turning to Borshay Liem: "She [the birth mother] says that although she is your mother, she only gave birth to you so you should really love and do everything you can for your adoptive parents. ... She wants you to be happy with your parents, your adopted parents." At this imperative, we see Borshay Liem wince. Having rejected her white mother, Borshay Liem, in turn, is rejected.

According to her Korean brother, who speaks on behalf of the Kang family (the father having died), Borshay Liem was sent away for a "better life." "It's not that important anymore. We are not very proud of what happened. She really needs to consider the cultural differences between us. Only then will she understand us," he rationalizes. "We have been apart for thirty years. It would be easier to close the gap between us if we spoke the same language. However, our cultural differences are difficult to overcome." Configuring her adoption as both an alienation from her "native" Korean culture and a gain, a "better life" for Borshay Liem in the United States, the Korean brother's attitude is remarkably similar to that of Donald Borshay insofar as neither man is capable of recognizing Borshay Liem's emotional injuries or needs. They cannot acknowledge her inability to negotiate the affective losses of her transnational exchange. (Tellingly, Borshay Liem does not state that "there wasn't room in my mind for two fathers.")

In *First Person Plural* affective responsibility is highly gendered, a psychic dynamic of which the mothers are not only aware but also for which they are both finally held accountable. "She [Borshay Liem] is filled with heartache," the Korean birth mother recognizes, "so I am very sad." Though she is "unable to express" this sadness in adequate ways, having "no words to describe the agonizing years" after she relinquished Borshay Liem for adoption, the Korean birth mother, like Alveen Borshay, must tend to the affective dissonance of the event, assuming blame for the situation. The Korean birth mother thanks the white mother for raising Borshay Liem, and in this way her sorrow and gratitude become, in the words of Alveen Borshay, "our joy." As such, Borshay Liem's "reunion" and fantasy of return disturb the notion of completion and closure, revealing in the process the asymmetry separating women in Third World nations who relinquish their children and those in First World nations who receive them. This racialized asymmetry between First and Third World comes to underpin the gendered dilemma of maternal melancholy delineated by Freud. That is, the endless cycle of maternal vilification is compounded by racial disparities that ultimately force a rethinking of the category of the "real" as well as Klein's notion of the good and the bad mother.[29]

Psychically pushed and pulled away by both her Korean mother and her American mother, Borshay Liem is unable to create space in her mind for two mothers. While there is a proliferation of multiple sites of the "real" in this reunion, there is nevertheless absolute psychic fidelity on the part of everyone involved that the position of the "real" mother can be only singular and not multiple. Indeed, the predicament of Borshay Liem's maternal melancholy, compounded by the dissonance of the "real" (Korean or white) mother, ultimately renders the question of the "real" impossible.

That is, Borshay Liem ultimately does not have space in her mind for *any* "real" mother at all. In Klein's vocabulary, while she cannot have room in her mind for two good mothers, she does indeed have room in her mind for two *bad* mothers. One—the Korean mother—is blamed for abandoning her to her fate; the other—the white mother—is blamed for being unable to mirror her emotional (racial) predicaments. Hence, Borshay Liem cannot create a beautiful picture from either, rendering the question of reinstatement extraordinarily tenuous. Rejected by both mothers she, too, must reject them. (Here let me gesture to Gail Dolgin and Vincente Franco's 2002 *Daughter from Danang*, another recent documentary exploring transnational adoption in the wake of the Vietnam War. The film is an elaborate disquisition on adoptee Heidi Bub's successive rejection of two "bad" mothers—first her adoptive mother and then her birth mother.)

The singularity of the "real" mother, as well as the question of blame, continues to haunt Borshay Liem through the very end of *First Person Plural*. Confessing that, with her parents in the room, she felt more like a "temporary visitor" with her Korean family, Borshay Liem admits that "the only way I can actually be closer to my Korean mother is to admit that she's not my mother anymore. The only way to be close to her is to acknowledge that she hasn't been my mother for over thirty years, and that my other mother has been my mother for—in a way my real mother." Borshay Liem's speech expresses the will to move forward psychically, but it is riddled with ambivalence and continues to be marked by the notion of singularity, origin, and return—the need to choose between the two mothers. Responding to Alveen Borshay's statement that "after all, that's your real mother [the Korean mother]," Borshay Liem attempts to broker a truce, stating cautiously, "I think you're my real mother." "Well, I feel that way," Alveen Borshay responds, "I really do." Again, we witness a certain asymmetry between mother and daughter, between language and emotion. While Alveen can affectively *feel* like Borshay Liem's mother, Borshay Liem can still only *think* this possibility.

The question of the singularity of the "real" mother is not only the kernel of the psychic dilemma of two mothers but also the key to imagining a poststructuralist theory of family and kinship predicated not on origin but on destination. However, this moving beyond fidelity to the singular, this moving forward from the fixity of the "real," is complicated by two powerful and compelling fantasies of return that simultaneously underwrite the psychic dynamics of transnational adoption: the return to the birth mother and the return to the motherland. In transnational adoption's crossing of sexuality and diaspora, we are presented with both the desire to return to the "real" mother and the desire to return to the place of origins. These intersecting discourses of return underwrite a personal narrative of self-realization, completion, and closure that, as *First Person Plural* illustrates, is not only an impossible task to accomplish but also creates fragmentation and further displacement rather than wholeness. In returning to Korea for her "reunion," Borshay Liem is forced to acknowledge the fact that confronting the past is always double-edged, challenging any sense of recoupable stability. On the social level, these discourses of return resist notions of authenticity and belonging that support conservative notions of diaspora. Configuring diaspora in terms of heterosexuality, filiation, and ethnic purity, discourses of return as "completion" and "recuperation" deny issues of queerness, affiliation, and social contingency at the heart of contemporary formations of queer diasporas, new global families, and flexible kinship.

Following this family "reunion," Borshay Liem admits that she has given up "that childhood fantasy of returning to my family," of "somehow be[ing] sent back to Korea." Although Borshay Liem recognizes that she must "develop another relationship, a different relationship with my Korean family," the conclusion of *First Person Plural* does not seem to endorse such a moving forward. Indeed, the documentary ends with Borshay Liem's marriage ceremony and the birth of a son, Nick. The sentimental "resolution" to Borshay Liem's social and psychic predicament is an entified Oedipal structure legislating only one privileged place for mother, father, and child. Hence, Borshay Liem's "cure" to her dilemma of two mothers does not move beyond either notions of the singular or the traditional structures of family and kinship. Rather, this marriage allows her to create and to inhabit a conventional nuclear family structure of her own, to make good on what she believes she never had. While Borshay Liem's marriage to her Korean husband, Paul Liem, complicates questions of return to cultural origins, the final image Borshay Liem leaves us with in *First Person Plural* comes in the form of a family photo of this naturalized Oedipal trio. Ironically, this compensatory Oedipal trio subscribes to the very psychic and material structure at the heart of Borshay Liem's maternal and diasporic predicament.

Here, let me conclude by way of my own return to the negative Oedipus complex. In "Girl Love," Kaja Silverman reminds us of Freud's insistence that it is only by accessing a woman at the level of her negative Oedipus complex that a man can love her. "It is in this identification," Silverman quotes Freud, "that she acquires her attractiveness to man, whose Oedipus attachment to his mother it kindles into passion." Silverman then observes that "so long as the negative Oedipus complex remains hidden from the female subject herself, she will not be able to respond to the desire it arouses in the male subject."[30] Hence, the melancholy to which the female subjectivity typically leads is based not just upon the impossibility of any reciprocal relationship between the sexes; it is equally based upon the loss of the loved mother, the forfeiting of a realm of extraordinary affective intensity, and the closing down of the possibility of any redemptive form of female love. The castration crisis inaugurates this form of pathological sexuality in the little girl who, like her lacking mother, finally becomes a subject who cannot love and a subject no one else could love.

What would it mean for the little girl to have access to the passionate psychic intensity of her negative Oedipus complex? What would it mean for the little girl, like the little boy, to have equal and reciprocal access to the affective realm of the loved mother, to refuse to devalue the negative-Oedipal mother, to repudiate the logic of maternal blame and recrimination? It would mean, of course, that she would have room in her psyche for two good mothers. Silverman proposes that the symbolic recovery of the affect associated with the negative Oedipal mother is indeed possible, not just for men but for women, too, in a signifying process she labels "girl love."

In both *The Interpretation of Dreams* and *The Unconscious*, Freud maintains that every signifying act in a given subject's life refers back in some ultimate sense to a primally repressed term, which, as we witness in *First Person Plural*, is still primarily the mother. But, while she is configured as our ground of desire, the mother in fact provides the first signifier for a more primordial loss: the loss of what Jacques Lacan variously calls "presence," "being," or the "here and now." Silverman writes:

> Unlike the other signifiers of the *hic et nunc*, though, she has nothing to refer back to. What she stands in for psychically cannot provide this function, since it is precisely what escapes signification. Although serving as the support for libidinal symbolization, the mother is consequently devoid of semantic value. It is not she who gives all of the other signifiers of desire their meaning; it is, rather, *they* who determine what *she* can mean. To go "backward," libidinally speaking, is also not finally to touch "ground"; it is, instead, to apprehend the groundlessness of all signification.[31]

"Girl love" represents a signifying process whereby one recuperates the loved and lost negative-Oedipal mother not by moving backward toward the recuperation of origins but by moving forward, "to symbolize lack in a way that is utterly our own."[32] It is a signifying process that is quickening of disparaged creatures and things, that endows devalued others, the bad Korean and the bad white mother, with new and alternate meaning. "There is nothing primordial about this relationship," Silverman writes. "It does not represent a continuation of the female's early love for the mother, but rather its symbolic recovery from a later moment in time, and there is no limit on when that can occur."[33] Like Silverman, what I am proposing here is not the recuperation of a lost origin in the recaptured figure of the negative-Oedipal mother, but the deployment of the affective intensity associated with this loved figure for a forgotten though crucial new form of symbolization.

Were it not for the castration crisis, Silverman concludes, we would all, men and women alike, have permanent access to the affective intensity of the negative Oedipus complex. "Girl love" thus recuperates a lost form of symbolization represented by the negative Oedipus complex, where libidinal "openness" rather than fixity reigns, and where words rather than binding affect come under the influence of their unconscious desire. By symbolizing lack in highly personalized and alternate forms we can create psychic space for two *good* mothers. While our words would still induce the "fading" of being, they would also induce a kind of "second coming." They would not only open psychic space for but also lend symbolic sustenance to two good mothers—two *"good enough"* mothers, to borrow from the language of D. W. Winnicott—not just the mother of lack but the mother of love, not just the Korean mother or the white mother but, indeed, both. The maternal resignification facilitated by "girl love" thus provides a crucial corrective to conservative (hetero)sexual and diasporic politics. We return to mother and motherland not by going back but by moving forward. We do not bring the present into the past. Rather, we bring the past into the present. In fact, we keep the past alive in the present by signifying and quickening through our desire those creatures and things that conventional culture would disavow or bury.

In the introduction to this essay, I stated that while we have numerous poststructuralist accounts of language, we have few poststructuralist accounts of kinship. Why is this so? I have spent some time analyzing the material and psychic contradictions of transnational adoption in *First Person Plural*, for I think the practice manifests the broader paradoxes of globalization and contemporary crossings of sexuality, racial formation, economic exploitation, and nation on both an international and a domestic level. As an instance of globalization and its discontents, transnational adoption also opens upon the difficult affective terrain of poststructuralist notions of family and kinship. While the age of late capitalism has given rise to numerous material reconfigurations of family, I fear that these new forms of kinship and social identity do not have any concomitant psychic support.[34] To the extent that the transnational adoptee functions as guarantee to conventional ideals of the white nuclear family, and to the extent that she cannot in turn create space in her mind for two good mothers, the possibility of a poststructuralist kinship is dubious at best. To the extent, however, that transnational adoption allows us to denaturalize powerful myths of return animating (hetero)sexual and diasporic politics in a global age, we are left with several possible alternatives.

As a contemporary phenomenon, transnational adoption installs racial alterity and otherness squarely into the privatized space of the white American nuclear family, even as our national borders continue to be sealed in unprecedented ways. The contemporary formation of interracial First and Third World families represents a tremendous opportunity to question the conservative impulses of (hetero)sexuality and diaspora. In the context of *First Person Plural*, the disjunctive experiences of the transnational adoptee open upon a painful though potentially productive social and psychic terrain exceeding the privatized boundaries of the family unit. There is no smooth translatability, that is, between the ideological demands of the white nuclear family structure and the adoptee's disjunctive affect, her psychic protest. By creating new global families and racial formations at once, the presence of the Asian child in the space of the white family necessarily erodes the boundaries between the public and private spheres, between public and private histories. If, as Lauren Berlant contends, the political sphere has been largely contracted into private life, then the practice of transnational adoption provides one crucial site to reengage with questions of the political.

Under the shadows of globalization, this erosion of boundaries separating public from private, calls for a broader response to racism, gender subordination, and economic exploitation that goes beyond, in Anagnost's words, "merely asserting one's entitlement to be a [transnational] parent."[35] Parents of transnational adoptees should not be held any more accountable than the rest of us to the political, economic, and social vicissitudes of globalization. Nevertheless, the practice of transnational adoption presents an exemplary—perhaps radical—opportunity for white, middle-class subjects to confront and to negotiate difference ethically within the social configurations of the new global family.

Restoring collective history to the process of a transnational adoptee's social and psychic development is crucial to the survival of the global family. It is also crucial to an ethical multiculturalism that rejects the model of the white heterobiological nuclear family as the standard against which all social orderings must be measured. Positing such an ethical multiculturalism may not just lead to powerful alliances for a progressive politics but could conceivably cut across historically constituted divisions of gender, race, and class to create important international and domestic political coalitions. In the process, it may also help us to create new material and psychic structures, a poststructuralist account and accounting of family and kinship, and of identity, community, and nation. Reimagining family and kinship, as well as recasting diaspora, in these terms offers a host of political opportunities, economic responsibilities, and cultural commitments.

Here, let me return to queer diasporas—to the John Hancock commercial and two dykes and a baby. We exist in a time when transnational adoption of Chinese baby girls by white lesbians can be aired on prime-time television during the Olympics. In this representation lies a nascent possibility, the possibility that this child might grow up to exist in a world where the psychic structure of two—indeed, three, four, five, or perhaps no— mothers of various races could be accommodated. Let us try to imagine— indeed, to live—these other possibilities, these other possible structures.

Acknowledgments

I thank the following friends and colleagues for their insightful feedback and support: Shinhee Han, Fred Moten, Mae Ngai, Teemu Ruskola, Mari Ruti, Josie Saldaña, Kaja Silverman, and Leti Volpp. I have been fortunate to present this essay to various university audiences and seminars at Harvard University, Dartmouth College, the University of Illinois at Urbana-Champaign, and the University of California at San Diego. I thank Brian Axel, Donald Pease, Robyn Wiegman, Martin Manalansan, Catherine Prendergast, Kent Ono, Lisa Lowe, Judith Halberstam, and Gavatri Gopinath for being ideal hosts as well as rigorous interlocutors. I also thank the *Social Text* collective, especially Brent Edwards and Cindi Katz, for their helpful comments.

Notes

1. Deann Borshay, dir., *First Person Plural* (San Francisco: National Asian American Telecommunications Association, 2000).

2. Amy Kaplan, introduction to *Cultures of United States Imperialisms,* ed. Amy Kaplan and Donald E. Pease (Durham, NC: Duke University Press, 1993), 16.

3. See *Social Text* no. 74, 21.1 (spring 2003) for a special issue on transnational parenting curated from the disciplinary angle of anthropology. My chapter, in part, is a response to what I see as a necessary critical reframing of current approaches to analyzing transnational adoption ethnographies and memoirs, as well as the broadening of the political, economic, and cultural issues they raise.

4. For an elaboration of the concept of "queer diaspora," see JeeYeun Lee, "Toward a Queer Korean American Diaspora," in *Q&A: Queer in Asian*

America, ed. David L. Eng and Alice Y. Hom (Philadelphia: Temple University Press, 1998); David L. Eng. "Out Here and Over There: Queerness and Diaspora in Asian American Studies," in *Racial Castration: Managing Masculinity in Asian America* (Durham, NC: Duke University Press, 2001); Cindy Patton and Benigno Sanchez-Eppler, eds., *Queer Diasporas* (Durham, NC: Duke University Press, 2000); and Arnaldo Cruz-Malavé and Martin F. Manalansan IV, eds., *Queer Globalizations: Citizenship and the Afterlife of Colonialism* (New York: New York University Press, 2002).

5. See Gayle Rubin, "The Traffic in Women: Notes on the 'Political Economy' of Sex," in *Toward an Anthropology of Women,* ed. Rayna R. Reiter (New York: Monthly Review, 1975); and Claude Levi-Strauss, *The Elementary Structures of Kinship,* trans. James Harle Bell and John Richard von Sturmer (Boston: Beacon, 1969).

6. Judith Butler, *Antigone's Claim: Kinship between Life and Death* (New York: Columbia University Press, 2000), 29–30.

7. Butler, *Antigone's Claim,* 70.

8. John Hancock Financial Services (Agency: Hill Holiday. Region: North America), 2000. To view this commercial, go to www2.conimercialcloset. org/cgi-bin/iowa/portrayals.html?record =216.

9. See "Hancock Ad Raises Alarm in Adoption Communities," *Wall Street Journal,* 14 September 2000. After protests from right-wing conservatives, the commercial was reedited without the final exchange about being great mothers. In addition, fearing reprisals from Chinese authorities that lesbians were snatching up Chinese infants, John Hancock added an audio track stating that a flight from Phnom Penh, Cambodia, had just arrived.

10. We need to dissociate the relationship between economic entitlement and political rights. That is, the current practice of transnational adoption suggests that family is available to those gays and lesbians with access to capital. However, the legal treatment of this group by courts has by and large excluded them from the sphere of non-economic rights (adoption, marriage, inheritance, service in the military, consensual sex). As a legal matter, adoption is a privilege; hence, the contemporary reconsolidation of family by gays and lesbians has become an economic privilege and entitlement for few rather than a political right for all.

11. Ann Anagnost, "Scenes of Misrecognitin: Maternal Citizenship in the Age of Transnational Adoption," *positions* 8.2 (fall 2000): 389–421.

12. Leti Volp, "Dependent Citizens and Marital Expatriates," unpublished manuscript.

13. See Lisa Lowe, *Immigrant Acts: On Asian American Cultural Politics* (Durham, NC: Duke University Press, 1996), and Mae Ngai, *Impossible Subjects: Illegal Aliens and the Making of Modern America* (Princeton, NJ: Princeton University Press, 2005).

14. Of course, the question of availability is not absolute but a discursive phenomenon. For a controversial analysis of the supply-and-demand aspect of baby adoption, see Elisabeth M. Landes and Richard A. Posner, "The Economics of the Baby Shortage," *Journal of Legal Studies* 7 no. 2 (June 1978):

323–348. For a critique of Landes and Posner, see Patricia Williams, "Spare Parts. Family Values, Old Children, Cheap," *New England Law Review* 28 (summer 1994): 913–927; and Laura Briggs and Ana Ortiz's essay "The Culture of Poverty, Crack Babies, and Welfare Cheats," *Social Text 76,* vol. 21.3 (Fall 2003): 39–58. Briggs and Ortiz write eloquently on how the 1980s emergent discourse on "crack babies," damaged beyond repair, also fuels the desire to adopt "safe" babies from abroad.

15. For an excellent discussion of the politics of interracial white parents/ black child adoption, see R. Richard Banks, "The Color of Desire: Fulfilling Adoptive Parent's Racial Preferences through Discriminatory State Action," *Yale Law Journal* 107 (January 1998): 875–964.

16. Miranda Joseph, *Against the Romance of Community* (Minneapolis: University of Minnesota Press, 2002), 43.

17. In *First Person Plural*, Donald Borshay tells Deann: "You were so determined to learn. I guess to please us, whatever, I'm not sure. You actually made yourself ill and you became jaundiced. You got kind of yellow-looking. And the only thing we could think of was that you really tried too hard and were trying too hard."

18. See David L. Eng and Shinhee Han, "A Dialogue on Racial Melancholia," *Psychoanalytic Dialogues: A Journal of Relational Perspectives* 10.4 (2000): 667–700.

19. Homi Bhabha, "Of Mimicry and Man: The Ambivalence of Colonial Discourse," *October 28* (spring 1984): 126, 130; Bhabha's emphasis.

20. See Sigmund Freud, "Mourning and Melancholia," in *The Standard Edition of the Complete Psychological Works of Sigmund Freud,* vol. 14, ed. James Strachey (London: Hogarth, 1957), 243–258. Later, in *The Ego and the Id* (1923). Freud comes to revise this distinction between mourning and melancholia, noting that the ego, in fact, comprises its abandoned and lost objects.

21. See Raymond Williams, *Marxism and Literature* (New York: Oxford University Press, 1977), 128–135.

22. In another part of *First Person Plural,* Borshay Liem adds, "When I had learned enough English to talk to my parents. I decided that I should tell them who I really was. I remember going up to my mother and telling her 'I'm not who you think I am, I'm not Cha Jung Hee. And I think I have a mother and brother and sisters in Korea still.' And she turned to me and said, 'Oh, honey, you've just been dreaming. You don't have a mother. And you never had brothers and sisters. Look at these adoption documents. It says that you're Cha Jung Hee and your mother died giving birth to you.' And she said, 'You know what, this is just a natural part of you getting used to living in a new country. Don't worry about it. They're just bad dreams. They're going to go away soon.'"

23. Here, I draw on this argument from Anagnost, "Scenes of Misrecognition," 395.

24. Sigmund Freud, "Femininity," in *New Introductory Lectures on Psychoanalysis,* ed. James Strachey (New York: W. W. Norton, 1965), 118.

25. Kaja Silverman, "Girl Love," in *James Coleman* (Munich: Lebhachhaus München), 159. I am indebted to Kaja Silverman for a series of conversations on the negative Oedipus complex and "girl love" that have influenced my arguments on *First Person Plural*.
26. Freud, "Femininity," 102.
27. Ibid.
28. Melanie Klein, *The Selected Melanie Klein,* ed. Juliet Mitchell (New York: Free Press, 1986), 125; Klein's emphasis.
29. It also complicates the notion of the "gift" that often attaches itself to (transnational) adoption—a notion that the infant is a "gift" from the birth mother to the adoptive mother, a gift that can never be repaid. See Barbara Yngvesson, "Placing the 'Gift Child' in Transnational Adoption," *Law and* Society *Review* 36, no. 2 (2002): 227–256.
30. Silverman, "Girl Love," 159.
31. Ibid, 156–157; Silverman's emphasis.
32. Ibid, 166.
33. Ibid, 161.
34. See Ken Corbett, "Nontraditional Family Romance," *Psychoanalytic Quarterly,* no. 70 (2001): 599–624.
35. Anagnost, "Scenes of Misrecognition," 395.

CHAPTER 6

Parenting and the Narcissistic Demands of Whiteness

GAIL M. BOLDT

The purpose of this chapter is to explore social, political, and psychic investments and contradictions that are inevitably a part of parenting* within and across racial lines. My argument, simply put, is that adults make demands on children, their own children and other children, for how children are expected to perform race. In this chapter, in short, I will use the psychoanalytically informed concept of *narcissism* to explore these demands as *identity demands*. Working from a poststructural position, I do not read narcissism as an individual characteristic or flaw but rather as a feature of Western, bourgeois subjectivity. I argue that under the best circumstances, we may be aware of our own anxieties and needs regarding identity performances of race and we might learn to view children as others with legitimate claims to forging identifications and attachments different than our own or those we would choose for them (Hall, 1997). At other times, we may, without much reflection, indulge the narcissistic propensity for playing out our fantasies, needs, and fears about race via the identity performances we expect from children.

---

* In using the term "parenting," "parent," or "parents," I am not making any assumption about who may be playing the role of primary caretaker(s) for a child.

In this chapter, following Butler (1997), Cheng (2002), and others (for example, Britzman, 1998; Eng, 2001), I am taking up the tool of psycho-analytic theories because I find them to offer tremendously useful and apt descriptions of the Western bourgeois family. Taken from a Foucauldian perspective (1988), I assume that what psychoanalytic theory describes as human development can be understood without resorting to an essential nature; rather, we can view these as the result of the process through which the infant, child, and adult become interpellated over time (Althusser, 1971) as an intelligible member of a given culture. My argument about race, then, is that race preexists us in culture, and that it is experienced as highly personal—as identity—and it is carried out in the demands we make upon ourselves and one another in the big and little things that are the material of ordinary life. Race is neither outside, as in culture, nor inside, as an attribute of the human. Race exists in a psychic-social space; it is something that we demand of ourselves and each other to stabilize the psychic-social contexts of our day-to-day lives. In the case of parent-ing, I turn to the psychoanalytic record as one potentially helpful tool for considering how and why we make identity demands of ourselves and the ones we love and care for and how these identity demands are expressed through race. Following the work of Judith Butler, I am trying to under-stand, "What is the psychic form that power takes?" (1997, p. 3).

From the outset it is important to note that the reader would be right to be suspicious of over-generalized claims about the nature of adult-hood, childhood, and race. The specificity of the adult's or the child's par-ticular racialized experiences and proximity to dominant and powerful discourses cannot be viewed generically. This chapter is specifically an exploration into one way that whiteness can play a role in parenting, and more specifically, about white mothering, and more specifically yet, about the potential of whiteness to exist as a demand that inflicts narcissistic injuries that move between adults and children across and within racial boundaries and generations.

In one important way, this chapter is yet even more specific; my child, now seven years old, is mixed race. Like his father and his paternal grand-parents, he was born in Hawaii and is of Japanese ancestry. On my side, he is the fourth generation of German-Americans to live (as we have since he was four years old) in the American Midwest. Central to this chapter is an exploration of demands that whiteness makes and that indivduals might make on whiteness, and how these demands inflict injuries that return to us as racial fantasies. Viewing the demands that parents make on their children to perform and embrace certain identifications as an attempt to repair the parents' narcissistic injury, I draw on personal narrative to think about how whiteness moves across generations. Because my child is mixed race, the issue of how racial fantasies and the desire to use the fantasy of race to repair narcissistic injury come into particular focus. My argument, however, is that the same mechanisms exist in families that identify as only white, but in more hidden ways. In taking the risk of putting my own parenting "on the couch" in such a public way, I hope that the investigation of my anxieties will be read as a useful example of much larger social conflicts and contradictions. For this purpose, psychoanalytic theory contributes to an exploration of how parents' anxieties and desires become translated as social identity demands made on children. It turns out that psychoanalysis has much to say about why identity matters so much in parent/child relationships; according to Freud (1923), the account of identity is, ironically, also an account of love.

A Psychoanalytic Account of Identification

A primary assumption of infant development offered by psychoanalytic theories beginning with Freud (1914) is that in the beginning infants have no need for identity or identification because they experience themselves as continuous with their parents. This is a narcissistically complete world in which the parent exists only as an extension of need satisfaction (Fink, 1996, 1997; A. Freud, 1953; Shapiro and Stern, 1989). At some point, however, the child experiences anxiety and doubt in his or her certainty of narcissistic completeness; there is a crisis in the relationship with the parent that leads to an awareness of separation. This is what many psychoanalytic theorists identify as the primary or founding crisis. It is our first awareness of need and of uncertainty over whether our need will be met. Psychoanalyst Jacques Lacan argues that it is the awareness of doubt and therefore vulnerability that drives us into language and sociality; children need to find ways to respond to the fact that they may or may not get what they want or need (Fink, 1977).

Desires and needs are twofold: there are the literal needs for food and care, the things that keep the child alive, and these are the needs that Freud calls "anaclitic"; and there are the narcissistic needs, the needs for love, admiration, belonging, comfort, and so on, the reassurances that soothe the anxieties caused by the awareness of one's own vulnerability and harkening back to the earlier fantasized completeness (1914). Narcissistic needs express themselves through identifications; that is, through introjection (internalization), we identify with and make our own those ideas and representations of people that we have found confirming or comforting.

Freud writes that the child's awareness of separateness and, therefore, vulnerability often causes the child to feel rage, grief, fear, and loss (1914).

These feelings can be threatening to the young child, raising the possibility that the child's feelings will cause the loss of the parent's love, that their feelings might actually kill the parent, or that the child's rage against the parent is mirrored in the parent's own punishing rage against the child. Often, the threatening and threatened feelings are introjected and split off from the child's conscious feelings toward the parent, leaving the child only with consciousness of loving and depending upon the parent. In an attempt to guarantee that the parent continues to meet the child's anaclitic and narcissistic needs, now conceptualized as love, the child comes to identify with the parent, taking on many of the parent's identifications, beliefs, and desires as its own. Our first identifications, therefore, are with our parents and are forged through fear and love. This is the point that Judith Butler (1997) makes when she states, "The Foucauldian postulation of subject as the simultaneous subordination and forming of the subject assumes a specific psychoanalytic valence when we consider that no subject emerges without a passionate attachment to those on whom he or she is fundamentally dependent" (p. 7).

As the child becomes more and more aware of adult expectations, the child learns the rules of sociality, what Freud (1916) called *the reality principle* and Lacan (1977) called the *Nom de Père* (the Law of the Father). A fundamental rule of the reality principle is that children can find limited companionship and narcissistic gratification only from the parent. This is what Freud describes as the Oedipal crisis. It is the second loss, children's frightening and rage-provoking realization that they cannot get the satisfactions they want and need from their parents. Children learn to look beyond the parent for satisfying, loving relationships. In this account then, social interest, group identification, and love are all born from the need to escape the terror of incompleteness, of vulnerability. Through identifications and relationships, we work to build the security, comfort, and assurance that will gratify our physical and our narcissistic needs.

But what are these identifications that we take on to cope with loss, vulnerability, disappointment, and fear? Butler (1997) explicitly moves the account of identification into a social arena when she says:

> Although the dependency of the child is not political in any usual sense, the formation of primary passion in dependency renders the child vulnerable to subordination and exploitation.… Moreover, this situation of primary dependency conditions the political formation and regulation of subjects and becomes the means of their subjection.… The desire to survive, "to be," is a pervasively exploitable desire. (p. 7)

This child subject, then, can be conceptualized as being formed in submission to power. The child who needs protection and sustenance moves into language and subjectivity, ultimately accepting the reality principle, the rules of culture. To posit that we become plausible social subjects via our acceptance as very young children of language, sociality, and the reality principle is to argue that as infants and young children we have to learn what it means to be specific proper subjects, or in other words, to perform normative identities (Boldt, 1996; Butler, 1990, 1993). Structures of language, expectations for acceptable sociality, and the reality principle are all discursive mechanisms of power that precede us.

Race as a Passionate Attachment

In essence, I am following Butler's work to try to elucidate how and why human beings develop passionate attachments to identities, including identities that we later come to recognize as less than admirable. We accept our submission to the reality principle in order to survive, and in our passion to survive we develop passionate attachments—love—to those objects in our environment that feed our narcissistic and anaclitic needs. Butler (1997) acknowledges the psychoanalytic account in saying that this submission happens when we are too young to know better. We may well have loved people—and ideas as representatives or sublimations of those people—whom our adult selves would rather we hadn't loved, people and ideas who are not, in fact, worthy of love, but we could not help ourselves. Because children need love in the form of literal and narcissistic sustenance, we, as children, often develop sublimations that take the form of racial and gender identities, things that helped us at one time to experience acceptance and approval from the adults upon whom we depended.

In some ways, then, the identifications develop through love. In fact, Anne Anlin Cheng (2002) argues that in Freud's writing, there is very little difference between falling in love and identifying with a group. The difference turns out to be simply the degree with which the relationship becomes invested with the sexual drive. Both identifying with groups and falling in love, she argues, are attempts at filling that desire for a fantasized authenticity and wholeness. Racial identification, Cheng argues:

> is not something that can be located on the inside or the outside, in the psychic or the social but rather is something that transcends or refutes the dichotomy itself. It is this idea of race—not as the unconscious or prehistoric inheritance but as the product of a relationship designed to bridge or naturalize the inherent gap

between individual and collectivity—that renders racial identification such a political activity. (p. 155)

For Cheng, as for Butler, racial identification is one way to fill the need for security and the assurance of love through immersion in group acceptance. Given that racial identifications—one's own identifications and the identifications one assumes or insists upon for others—are conferred with social privilege and social inequity, Cheng understands this identification as more than just a personal act. It is usually felt first and foremost as a personal experience, but Cheng argues that it is identification with power.

What might these passionate identifications look like? In my case, I grew up in a rural, Midwestern community that was homogeneously white, working class, and religious. A love of and sense of privilege about whiteness and a fundamental racism, while not identified as such, were absolutely central to shared local identity and embedded in our everyday practices and ways of making meaning about the world. While this is an identification I came later to reject, the psychoanalytic account provides me with a way to acknowledge that, as a child, I desperately loved and needed my parents and the other adults in my local community. Whiteness and racism were part of how I survived and even prospered. I sustained my life through being part of this community with all the promise and all the ugliness that entailed. In understanding the power that racialized identities have over us, it is important to consider that, like many others, as a child I did not simply tolerate a racist identity; I embraced it, finding in it the promise of life. Racialized identities can feel like a matter of life or death because this is exactly how they can be experienced, as the promise that allows us to feel the safety and comfort of belonging.

In American culture, we are not given any choice about whether or not to undertake racial identification. It is framed both as a social demand and a psychological necessity. As Butler (1990, 1993) argues about gender, identification is presented as the promise of meaning; failure to properly identify within socially recognized categories carries the price of social reprisal and loneliness. Cheng puts it this way:

> ... for Freud, one's investment in the act of identification, of taking on a certain identity, is conditioned by fear and is, by extension an identification with power. The individual, with what I call the deer caught in the headlights syndrome, is impressed into mirroring the group via fear, paralysis, even love. Thus power facilitates identification: an identification that is both paralyzing and exhibits the unlimited devotion of someone in love. Freudian identification describes the power of communal seduction. (p. 156)

Thus, Cheng moves both love and identification firmly onto social/ political ground. Whether one is falling in love with a person or with a group, falling in love is falling into ideology: "Ideology provides the very foundation for an individual to conceive of him/herself in relation to a community" (pp. 156–157). Ideology, love, and identification provide us with nothing less than the promise of a self.

Like many academics investigating the political and social processes of identification, Cheng cites the work of Louis Althusser, who described a process he called "interpellation" as the mechanism through which social meanings and legal demands come to constitute us as subjects in a given culture (1971). Althusser's famous image is that of the person hailed on the street by a police officer. The officer calls out, "Hey you!" and in the moment of acknowledging the hail by turning to it, we are both constituted as and acknowledged as subjects of the law. A common use of Althusser's description reads this social interpellation into subjectivity as a bad thing (or *only* a bad thing), a coopting of an originally good or pure self into ideologies that support our own oppression or the oppression of others; however, psychoanalytic theory articulated through a poststructural lens posits that interpellation is in fact the necessary process through which we become recognizable as plausible people in the world (Butler, 1997; Cheng, 2002; Eng, 2001). Discipline from this perspective is not a corrupting of an original human nature, what we were like before society wrecked us, but rather it is the imposition of the very possibility that one can participate in society (Ball, 1990). From the psychoanalytic perspective, the person who cannot be interpellated into society ends up labeled psychotic and has severely constrained possibilities for the pleasures and powers that are attached to social recognition and approval.

A Story of Whiteness

As a young adult, identification with my rural community became increasingly intolerable for me. In rejecting identification with my local community, I also began the intellectual effort of rejecting racism. To ask which came first—a socially and intellectually motivated rejection of racism that led to emotional alienation from the community, or an emotional alienation from the community that was then justified by an intellectual rejection of racism—is to miss the point of this analysis. That is, what I am attempting to point out is the inadequacy of understanding identities as either/or, either social or emotional. Just as there is no individual outside of the social, likewise there is nothing that is the social outside the embodied enactments of sociality through individuals.

Bringing Cheng's psychoanalytic reading of love and need together with Foucault's (1977, 1988) writing on the power relations present in the internalization and policing of group identity has been especially helpful for me in creating a narrative explanation for the fear and despair I have felt in negotiating the alienation from my roots in what I stereotype as rural, working-class whiteness. Foucault argues that the boundaries of proper signification of one's allegiance to the group are established in part by identifying those entire groups of people who are "not us," but also by identifying *within* a given group those people who *should* be part of the group but who are not due to some sort of deviance or disloyalty. Members of the identity group police one another to assure allegiance to the rules of group membership, and at the same time, because our own subjectivities are formed through the identity, we also police ourselves. Central to Foucault's argument is that we experience these identities as the truth of who we are or who we should be. The fear and urgency with which we police ourselves turns out to make use of what psychoanalysis describes as some of the most powerful affects known to humans—guilt, humiliation, and shame (Freud, 1923; Sedgwick, 1995).

Growing up, I *believed* that my family, church, neighbors, and schools were all homogeneously white, rural, conservative Christian, heterosexual, and working class, or that everyone should be, must be. Within that sameness, difference was marked with a vengeance, whether it was the deaf girl who lived next door to me who was sent away to boarding school, the boy in my high school who spoke with an impossibly high pitched voice, or whether it was me, the fat girl. As a child and a teen, I tried to turn to the hail of local interpellation, "Hey, you, pretty white girl" and what I got back was, "Oh my god, you didn't think we were talking to you, did you?" In my failure to achieve the norms of white, rural, working-class femininity, the public humiliation I suffered was rivaled only by my self-accusations. I now understand that these very public and humiliating rejections worked to establish privilege for some by marking the boundaries of proper, white, working-class, heterosexual femininity. I marked one set of the internal boundaries of the group; there were of course all the others—not white, poor or wealthy, urban, not Christian, lesbian, not American—who marked the outside of the group, thereby allowing the identity to have meaning by creating an "us" and a "not us." My sense of alienation from rural, working-class whiteness could be understood as a defensive act of self-preservation in the face of cruelty and public rebuff. As an adult, I was able to understand that the injury inflicted went far beyond me when I came to understand the narrowness of privilege granted within that identification as racism, sexism, and heterosexism.

Freud (1912, 1923, 1936) argues that when a reality intrudes with ideas that are unacceptable to our ego, one of the ways to deal with this threat to our self-image is through splitting. The idea and the affect are split; the idea is banished and the affect is pushed into the unconscious. The energy or anxiety of the affect can continue to provoke us, a thorn in the side, but as long as it is unattached to an idea, it cannot be released. Unmoored from the original meaning it held for us, the energy attaches to other ideas; the repressed returns. In other words, Freud tells us that while we may intellectually reject what were once passionately held identifications, it is possible (though certainly not inevitable) that if we repress the affective fall-out of this, the repressed will return in all sorts of disguised and not so disguised ways.

In my example, when I could no longer embrace the rural whiteness that meant belonging and safety to me, this was experienced as a traumatic loss. At least three ideas were intolerable to my ego. One was I desperately loved people who did not return that love in the way I needed it. A second was that I ever loved and shared identity with those in my local community whom I had come to distrust. The third was that the loss of this community was in fact a real loss, a loss of safety, love, belonging, and reassurance. The idea, "I loved you and I lost you," was split from the trauma of the loss. The affect was repressed and then attached to the idea, "I never loved you." I fervently rejected that I had ever really cared for these people, and at the same time I repressed the fact that I ever was truly one of them or at least wanted to be one of them.

As a young adult, I sought relief from the humiliation of my failed femininity in relationships with men who were not white. In order to allow myself to believe that any man could ever be interested in me, I drew comfort from the racist fantasy of the desirability of white women to men who are not white. In living twenty years (thus far) with my son's father, I believed that the evidence that I was different from the people I grew up with was obvious. Both my marriage and my child existed as testimony to all the ways that my past community was wrong about racism and about me. I expressed desires about how I wanted my son to perform a racialized identity; through these identity demands, I attempted to concretize, for everyone to see, that my present was in no way related to the lost and unmourned (but deeply mourned after) past.

At some point, however, I became uncomfortably aware of the idea that perhaps in asking my child to perform the identity of "not white" on my behalf, I had not made such a clean break from racism as I had thought. It was easy to identify the kind of racism in which hatred, slander, fear, suspicion, violence, and revulsion are obvious manifestations. But what did it mean that I was more invested in my son recognizing himself and being recognized as not white or not only white than his not-white father was? I began to realize what analysts have understood for a long time: that rejection and desire are often two sides of the same coin.

Race and Desire

In what sense are rejection and desire related? Cheng describes it this way:

> Dominant white identity in America operates … as an elaborate identificatory system based on psychical and social consumption-and-denial. Both racist and white liberal discourses participate in this dynamic, albeit out of different motivations. The racists need to develop elaborate ideologies in order to accommodate their actions with official American ideals, while white liberals need to keep burying the racial others in order to memorialize them. (2002, p. 11)

For both racists and liberals, the racial other has no being and no grounds for self-definition, but exists as a prop in white self-definition (see Fanon, 1967). Whether the insistence is that the racial other is deviant and threatening or beautiful, racial fantasy demands that race is real and demands the right to define what it means.

In what ways have I placed racialized identity demands on my child? Here, the specificity of cultural stereotypes announces itself. Taking up an essentialized, often banal and stereotyped vision of Japanese American- or Japanese- Hawaii-born American identity, I turned to food, clothing, language, and pop culture to ask him to mark difference. I pointed out to him that almost all of the cartoons, video games, and comic books that he and his friends preferred were from Japan. I looked for Japanese restaurants and tried to interest him in Japanese and Japanese American history and culture. He would announce that he wanted to get a t-shirt from the local college football team, and I would immediately get on the Internet and say, "Look at these cool surf t-shirts from Hawaii." Three years after leaving Hawaii* I continue to offer him favorite local Hawaiian foods, to help him make leis for important occasions, to use common Hawaiian Creole words, and to remind him through our reminiscing about his family, friends, and experiences there. In contrast, the German part of his heritage receives no attention; it is marked for good or for ill in no way at all.

---

* I am conscious that my romaticization of life for an Asian-Caucasian child in Hawaii threatens to disguise the troubled history of native Hawaiian fortunes in the face of Asian and Caucasian immigration to the Hawaiian Islands (Fujikane and Okamura, 2000).

In many ways, this is the day-to-day stuff of most parent/child interactions. Parents want their children to dress in certain ways, enjoy certain things, and have some friends or interests and not others. This is not different because I am a white mother raising a mixed-raced child. What is different is that the desires I express are noticeable because they are so clearly marked as "foreign" or "exotic" in our Midwestern community, and they are in fact exotic in my mind as well. Racial desire and the demand that my child perform a racial identity is therefore visible in a way that it would not be if he were only white or if I were wanting him to identify as white. This situation makes it blatant that as a parent, I am demanding a performance of racial identity of my son, but my argument is that the desires and demands that most parents express toward their children articulate racial identifications, whether these are so blatantly visible or not. Nonetheless, even if these demands are not particularly different in quality from the kinds of demands and desires that parents hold for their children all the time, because of the histories of racism in our culture, the demands made in cross-racial parenting take on a particular weight.

When I insist that my child and others be aware of his marking as "not white," I am walking on a slippery path. On the one hand, it is not as if in the absence of my efforts, my child would (or should) pass as white. While white parents of adopted Asian children have said to me, "Race means nothing; I don't even see it and we don't talk about it," I understand that race is one of the primary categories through which we make meaning in life, for good and for ill, and to ignore my child's race would be to ill-serve him. White children in the United States often grow up with no understanding of whiteness as anything other than that which is natural and therefore needing no thought or critical exploration, while "race" becomes synonymous with that which is not white and is therefore unnatural, strange, exotic, titillating, and/or dangerous (Savigliano, 1995). But of course, herein lies the rub; it is that in my need to deny the ongoing centrality that whiteness plays in my own life, I have made strange and exotic my own child. Fascination with the racial other, every bit as much as whiteness and racism, must be understood as a failed attempt to negotiate loss and injury. I had not overcome an essentializing racism but was simply playing to the other side of the coin. On the one side—race is not white and it is ugly, dangerous, and foreign. On the other side—race is not white and it is beautiful, titillating, and foreign.

Perhaps because I experienced abjection in relations to the demands of whiteness, I came to see whiteness as an identity that is cruel in its exacting of loyalty and solidarity (Hayes, 2001). The performance of whiteness requires the constant policing of self and others, while simultaneously requiring repression of the possibility that the identification has come at a cost. To perform whiteness as a desirable, successful, complete identity means to deny that identity itself is founded in loss. If we cannot admit that whiteness is not a natural attribute but an identity and a group membership taken on to compensate for the fear and incompleteness of human existence, then we cannot mourn our losses. The injury that founds whiteness is split; awareness is repressed, injury is denied, and the repressed returns through the enactments of racism. Racism and the denials that sustain it foreclose the possibility of companionships that might be forged through the shared awareness of our essential human vulnerability.

Insofar as I insist upon denying that I have been hurt by demands and failures of whiteness, I act on that which I have repressed, passing that narcissistic wounding on to those whom I love the most. My child and other children who are not white (or not only white), marked as representing race sometimes by those who love them and often by those who don't know them, bear the burden of return of race as injury. So, what is it like to be seven years old and bear so much weight of history—my history and America's history? Given that my child's race will be a defining factor in his life whether I demand it to be so or not, does my piling on of stereotyped identity demands make things better or worse?

Learning from Narcissism

To address these questions, it is useful to examine what psychoanalysts have said about narcissism. From an analytic perspective, our perspectives on other human beings are always influenced by narcissism. We may think that the desires we feel toward others and the demands we make upon them are selfless or for the other person's good, but for analysts, the ability to do anything that exceeds narcissism grows from a deliberate and ethical stance rather than a natural stance. A few analysts (Benedek 1959; Bibring, 1959; Ornstein and Ornstein, 1985) have specifically worked to understand the narcissistic demands that parents make on children. They argue parents have transferences to their children and make demands on their children that arise from the parents' narcissistic needs. Drawing parallels between children and racial others as objects of our narcissistically driven fantasies and demands, I will conclude by suggesting an ethical stance from which we might begin to reflect on different possibilities, limits, and hopes.

Narcissism is not, in psychoanalytic theory, a negative thing. It is, in fact, an absolutely necessary prerequisite to the possibility of loving or even being able to perceive others. Narcissism is the possession of an internal self that allows us the possibility of connecting externally or, in other words, of having a relationship. As Grunes (2002) explains:

> For the external world to have impact on an individual there must be internal objects to use for this communication. The internal world is likened to a flashlight that is always searching outside for something to attach to. Some person or situation will seem *as if* it is the same person or situation that already exists in the internal world. To get into the mind and to be intelligible, something outside must be similar enough to something that exists inside. Internal objects are not just a lens for how one will go on to experience new situations but the actual passageway for the powerful force of the unconscious to connect what is internal to what is external. This is how events in the external world are attached onto the internal objects. And this is the reason that events in the external world can have profound internal effects. (p. 6)

In this psychoanalytic description, we are able to love because the narcissistic self mistakes someone or some thing in the outside as the same as the internalized parent who first (in fantasy) perfectly fulfilled all our needs.

However, it is not enough to see others as only blank canvases upon whom we can paint our own desires, needs, and fears, whether positive or negative. Grunes goes on to write that while love is narcissistic and transferential, it is not only this. That is, it is true that "we love others because they remind us of something in us, but that 'something in us' is the attachment as well as the identification that at one time really existed in the real external world" (personal correspondence, June 14, 2004). In other words, the reality of the other person and the other person's own personality, identifications, and desires should bound our transferences onto them. Others are not only or even primarily what we imagine and want them to be. An ethical and healthy narcissistic love is one that consciously and actively reminds itself that others have their own being, that their needs may be different and even contrary to our wishes, that they have legitimate claims to forging identifications and attachments different from our own or those we would choose for them.

Because our children are vulnerable to us in ways that exceed other relationships, we have an especially charged responsibility to reflect on the impact of our transferences to them. "Parental love, at its roots, is narcissistic love," write Ornstein and Ornstein (1985). "It is the parent's self-object tie [narcissistic investment] to the child that assures adequate parental love" (p. 200). They go on to write that it is the narcissistic investment in our children that creates the opportunity, whether we take it or not, to learn to become better, more responsive and empathetic parents and, by extension, human beings (p. 201). This reflects Freud's (1916) position that narcissism motivates not only love of external objects but also our ego ideals, our commitments to society, morality, community, art, and so on. It motivates us in our commitments to be the best we can be, in whatever form that takes.

Ornstein and Ornstein's definition of empathy in parenting does not assume that the empathizer necessarily understands or even agrees with the child's perspective. Like Grunes, Ornstein and Ornstein write that an ethic of parenting demands that we not allow our transferences to take precedence over the conscious acknowledgment of the child's entitlement to his own feelings, ideas, desires, and emotional history (1985). At the same time, this ethic does not assume empathy is something that we achieve; it is, rather, a constant stance of inquiry that sees the parent/child relationship as a reciprocal one. In accepting that the child has a right to his or her desires or behaviors, the parent may discover that that the parent is the one who needs to change, that the child's stance may have broadened the parent's perspective for the better. The parent may also find a more expansive ability to love that does not demand identification and sameness. It is from this understanding of narcissism that we can begin to build an ethical stance.

Binding Narcissism: An Ethical Beginning

The psychoanalytic account insists that we work deliberately to view others as having a right to an existence separate from ourselves, and that the existence of others should have the potential to move us and to change us. While it is not the only legitimate perspective on relationship, bringing it into tension with reflections about my own transferences onto my child creates a space that offers potential for me to take an expanded view on the importance of my child's efforts to name his own experiences and, to the extent that any of us can, to determine his own experiences. At seven, my child already has beliefs, interests, relationships, and ideas that are his own. In accepting this as right, I can acknowledge that what is disguised by the romantic notion that the family is the best or only place for children to develop meaningful identities is how many of us feel we found the most caring homes and our best selves outside of our families of origin and often outside the traditional family structure. While I hope to provide my child with a loving relationship he can count on throughout his life, the psychoanalytic emphasis on the importance of children developing boundaries and turning outside the family is, at least potentially, simultaneously personal *and* political because the identifications adults demand from children are likewise simultaneously personal and political. The same might be said of the importance of parents developing boundaries that are separate from their children.

Psychoanalysis suggests that all our hatreds and loves are narcissistic. Our capacity to love and to hate is founded at least in part in fantasy and desire, in fear and loss, and in the impossible longing for completion. While some might find this perspective too pessimistic, for me it is a source of relief and even of invigoration. I cannot help but view others through the veil of narcissism, and this means that I will project onto others what I take to be the meanings of their identities. The understanding that we place unseemly, impossible demands upon one another through love, hate, identification, and ideology can be the starting point for reflecting on ethics and responsibilities. My narcissistic desire to do better as a parent and as a human being means that I have to think differently. I must learn to be aware and critical of the propensity to use others as a blank screen against whom I play out my own desires.

Practically speaking, as my child grew older and began to express his own desires, I grew curious about the desires I felt for him and particularly about the way they seemed often to announce a stereotyped version of race. In coming to grips with the psychoanalytic emphasis on the creation of boundaries between parents and children and the insistence that parents respect the child's right to be acknowledged as separate, I came to think of desires and of boundaries as simultaneously personal *and* political because the identifications adults demand from children are simultaneously personal and political. In some ways, this is about bounding parental fantasies and demands and in other ways it is about bounding racial fantasies and demands.

Cheng (2002) writes, "In a world defined by sides, where everyone speaks in the vocabulary of 'them' versus 'us,' not to take a side means to exist in an insistent, resistant middle ground that is also nowhere. The perspective that sees beyond the self is also the perspective that takes on the view of the other, which is also an impossible perspective" (p. 194). To try to see beyond the self, I am suggesting, is to try to understand the fact of our own narcissism, of our own transferences, and to refuse to assume that we know the meanings of others' lives. This is, Grunes (2002) writes, the position of the analyst, who deliberately looks to understand not his or her own interpretations of meaning but rather the meaning the patient has internalized. Being conscious of my own needs and transferences means that I might now understand that my own perspectives are only the beginning step in a discussion that holds the potential for both me and for the other. I can learn to begin to listen for the meanings others claim and not just for confirmation of my own meanings. I am learning to be more critically circumspect about the demands I make upon others and especially upon my child, who is bound and especially vulnerable to me through love. Psychoanalytic theory helps me to consider what I do not readily want to think about; in coming to imagine these things either I can turn away or I can accept the challenge to take on more carefully reflective, attentive, and present relationships with those who are intimate and those who are distant.

Acknowledgment

I owe a particular debt of gratitude to Aimee Mapes for support throughout the various drafts of this chapter.

References

Althusser, L. (1971). *Lenin and philosophy and other essays.* B. Brewster (Trans.). New York: Monthly Review Press.

Ball, S. (1990). *Foucault and education: Discipline and knowledge.* New York: Routledge.

Benedeck, T. (1959). Parenthood as a developmental phase, *Journal of the American Psychoanalytic Association, 7,* 389–417.

Biring, G. (1959). Some considerations of the psychological processes of pregnancy. *The Psychoanalytic Study of the Child, 14,* 113–121.

Boldt, G. (1996). Sexist and heterosexist responses to gender bending in an elementary classroom. *Curriculum Inquiry, 26*(2), 113–131.

Boldt, G. (2002). Oedipal and other conflicts. *Contemporary Issues in Early Childhood, 3*(3), 365–382 [On-line]. Available: http://www.triangle.co.uk/ciec/content/pdfs/3/issue3_3.asp#5.

Britzman, D. (1998). *Lost subjects, contested objects: Toward a psychoanalytic inquiry of learning.* New York: State University of New York.

Butler, J. (1990). *Gender trouble: Feminism and the subversion of identity.* New York: Routledge.

Butler, J. (1993). *Bodies that matter: On the discursive limits of "sex."* New York: Routledge.

Butler, J. (1997). *The psychic life of power.* New York: Routledge.

Cheng, A. (2002). *The melancholy of race: Psychoanalysis, assimilation, and hidden grief.* London: Oxford University Press.

Coffel, C. (2004, Spring). Raising my son righteously up: On reading Jewish children's books in Iowa. *Reader: Essays in Reader-Oriented Theory, Criticism, and Pedagogy, 50.*

Eng, D. (2001). *Racial castration: Managing masculinity in Asian America.* Durham, NC: Duke University Press.

Evans, D. (1999). From Kantian ethics to mystical experience: An exploration of jouissance. In D. Nobus (Ed.), *Key concepts in Lacanian psychoanalysis.* New York: Other Press.

Fanon, F. (1967). *Black skin, white masks.* New York: Grove Press.

Fink, B. (1996). *The Lacanian subject: Between language and jouissance.* Princeton, NJ: Princeton University Press.

Fink, B. (1997). *A clinical introduction to Lacanian psychoanalysis: Theory and technique.* Cambridge, MA: Harvard University Press.

Foucault, M. (1977). *Discipline and punish: The birth of the prison.* New York: Pantheon Books.

Foucault, M. (1988). *The history of sexuality: An introduction.* New York: Vintage Books.

Freud, A. (1953). Some remarks on infant observation. *The Psychoanalytic Study of the Child, 8,* 9–19.

Freud, S. (1912). A note on the unconscious in psycho-analysis. In J. Strachey (Ed.), *Standard edition of the complete psychological works of Sigmund Freud* (vol. 12). New York: Norton, 2000.

Freud, S. (1914). On narcissism. In J. Strachey (Ed.), *Standard edition of the complete psychological works of Sigmund Freud* (vol. 14). New York: Norton, 2000.

Freud, S. (1915). Instincts and their vicissitudes. In J. Strachey (Ed.), *Standard edition of the complete psychological works of Sigmund Freud* (vol. 14). New York: Norton, 2000.

Freud, S. (1916). Introductory lectures. In J. Strachey (Ed.), *Standard edition of the complete psychological works of Sigmund Freud* (vol. 15). New York: Norton, 2000.

Freud, S. (1917). Mourning and melancholia. In J. Strachey (Ed.), *Standard edition of the complete psychological works of Sigmund Freud* (vol. 14). New York: Norton, 2000.

Freud, S. (1923). The ego and the id. In J. Strachey (Ed.), *Standard edition of the complete psychological works of Sigmund Freud* (vol. 19). New York: Norton, 2000.

Freud, S. (1936). *Inhibitions, symptoms, and anxiety.* London: Hogarth Press.

Fujikane, C., & Okamura, J. (Guest Eds.). (2000). Whose vision: Asian settler colonialism in Hawaii. *Amerasian Journal, 26,* 2.

Grunes, D. (2002). The psychodynamics of suicide. Unpublished lecture, presented at Loyola University, Chicago, IL.

Hall, S. (1983). The problem of ideology: Marxism without guarantees. In B. Matthews (Ed.), *Marx: 100 years on.* London: Lawrence & Wishart.

Hall, S. (1996). Who needs "identity"? In S. Hall & P. du Gay (Eds.), *Questions of cultural identity.* London: Sage.

Hayes, M. (2001). A journey through dangerous places: Reflections on a theory of white racial identity as political alliance. *Contemporary Issues in Early Childhood, 2*(1), 15–30 [On-line]. Available: http://www.triangle.co.uk/ciec/.

Lacan, J. (1977). *Ecrits: A selection.* New York: Norton.

Ornstein, A., & Ornstein, P. (1985). Parenting as a function of the adult self: A psychoanalytic developmental perspective. In E. Anderson & G Pollock (Eds.), *Parental influences in health and disease.* Boston: Little Brown.

Savigliano, M. (1995). *Tango and the political economy of desire.* Boulder, CO: Westview.

Sedgwick, E. (1995). *Shame and its sisters: A Silvan Tompkins reader.* Durham, NC: Duke University Press.

Shapiro, T., & Stern, D. (1989). Psychoanalytic perspectives on the first year of life: The establishment of the object in an affective field. In S. Greenspan & G. Pollock (Eds.), *The course of life,* vol. 1: *Infancy.* Madison, CT: International Universities Press.

INTERLUDE IV

The Child's Question

Film: *Ponette*

Paired chapters: *Sigmund Freud, Melanie Klein, and Little Oedipus: On the Pleasures and Disappointments of Sexual Enlightenment* by Deborah P. Britzman
On Knowing and Desiring Children: The Significance of the "Unthought Known" by Michael O'Loughlin

In these chapters, Deborah Britzman and Michael O'Loughlin describe the work of children to articulate the questions that will help them to make meaning of their worlds and their place in it. Through clinical case study, the authors narrate stories of children's struggles to locate themselves in their social worlds through *symbolization*, bringing into consciousness and language those feelings and unconscious forces that shape desire and response. Michael O'Loughlin draws from his psychoanalytic practice with children and introduces us to the concept of the "unthought-known" to detail situations wherein children have experiences or knowledge at an unconscious level, but do not have the capacity to symbolize them in linguistic terms. Deborah Britzman, drawing from the clinical work of

Melanie Klein, explains that the questions children are trying to ask have at their core problems of existence, of their place in their parents' lives and in the larger world. In these chapters we see children grappling with their questions through developing both theories and symptoms that collapse the adult distinction between fantasy and reality. What both authors make abundantly clear is that as adults we are terribly misguided in so far as we see it as our duty to dissuade children of their fantasies and of the worth of their questions of existence in favor of bringing children, as O'Loughlin says, into the world of "rational, explicit, and memorable forms of knowledge."

These issues are poignantly portrayed in the film that we have paired with the chapters, the 1996 work *Ponette*, directed by Jacques Doillon. In this film, a four-year-old girl waits for the return of her mother who has just died. Doillon opens this film with the very young Ponette (played by four-year-old Victoire Thivisol), hospitalized and sucking her thumb, her arm in a cast as a result of the automobile accident, which we learn, killed her mother. Ponette is incapable of accepting her mother's death, and cannot bear the irremediable loss of her mother's body.

Visually and through the dialogue, Ponette's loss and her need for the physical body of her mother is overwhelming. Ponette clings to her father as he caresses her, telling her that her mother is dead, "Elle est toute cassée." Throughout the film, Ponette and her cousins with whom she goes to live are in constant bodily contact, touching and kissing one another. Being held in the comforting arms of her aunt, Ponette sniffs her breasts, seeking the comforting smell of her mother. Ponette explains to one of the other children that when she is sick, she loves a particular cream rubbed on her body. Her gestures repeatedly convey the intimate bodily contact with her mother that Ponette has lost, and that she seeks to reclaim.

Ponette's intensely felt body hunger points to the key question with which she struggles throughout the film: Where is the mother's body? Deborah Britzman tells us that in the work of Melanie Klein, the child is driven to know the mother's body as a means to secure the child's understanding of her place in the parents' lives. Ponette's loss of her mother is a traumatic unmooring from the reality and the consolation she has constructed against the uncertainty of her existence; without this, she is left adrift. In an attempt to anchor her life once again, Ponette clings to the certainty that her mother will return to life. She looks for her everywhere, seeking out some sign that her mother is in fact alive.

Ponette's inconsolability frustrates her father who is consumed with his own grief and bitterness. In an early scene, we see him taking Ponette from the hospital and as he drives her to the home of her aunt, he berates his wife for causing the accident by driving recklessly, all the while driving at a ragged pace that threatens to recreate the accident. He has not yet told Ponette that her mother is dead and when he finally stops the car and tells her, he makes her promise that she will never die. He is not able to do, in the face of this devastating traumatic loss, what O'Loughlin urges: To set aside his own trauma for long enough to reassure Ponette that she is not responsible for fixing this sudden upheaval. Ironically, after extracting Ponette's promise that she will not abandon him through her death, he abandons her at the home of her aunt; unable to tolerate anguish of Ponette's loss, he leaves her to work in a distant city.

Ponette's aunt and her young cousins attempt in their own ways to connect to Ponette and to offer her consolation. In contrast to her father's decidedly anti-religious explanations, her aunt answers Ponette's need with her own need for consolation through telling Ponette stories about Jesus. Her cousins offer her play and physical consolation, and in the context of their play, they offer her their own brand of metaphysical advice. This begins Ponette's quest to talk to God in order to determine when her mother will be returned to her. It is a quest that Ponette carries forward as she and her cousins move into boarding school, where they are left to work through their confusions on their own, away from the (mis)guidance of adults.

At boarding school, Ponette is able to engage in the serious work of symbolizing her losses and needs as the children minister to Ponette through games, rituals, and imaginative discussions. In an uncanny echoing of O'Loughlin's (cited from Davoine and Gaudillière) comment that "when children hear the voices of the dead, they are most often those dead who died without burial, without rite," one child teaches Ponette the rituals that will allow her to speak to God about her need to be with her mother. We see Ponette work through one ritual after another, one hypothesis after another, constantly testing her understanding of the world against her great need. Eventually, Ponette achieves reconciliation to the loss of her mother through a striking gravesite visitation from her dead mother. This imaginary moment marks Ponette's success at finally memorializing her mother, a gesture to re-locate her mother in Ponette's present and ongoing life.

Reading Ponette alongside Britzman and O'Loughlin, readers may be struck by the insistence of the children's questions and the gap between what matters to adults and what matters to children. In one brief but particularly striking scene, Ponette and her classmates are forced to abandon the significant conversation in which they are engaged in order to attend to the business of curriculum. O'Loughlin draws from the Lacanian understanding that adults impose their wishes, anxieties, and desires on children in the name of parenting. As Britzman so strongly reminds us, we also do this under the name of "education" and what counts as good and bad knowledge.

This turns us, then, to the classroom. Both Deborah Britzman and Michael O'Loughlin raise the questions of what it is that educates and what it is that is worth knowing. The adults in Ponette's life, and in the lives of many of the children about whom O'Loughlin and Britzman write, consistently miss the point of children's questions and desires. Britzman argues that we are dedicated to the enlightenment project of mastering anxiety through the fantasy of knowledge and education. Knowledge as it is structured in schools is often a defense against the anxiety of all that we do not know, that we can not know, about the intractable mysteries of existence. In this perspective, the questions of children and those of adults are not different, but so often the dreams of teaching and learning disguise all that as adults we don't know and we can't control. O'Loughlin argues that as long as we continue to impose our needs upon children in this fantasy of mastery, we lose the potential of the classroom that is openly emotionally evocative to release the power of imagination and the desire to connect with the world. O'Loughlin does not expect teachers to fulfill the role of the analyst, but he calls on his clinical practice to illustrate how play can usher children into speech, and the vital role that adults can play by learning to listen for the questions that matter. Decrying the drive to reduce every classroom interaction to measurable learning outcomes, O'Loughlin urges teachers to make space for fantasy, pleasure, play, desire, and curriculum in which children are supported to identify the things they desire to know and be in the world.

CHAPTER 7

Sigmund Freud, Melanie Klein, and Little Oedipus

On the Pleasures and Disappointments of Sexual Enlightenment

DEBORAH P. BRITZMAN

"Psychoanalysis is about the unacceptable and about love, two things we may prefer to keep apart, and that Freud found to be inextricable."

Adam Phillips, *Terrors and Experts*, xi

Let us begin with the assumption that one of the most controversial, difficult, and even murky relations in the history of both education and psychoanalysis concerns matters of imagining love and hate. And let us assume that the difficulties of these matters cannot be understood with any certainty. Nor can their contours be anesthetized with logical, unaffected thought because matters of love and hate are impressive; they are magnetizing and affecting, even contagious. And let us also imagine that love and hate occupy, through personification, an internal world of object relations.[1] Indeed, inquiry into these things called love and hate requires gigantic narrative detours, novel imaginative leaps, fantastic speculations, and the suspension of all credible things. Our epigram gives us more than a hint of the range of thinking needed. Psychoanalysts are no strangers to these views: theirs, too, follow curiosity toward love's migration to "unacceptable" conditions, situations, fantasies, objects, and breakdowns. All in the name of love one can find crimes of passion and seduction, scenes of jealousy and envy, aggression and violence. These vicissitudes of love are our own and, to clear them from the rubble of social convention, also allows us to ask surprising questions about the nature of meaningful existence. In fact, if love has no alibi, it does permit our susceptibility to psychical and epistemological reverberations. In love, selves are crafted and deferred, objects are lost and refound, thoughts become poetic and absurd, and from these internal experiences knowledge is made.

Our beginning dilemma is this: that this concept of love—the one that so easily finds its way to the unacceptable, the one that crumbles into a thousand tiny suspicions and scatters broken hearts here and there, the one that seems to persist and find its own way in spite of pleas to let it lay dormant, to wait until one grows up, or to forget homosexual yearnings, and the one that startles the language of poets and novelists, yes, this cacophonous complex of love, for psychoanalysis and education—frays credibility and our logical foundations. Indeed, the story of love psychoanalysis tells is incredible, for it begins with views that love is not the absence of aggression, that our parental love and love for our parents involves sexual feelings, and that infantile sexuality is the basis for all that follows. Psychoanalysis places what Phillips (1996) noted as "the unacceptable" within an allowance of love's working and its own methods for cure: the transference of love. For any educator, this type of inquiry will be a curious undertaking because what educates is not the person but an emotional experience of relating that becomes the basis for furthering meaning. Freud (1916) hinted at this uncertain relation when he suggested love's influence: "Side by side with the exigencies of life, love is the great educator" (p. 312).

This chapter narrates an unusual psychoanalytic love story, having at its center peculiar relations in love, hate, and knowledge. From this admixture I explore the affective underpinnings of philosophical reasoning because any education must contain, however implicitly, ideas about the workings and breakdowns of good and bad knowledge and of processes of deciding which knowledge shall be loved and which knowledge shall be hated. Let us set aside the narrow, instrumental view of education as an application of knowledge onto the body of a student and as material set in stone. Think instead of what else we do with one another when we go about a particular relationship of trying to learn. Representing love will take us into discussions of philosophy and psychoanalysis and what each gives away for education. Whereas philosophers, recognizing the dilemmas of existence as the central human preoccupation, pondered this problem through reason and judgment, psychoanalysts realized that what is immanent for this question to be asked is love and hate, which is there for all of us from the beginning. It would take the child analysts to see in this question of existence something startling in the child's work of learning to live with others. To make this argument, I take some detours through past and present speculations on learning to live found in a series of psychoanalytic archives,[2] both contemporary and anachronistic. I use them to suggest that without a complex conception of love as a meaningful experience, there is no way into any understanding of our inner world, its passionate currents, and how love constitutes learning and thinking. And, by bringing into relief the problem of meaning from the inside out, I begin with a style of thinking that wonders about the work of psychological significance, when our minds and bodies feel recognized and meaningful. Psychoanalytic stories of learning assume many difficult names: the Oedipus Complex, the drive, infantile sexuality, and insight. Education, too, contemplates these conflicts through terms such as influence, authority, autonomy, curiosity, and affection. In our attempts to know the depth of our world, we become entangled with our own phantasies of knowledge and resistance to this knowing. This erotic epistemology, composed from putting all these urges into words is the condition, not the guarantee for psychological significance.

What then can knowledge mean for understanding desire, satisfaction, ignorance, and our relations with others? This old question preoccupied eighteenth-century philosophers of the Western European Enlightenment. They, too, would write about education to tie it to child rearing, to the work of emerging from dependency and immaturity and to clarify the responsibilities of thinking. And these philosophers, peddlers of rationality, so to speak, saw salvation and hope in public discourse, seeing talk with others as the equivalent to becoming influenced and influencing others. In the beginning of the twentieth century, the field of child psychoanalysis would try to borrow from philosophy a faith in rationality. Analysts named this rationality sexual enlightenment. Having faith in the truth of sexual knowledge to enlighten and liberate, analysts felt that if they just told children the truth about sexuality, they could leave their neurotic trends behind. Eventually, child analysis left this logic when it began to listen to children without recourse to a didactic instruction or to sensitive pedagogy. These were the unsatisfying choices made available to them through their insistence on sexuality enlightenment as the cure. How these choices came to be so unsatisfying is part of the story. The other part is how analysts came to see the vicissitudes of love as infused and thereby transformed with themes of existence and psychological meaning. And we will see how this mode of listening moved some psychoanalysts to pursue questions of love and hate in order to encounter an inner world.

Readers will meet the early theories of psychoanalysts, notably those of Sigmund Freud and Melanie Klein, through their disagreements over the work of love in thinking and in education. I consider some pedagogical and existential dilemmas in two of their early case studies: Freud's (1909) "Little Hans" and Klein's (1921) report on "Fritz." While about fifteen years separates their publication, in the strange chronology of psychoanalytic knowledge, they are also contemporaries. If each case represents both an initiation and a rupture in thinking psychoanalytically, their commonality resides in the fact that these case studies also prepared the ground for significant revisions to child analysis and, more generally, to psychoanalytic theory with adults. My psychoanalytic approach moves from the philosopher's problem of enlightenment to the analyst's problem of sexual enlightenment.

Early Years

Melanie Klein was in the second generation of psychoanalysts. As one of the founders of the field of child psychoanalysis and object relations theory,[3] Klein's views of psychoanalytic interpretation—what should be interpreted, how interpretation works, and what is the nature of conflicts it may animate—developed with her work with very young children. Freud's clinic was with adults and their psychoanalysis began with reconstructing a childhood that had already past. Whereas Freud's view of the child was primarily made from an adult's reconstruction, an adult trying to look back on experiences that were hardly remembered but terribly memorable, Klein came to a view of the child that challenges linear, sequential notions of development. This untimely insight developed from her observation of children engaged in play and drawing. In her practice she witnessed children constructing something unanticipated, a time before adult meanings could work to ease anxiety through the imposition of a misleading coherence, a time when phantasy, as the representative of an inner world of object relations, worked overtime. This surreal timing may be thought of as a misstep of chronology that has tripped upon its own desire. Certainly, analysts overheard an unexpected language that expressed children's internal worlds. What Klein suggests, then, is a creative relationship of listening and speaking. Her task as an analyst was not to love the actual child or to teach the child to love. Her work became focused on the child's conception of love and hate. Within the child's speech, Klein would overhear intimate and involuntary worlds of object relations as they played—sometimes aggressively, other times poignantly—with the child's theories of inner life and with her or his projected relations into others. And what Klein listened intently for were affects of love and hate.

In these earliest years, however, Klein was caught in a conundrum: while having a faith in cure, in reason, in rational persuasion, and in the analyst's educative efforts, analysts kept meeting or having to pursue the estranging psychological meanings of hopelessness, inhibition, and anxiety. If one side spoke to cure, the other side had to learn to listen without idealization. When working within a developmental framework, analysis was conceptualized as a progressive march from repression, to memory, to consciousness, and efforts were corrective. At first it was thought that realistic knowledge of sexuality and desire, or in other words, sexual enlightenment, creates new catharses, thereby allowing attachment to and curiosity toward the actual world of others. They thought that once the proper representatives were supplied, or found, or remembered, the neurosis and its symptoms would diminish.

One small admission in the early history of child psychoanalysis cast doubt upon the progression of knowledge as a mechanism for cure. Even as child analysts assumed, in the beginning, the goodness of knowledge to affect rational thought, there was some difficulty understanding what made knowledge good or bad. This uncertainty emerged from analysts' explorations of the underside of education, since so many of their young analysands could not bear going to school. There was also, then, the idea that education itself made the child and the adult nervous, contributed to inhibition or the cessation of thinking and enjoyment, and created its own learning difficulties and problems with authority (Britzman, 2003). In education, little scenes of civilization and unhappiness were being played out. There does not seem to be, in contemporary education, a comparable sense of doubt toward its own motivations and goals. I think this may be the case for a number of reasons. Our educational efforts may not have a theory of the inner world or of emotional life. Second, given that mainstream education is so enamored by brain theory and theories of cognition, resistance to thinking of emotional life as the grounds for thinking itself—both from the perspective of the teacher and student—is even left unthought. And third, the chilling effects of the testing industry contribute to an instrumental, repressive orientation to knowledge. The procedures of content, comprehension, and skills dominate pedagogical interactions, and there is hardly time for curiosity into the mysteries of being.

By the time of Klein's disagreement over the nature of psychoanalytic education, the skeletal outlines of psychoanalysis were in place. Freud (1900) had already published his inaugural text, *The Interpretation of Dreams*. Working from his own self-analysis, Freud speculated that psychical life was governed by the pleasure principle and its myriad wishes, that dreams unfettered by conscious censorship were the royal road to interpreting unconscious wishes, and that the dream work itself, or the particular operations dreams employ to distort representation and maintain some sleeping state, reworked unconscious wishes through representations in the form of displacements, reversals into opposites, substitutions, and condensations of meaning. In this strange scene of otherness, words turned into images. And dreams, so linked to the wish, were unapparent knowledge. In this complexity, love, hate, and knowledge could be barely distinguished. From this dream theory, symptoms of distress could be traced to a repression of pleasure, to a libidinal fixation, and also to an actual trauma. This was the adult's progression.

The twentieth century ushered in the psychoanalysis for children. And with all new beginnings, the young field of child psychoanalysis looked to the future. It was tethered to an impossible promise to prevent the future of neuroses by lifting the veil of superstition and lies that obscured both the child's understanding of sexuality and the meanings of her or his pursuit of pleasure. As both a critique of societal hypocrisy toward sexuality and the damaging effects on development of repressing desire, child analysis heralded objective knowledge by telling children the truth. This is where the goal of sexual enlightenment as only an adventure with consciousness entered the picture: the child's supercilious theories of sexuality would be replaced by the adult's truthful knowledge.

Clinical work ruined the theoretical dream of a prophylactic analysis that emphasized education. Theory followed not far behind. Freud found something beyond pleasure. By 1920, Freud would rethink the structure of psychical life not through pleasure and unpleasure but as a great conflict of pressures, investments, and desires organized by the life (Eros) and death (Thanatos) drives. The life drive would become a metaphor for psychical binding and integration through qualities of Eros. The death drive would work in the service of unbinding, through the accession of aggression and its only reason: the reduction of all tension. There would then be a negativity at the heart of psychical life. Freud began to understand that what he called "the cure of love" would be a terrific battle: people do not give up their symptoms easily; consciousness is too fickle, even inattentive, to affect itself; and, there would even be a secondary gain from illness. From these limits came a focus on resistances to analysis. Constructions then were made for the sake of insight into more general existential problems of having to create meaning from the fact of existence.

Melanie Klein, when she listened to children, stretched all of these new views to their farthest outpost. Mrs. Klein took the problem of hate and love so seriously that the reasons for these emotions, why we have them at all, became strangely unmoored from a love of reality and from the original goal of child analysis, sexual enlightenment through didactic education.

Enlightenment and Its Discontents

The early goals of child analysis were influenced by the philosophy of the Enlightenment. Indeed, to understand something of the reach of the question of sexual enlightenment and why it was so central to the early psychoanalytic archive, we must go further back in time, to the eighteenth century, and consider a problem Kant (1999) raised when he wrote his 1784 newspaper editorial, "An answer to the question: What is Enlightenment?" His enlightenment was intimately shaped by his idea of education and why we have it at all. Kant stated his reasons directly in another of his essays, first published in English in 1899, and titled, "On Education." There, Kant (2003) begins: "Man is the only being who needs education. For by education we must understand nurture (the tending and feeding of the child), discipline (*Zucht*), and teaching, together with culture" (1). Kant's turn to natality and the fact of dependency as justifying adult responsibility to the child occurs at a time when many continental philosophers were preoccupied with humanist concerns about the human nature, what it means to become a human, how to conceptualize needs and desires, and how judgment, autonomy, and action in the world come to influence development (Todorov, 2002).

For Kant, enlightenment depends upon the acquisition of education and literacy. That is, in order to think for oneself, one has to have something to think about and education provides this material. Kant asserts that publicly performing one's reason is essential: he writes, "But by the public use of one's own reason I mean that use which anyone may make of it *as a man of learning* addressing the entire *reading public*" (p. 55, original emphasis). Unfortunately, this address can become confused because the learning man is not a man of learning. This misrecognition is hinted at when Kant defines enlightenment as "*man's emergence from his self-incurred immaturity*" (p. 54). Kant defines immaturity as the inability to understand and think for oneself. Kant's unthought problem is an aggressive faith in education as a representative of knowledge capable of transcending what he saw as "the second nature," or adult immaturity (p. 54). Kant's faith cannot account for why people refuse to think, why they hold fast to "passionate ignorance."

Almost two hundred years later, Kant's question became variegated when it found its way into an early debate in psychoanalysis. By the early twentieth century, knowledge and love became part of the discussion of psychoanalytic orientations to education and thereby made a new question: what is sexual enlightenment? Despite our leap in time, despite the nearly two hundred years between the Kantian and Freudian question, both began with the problem of a body: that its archive of desire is not in correspondence with its index of conscious knowledge. Psychoanalysts eventually came to the idea that in order to even understand something like the desire for sexual enlightenment, one must be willing to meet the limits of what we are willing to think, or in other words, Kant's regression from maturity to immaturity. For Freud, this limit led to speculation of human drives. In what way might Freud's concept of the drives illuminate Kant's concern about this regression?

The concept of "the drives" is a psychoanalytic metaphor to speak of the human's motivations for living and dying. Sometimes, the drives are spoken of as instincts, biological entities that attach to representations. More generally, the drives signify simply a bodily demand. They are inner excitations that seek release, that seek objects, that exert force, and that have a source. The drives demand both notice and meaning, and Freud used them to characterize how psychical life drew its force, its susceptibility to the world, and its capacity for representation. Two considerable problems previously unavailable to psychoanalysis emerge from Freud's theory of the drives as the urge that motivates psychical and social life. First, if sexual enlightenment was meant to enlighten sexuality, how is sexual enlightenment even possible if the sexual is related to the drive and the drive insists that it be noticed but cannot be represented? How can that which is not represented possibly be the source of sexual enlightenment? The drives allow a return to something primordial that resists enlightenment—what Kant noticed as "a self-incurred immaturity" (p. 54), which must be overcome if there is to be something like a second chance for Reason. Second, there is the problem of regression: why does the self return to this earlier state?

Modes of Knowledge

One of the unusual qualities of psychoanalysis is that it considers its object of knowledge in terms of its functions and structures and through the mechanisms required for its representation. How we come to know is not just an investigative procedure. The process of coming to know creates the self and knowledge. We know that psychoanalysis entangles knowledge with desire and posits that the first libidinal relationship with the mother is a "template upon which all later relationships are based" (Verhaeghe, 1999, p. 37). This template is actually an impression in two senses of the word. As an infant, the impression made upon me in the relationship with the mother is a sort of "theory kindergarten," a constellation of the infant's sexuality and its phantasies, conveyed and animated by projections and identifications. So my impressions of the world beyond me emerge from a world inside me. My impression is projected outside of me, but because it comes from me, I am tied to these objects through identifications. However, these impressions, or phantasies, can seem as if they are coming from the world, directed at me. More improbably, something must be taken in, introjected, to leave behind an impression. In the second sense, the impression is of an introjective nature, constituting a groove, or pleasurable indentation to which mesmerized knowledge migrates to and is magnetized by, but cannot fill the space between the mother and the child. This template, then, affected by our first mode in which we believed that we loved and were loved completely, must also mark the loss that occurs when we realize that we are not one with our maternal object. Too soon a flurry of knowledge is being made, things that cannot be understood yet still demand to know and to be known. One consequence is that we will use knowledge as a defense, as an attempt to settle the longing and emptiness. At the same time, resistance to knowing this emptiness will be the counterforce.

Freud wrote that there is "a thirst for knowledge" that has two conflicting sources. One emerges from infantile sexuality which allows for curiosity or the drive to know and that bestows its theories with omnipotence and grandiosity. The other source encompasses anxiety and internal danger, a pushing away of the distress from the original object. Curiosity, or thirst for knowledge, carries and is charged by tinges of anxiety and desire. This is because there is a certain delay in knowing that impresses itself within the very construction of knowledge: The child encounters experiences she or he cannot understand, and only later, with new knowledge placed over the old mysteries, does sexuality come to mean something different from what was first felt, thought, and encountered. For Freud, curiosity will be a shorthand for sexual curiosity. This curiosity is directed outward, resembling a sociological push to understand sexuality. The seriousness of inquiry is there, but it is distorted by an infantile phantasy of omnipotence, aggravated by an impossible wish to possess mother and father in order to give birth to the self. Curiosity will express itself through feelings of love and hate. And the research of the child, the particular knowledge of sexuality, will be affected.

Contradictions will then accrue. Donald Meltzer (1998), for example, in his discussion of Freud and Klein, finds ambivalence: "Since Freud's idea seems to be that this curiosity is fundamentally driven by anxiety and hatred, it is very puzzling that he should think of it as something that should drive the child in the direction of wanting to discover the truth"

(p. 67). This drive to know has some constitutive flaws: one both wants and does not want the truth. This problem leads Lacan to further complicate an understanding of the drive to know through what he called "the passion for ignorance," or the myriad ways our search for knowledge performs negations and resistance (Felman, 1987).

Melanie Klein (1928) takes this uncanny complex of desire, anxiety, and knowledge and gives it an even more precocious chronology. Not only that. She will insist that the drive to know pertains to internal affairs, wanting first to know the inside not the outside. And she will give it an awkward name, calling it an epistemophilic instinct, a drive to know the inside of the mother's body. This drive is aggressive, sadistic, and intrusive, tied to wanting to take possession of the mother by knowing her insides. Love and hate will be confused, protecting the inquiry, destroying the object, destroying the inquiry, loving the object. With Freud, Klein keeps the idea that the drive to knowledge is a defense against the anxiety of not knowing yet urgently needing to know. But unlike Freud, Klein sees this drive as if it were a desire for x-ray vision. That is, it is not the outside world that the child wants to know but the inside world. Why should the inside of the mother's body matter so much to the child? Klein speculated that the first object for the infant is the mother's body, while the first existential problem for the child concerns conceptualizing a time before birth (Meltzer, 1998). Moreover, Mrs. Klein used the concept of the epistemophilic instinct as a way to characterize the flora and fauna of the inner world of object relations. Meltzer's (1998) description of Klein's contribution is lovely:

> It took somebody like Mrs. Klein, listening to little children talking about the inside of their mother's body with absolute conviction as if it were Budapest or Vienna, as an absolutely geographical place, to realize that there really is an inner world, and that it is not just allegorical or metaphorical, but has a concrete existence—in the life of the mind, not the brain. (p. 98)

For Klein, internal reality would be like a crowded city in rush hour traffic, not the stillness of the archeological site of Freud's view of the psyche, but more active, more dynamic, more real. And the propulsion of affect would gain lightening-like force from this carnival world, creating, announcing, and addressing object relations.

The drive to know carries its own convictions, and it is the outside world, then, which seems absurd. In this confusion the adult's insistence for an accurate, unaffected knowledge is of no use because of the nature of the questions that a child must ask. Verhaeghe (1999) posits three questions that form the child's curiosity: "What is the difference between me and the other sex, where do children come from, and what is the relation between my mother and father?" (p. 127). As I will suggest later, sexual enlightenment fails because these questions posit a first nature, the infantile, which entangles its own nature with theoretical worlds of love and hate. If the questions pull us back to this first nature, their power resides in a question of existence, a lifetime pursuit. It was Melanie Klein (1921) who first theorized a strange "resistance to enlightenment" as a return of the infantile sexuality. She then stretched the idea of this resistance to the problem of having to be educated (Britzman, 2003).

"Little Hans"

For those of you who are not familiar with Freud's (1909) "Little Hans" case,[4] here is how Freud summarizes the presenting problem: "'Little Hans refused to go out into the street because he was afraid of horses. This was the raw material of the case" (Freud, 1926, p. 101). The horse, we learn, is not really a horse but a father whom he both feared and loved. So the conflict has a measure of ambivalence. And Freud (1926) distinguishes Hans's fear of having a horse bite him or fall down in front of him from a phobia with the simple statement, "What made it a neurosis was one thing alone; the replacement of his father by a horse" (p. 103). From here, Freud elaborates a theory of knowledge that resists its own unity. Meaning is unmoored from the sign and Hans creates "a horse father." This dream-like transformation harkens back to Freud's theory of what happens to meaning in dream work: meaning will be broken into bits and pieces and rearranged and reorganized through condensation, reversal into its opposite, substitution, and displacement. "As we see," writes Freud, "the conflict due to ambivalence is not dealt with in relation to one and the same person; it is circumvented, as it were, by one of the pair of conflicting impulses being directed to another person as a substitutive object" (1926, p. 103). Here then is the emotional logic that can assert without negation: "Yes, my father is a horse." But how does one make sense of this irrational reason?

Around 1926, Freud retracts his earlier meta-psychological speculation that repression causes anxiety and turns it around to the idea that anxiety, specifically an internal danger, creates repression. Now, repression will be an *after repression*, a secondary defense. But it will be known only if the repression has, in some sense, failed. The nature of the failure will be marked by a symptom, itself a placeholder for something missed (Freud, 1926). Hans, for example, may repress his hatred for his father, but the hatred does not go away. Rather, it returns in the symptom of fear of horses that fall down or bite him. The Little Hans case helps Freud understand this sequence when he traced the disjunction between an idea which is repressed and the affect which is not. Essentially, by splitting representation into the thing and the presentation, the idea may be shut out but the affect is carried over to another object. The affect continues to exert pressure on us but we refuse to know the idea that was the source of this pressure. The affect attaches onto another idea—it is no longer that Hans is ambivalent about his father but that he is afraid of horses.

Divisions, reversals, and dissociations of affect and idea are working models for understanding the symbolic procedures set in motion by a traumatic perception of helplessness, passivity, and loss. The ego must face two kinds of losses: the loss of that first maternal object and the threat of the un-representability of that loss. We return to Little Hans, the boy wanted his mother (the first object) and hated his father. Yet how can this phantasy be even spoken, how can his desire here be representable? What exactly did Hans want? I suspect that he wanted a fantasy of knowledge that would help him to contain the force of the loss of the first fantasy, the loss of maternal figure. Here, as stated earlier, knowledge will be a defense against this loss. An object has been lost, libidinal cathexes have been withdrawn, and a traumatic search for ways to symbolize this loss is set in motion.

In psychoanalysis, this remembering, repetition, and working through are also models for thinking and making theories: thinking over drive conflict, finding adequate symbols, and mourning the un-representable loss that the drive also animates. Hence what Freud (1914) called "working through" will now consist not of the recovery of memory but an encounter with one's own humanness: encountering and even taking pleasure from the gap between psychical life and historical life, and learning to love psychical reality and to accept that hatred is part of this world as well. The problem is that in this search for meaning, something primal, an existential agony, repeats. There is no way around this constitutive fault line. There is no way around the self-incurred immaturity—the passion for ignorance—that defends us from knowing the loss. Indeed, this agony that insists upon being felt may become our first resource. Knowledge, too, will carry this burden and Freud (1909) hinted at this conundrum when he called Little Hans, "our Little Oedipus." Who would have thought that phobias had something to do with love and its losses?

Little Hans is precocious and worried, ostensibly afraid of horses that would bite him or fall down. There are other worries, we might surmise, to be distorted glimmers of Hans's three concerns: that someone will see him making wiwi, that he will turn into a woman, and that his father's questions are somehow beside the point. These displaced occupations were also enactments of early attachments: Hans was afraid of crossing the street and thus leaving his mother behind. His solution is rather ingenious, for here is where Hans attempts to represent the drive and it is no mistake that he calls out for his mother. That first impression, what Verhaeghe (2001) will see as the way the drive is linked to the Other, will also mean that the existential realities of life are at odds with the drive to know. Freud (1909) observed this tension in his introduction to the case with an example of Hans wondering, at age three and a half, if his mother has a "widdler" like his father's. His mother replies, "Of course. Didn't you know that?" and to which Hans answers, "No. I thought you were so big you'd have a widdler like a horse" (pp. 9–10). Freud commented on this absurd mismatched exchange: "Thirst for Knowledge seems to be inseparable from sexual curiosity. Hans's curiosity was particularly directed towards his parents" (p. 9). And Freud also asked readers to remember the horse.

Let us take a closer look at Hans's worries in relation to the development of psychoanalysis for it was not just that Hans wanted sexual knowledge. He was also trying to figure out a chronology prior to his existence, and he was trying to do that through seeing if his own body meant anything to his fantasies of femininity. Would he give birth as well when he grew up? Hans could not figure out his hatred for his father and then, whether love and hate carried any significance at all. And the more his father explained, the more frustrated Hans became. There was something about Hans that Freud could not address, namely, the significance to the child and to psychoanalytic theory, of the child's phantasies of the mother and the unconscious register of these impressions. Klein will begin with these impressions.

Meltzer's (1998) thoughts on Little Hans suggest that Freud was not yet at a crossroad where love and hate would be more useful than a theory of instincts. For Donald Meltzer (1998), "Little Hans" also proposed something enigmatic about the thirst for knowledge: "that the thirst for knowledge is driven by anxiety, and that knowledge will inevitably be used for defensive processes" (p. 52). That is, entangled in trying to know the truth is also a fear of truth, and this makes for a confusion between good and bad knowledge. It also charges a certain regression, the Kantian "self-incurred immaturity," a defense never far away.

Fritz and Company

Klein's (1921) "The Development of a Child" endorsed sexual enlightenment as a goal of child analysis. In part one of the paper, Klein has a sharp critical wish: "We can spare the child unnecessary repression by freeing—and first and foremost in ourselves—the whole wide sphere of sexuality from the dense veils of secrecy, falsehood and danger spun by a hypocritical civilization upon an affective and uninformed foundation"

(p. 1). Readers are pulled inside the dream of sexual enlightenment, itself a "necessary repression" of the infantile stage.

Part two of the paper, written a few years later, discards this faith in the power of rational knowledge to overcome the symptom. Klein now considers naive her early insistence on the usefulness of a prophylactic psychoanalysis. In leaving this faith, it is almost as if Klein is asking, "If education cannot prevent the neurosis, then what is it doing?" Klein's difficult contribution was to wonder if there is a place where education cannot go, but where, nonetheless, knowledge can become. But this is a knowledge of a different order, the inexplicable reach to phantasy, which opens our educational archive to its own otherness, rewriting Freud's story of thinking as reality testing, reminding us that there is no thinking without phantasy.

Mrs. Klein began a psychoanalytic education with her son with the idea of enlightening him in what she called, "sexual matters." By answering any of his questions with honesty, she thought she could help him avoid the future of neurotic tendencies and also "deprive sexuality at once of its mystery and of a great part of its danger" (pp. 1–2).

Things get rather absurd. At one point, the five-year-old Fritz believes he is a gourmet cook, can speak French fluently, and can fix any object that is broken. While Mrs. Klein explains patiently that he does not yet know how to do any of these things—that he must learn—Fritz replies calmly: "If I am shown how just once, I can do it quite well" (p. 3). He holds tightly to this great refrain; it is his last word. Something about having to learn is being skipped, and Klein places what is missed under the ominous heading, "The child's resistance to enlightenment." It is possible, however, to wonder what precisely was being resisted, given the fact that other divisions of this early paper gather Fritz's struggle under the grand theme of existence. That is, Fritz wonders about the nature of reality and its judgments, the qualities of time, history, and memory, the definitions of his rights and powers, the future of his wishes and hopes, the meaning of birth and death, and whether there is a God.

Fritz's problems are exquisite, and they take us to the dreamy realm of efforts to symbolize our encounter with both reality and phantasy. And if Fritz is now sounding a bit like Kant, working to know things-in-themselves and all the while bumping up against the limits of trying to know, his questions force Mrs. Klein to move as close as she ever would to confronting her own wishes for enlightenment. From this confrontation there will emerge the question of phantasy and a Kleinian view of an infantile life that will speculate upon not a self-incurred immaturity, but a constitutive immaturity that will set thinking to work. Here is where Klein begins to think about infantile omnipotence differently, as both a defense against being small and helpless and as a mode of obdurate thought that, even if buried by having to grow up, is still preserved by way of our wishes for learning and existence.

Klein had difficulty figuring out the nature of curiosity—where it comes from, what it represents, how it loosens itself from its object, and also what it means to urge *this* facility. These questions animated something new in her own curiosity; Klein discovered, along with the child's resistance to enlightenment, her own resistance to what else the child asks. We are entering the psychoanalytic field of the transference: the exchange of unconscious wishes, the displacement of our first love onto figures of authority, and the transposition of symbolic equivalences of old and repressed conflicts onto the understanding of new situations.

Significantly, Freud (1912) writes of transference as a dynamic, as a relation, and as an obstacle, and he links its indelible signature to permitting an impossible investigation. In trying to know something new, our psychic archive is animated and perhaps agitated. The transference, Freud writes, emerges from "a compromise between the demands of [the resistance] and those of the work of investigation" (p. 103). Something within the very work of investigation resists and animates its own demands. And in psychoanalysis, this resistance may symbolize a paradox: there is mystery to sexuality, and knowledge cannot take this away. But there is also mystery to knowledge because we have sexuality. It is here that our elusive education, our elusive enlightenment, flutters and flounders.

It is useful to return to Verhaeghe's (1999) summary of the three questions that preoccupy the child: "What is the difference between me and the other sex, where do children come from, and what is the relation between my mother and father?" (pp. 127). Klein's study of Fritz offers us a sense of how chaotic, desperate, unreasonable, and insistent these questions feel. The breakdowns of meaning provoked by Mrs. Klein's sexual instruction begin to give us a sense of the profound mismatch between the needs and desires animated by sexual enlightenment. This passage also harkens back to the exchange between Hans and his mother:

> When I begin once more about the little egg, he interrupts me, "I know that." I continue, "Papa can make something with his wiwi that really looks rather like milk and it is called seed; he makes it like doing wiwi only not so much. Mama's wiwi is different to papa's" (he interrupts) "I know *that*!" I say, "Mama's wiwi is like a hole. If papa puts his wiwi into mama's wiwi and makes the seed there, then the seed runs in deeper into her body and when it meets with one of the little eggs that are inside mama, then that little egg begins to grow and becomes a child." Fritz listened with

great interest and said, "I would so much like to see how a child is made inside like that." I explain that this is impossible until he is big because it can't be done till then but that then he will do it himself. "But then I would like to do it to mama." "That can't be, mama can't be your wife for she is the wife of your papa, and then papa would have no wife." "But we could both do it to her." I say, "No, that can't be. Every man has only one wife. When you are big your mama will be old.... Your mama will always love you but she can't be your wife."... At the end he said, "But I would just once like to see how the child gets in and out." (p. 34)

It is no wonder Klein places this conversation under the sign, "The child's resistance to enlightenment." Fritz, like Oedipus, demands all of the positions: he is baby and father, son and lover; he is egg and seed, big and old. And these positions regard his mother's appeal to a future as ridiculous. The child cannot give birth to himself and cannot witness his own birth. Yet there was something Fritz needed to know: what is going on inside of the mother? This was how Fritz wondered about his own origin. Yet it was mistakenly answered through the mother's desire. That is, Mrs. Klein told the story of her love with Mr. Klein. And this leaves out little Fritz, who was not only not there during parental intercourse but whose parents could not have even thought of him at the time. How is Fritz to understand that he had no existence in his parent's sexual intercourse, that what had existed then was not him but the parental erotic love that excludes him? The enlightenment Fritz resists, then, is that his parents have a life without him and that Fritz cannot yet use the knowledge his mother offers to make sense of either his origin or his desire to know. We have reached the crevices of the Oedipus Complex, not so much the story of exclusion but the yearning for knowledge to complete the mystery of existence.

Mrs. Klein, too, is unsatisfied with the nature of her explanation, for she has not reached phantasy, nor even interpreted the anxiety that Freud spoke of as also being a part of the child's sexual curiosity. She is still early in her own education although she manages to link Fritz's persistent questions to an inner world where there is mental pain made from not understanding. Here is where Klein (1921) begins to grapple with the problem of thinking emotional worlds when she comments on how Fritz's struggles with his desires: "That a certain 'pain,' an unwillingness to accept (against which his desire for truth was struggling), was the determining factor in his frequent repetition of the question" (p. 4).

Where there is existence, there is a certain pain, an ambivalence that is also an impression. Here is where love and hate begin their efforts. The child's questions, Klein came to suspect, were an unconscious plea to possess both a history not yet formulated and to formulate something that can never be history, to have his own private enlightenment by answering the question of existence prior to his existence. Even more, Fritz already knew how babies are born. He wanted to know where he was before he was born, and this led him back to that first relation with his mother's body. Once Klein could give up on explaining the world as it was or, more actually, in a language she supposed her son would understand, she could allow herself to listen to the child's worries over existence made from wanting to know an inner world. The ethical turn is hinted when Klein leaves the drive to know and also her own drive to tell, and instead considers that range of love and hate in the inner world and what these feelings have to do with the child's theories and meanings.

Many years later, Klein (1946) would speak of psychical positions needed for thinking. She would see this inquiry as wavering between a paranoid-schizoid and depressive positions. The paranoid-schizoid position is a phantasy of knowledge, created from the splitting of good and bad and trapped by paranoid anxieties that this knowledge, which has been hurt by splitting, may take its revenge. Then there is the development of a knowledge of phantasy, what Klein would call "the depressive position," where pining, loss, and depressive anxiety may become integrated into the fact of existence. The infantile wish to give birth to itself, to possess the other, transforms into a concern for the other which includes feelings of loss and remorse. Rather than be left only with the Kantian subject, the "I-think-that-accompanies-all-of-my representations," we have what instead is an inner world, capable of thinking one's thoughts, of accepting ambivalence. In the depressive position archaic defenses of splitting, idealization, and envy give way to feelings of love, reparation, and gratitude. Love and hate, on this view, are never so far apart, but neither are they so close that each would lose their respective uniqueness.

Mind the Gap

Originally, Melanie Klein put great faith in the value of psychoanalytic education to cure ignorance, settle confusion, and perhaps, even, correct the mistakes of existence. *Bildung*, or moral training, is what Kant (2003) hoped education could become to create the conditions for reason. Reason then would ensure a move from self-incurred immaturity to autonomy and individuality. Both of these views of education sustain a phantasy of knowledge; that knowledge can, in and of itself, transform the self and its superfluous infantile theories. They do not yet reach a knowledge of phantasy or the Kleinian depressive position. The self-incurred immaturity that so worried Kant is emblematic of two demands whose conflict is the prerequisite for thinking: infantile sexuality with its wish to have no knowledge (the Lacanian passion for ignorance) and the drive to know one's own origins, fueled by the paranoid-schizoid position. Klein leaves us with a question as to whether enlightenment can even be useful to any working through of the phantasized events of the child with a theory. She also allows us to question the phantasies of that other theory: enlightenment. It was Klein who, in depicting a concrete inner world, relaxed the grip of enlightenment and turned to the tumult of love and hate. The movement is away from a belief in the phantasy of knowledge to overcome immaturity toward an analytic style whose only goal was a knowledge of phantasy. What her young analysands did with this new knowledge, and here Klein supports a very different sense of autonomy, was theirs to do with as they wished.

In more contemporary terms, Verhaeghe's (2001) summary of Lacan's view of knowledge brings us to the heart of the matter:

> The fact that the unconscious is not a thinking being, but first and foremost an enjoying being who does not want to know anything about it. This cannot be captured within a traditional articulated knowledge. Beyond the illusion of mirroring, then, there is a "relation to being" that cannot be known. There is a discordance, a cleft between being and knowledge on *our* side, that is, at the side of the subject where the latter is indeed not-whole. (p. 113)

Self-incurred immaturity may remind us of this not-whole, allowing us to pass over an interpretation of Enlightenment to one of the not-yet interpreted dream of existence. This mystery is what the drive may theorize but cannot complete because what else can the drive be but a terrific story of love and hate? It is this discord that the work of integration attempts to contain and that the work of thought must tolerate to go on thinking. And the discordance between being and knowledge, the one that philosophy may try to fill and that education may try to ignore, may be another way of thinking about love and hate. If education is to "mind the gap," it must consider the origins of its own workings, its own dream-work, but not mistake those workings as settling the research of either the child or the adult.

Notes

1. The concept of "object" as used in this chapter refers to one's feelings for things, people, and relationships. They may be whole objects or part objects. Melanie Klein derived this view from her observations of children playing with toys. She saw their passionate relation to these objects, where the toys became personified, having feelings for the child and being used as if

they were alive with as many complex feelings as the child may project onto them. From this observation, Klein speculated that these projected feelings lived in the mind of the child; these objects lived, died, and had the capacity to haunt and persecute. Paradoxically, objects contain congealed motivations, secrets, and minds of their own. There are, for Klein, good and bad objects, the first object being the breast. And these objects are given life by the child's fantasy. Object relations refers to the to and fro projections and identifications, the love, hate, and ambivalence that fantasies carry. For further discussion, see Hinshelwood (1991).

2. I am using the term "archive" in two ways. The first references a storage place where the documents of life are cataloged and housed. The second meaning is existential in that it references the phenomena of our own mind and its capacity to register, be affected by, and metabolize impressions of the world, creating memory and its workings. In this second dynamic meaning, the archive affects and is affected by its holdings.

3. Object relations theory begins with the view that from the beginning of our lives, the human is object seeking and object making and requires, for development, relations with others. Klein's idea is that from the beginning of life, the infant has an emergent psychological knowledge constituted from the anxiety of dependency. This is not a knowledge that has words, but rather is carried through feeling states that are projected into the world and identified with. One of the interesting paradoxes that Klein presents us with concerns the idea that while the human is object seeking, the objects carry the burden of the self's fantasies of good and bad.

4. Freud's original title for this case was "Analysis of a Phobia in a Five-Year-Old Boy." He wrote the Little Hans case seventeen years later, and in his structural phase of psychical life, where now he is concerned with what he perceives as the profound conflict between two drives—Eros and Thanatos.

References

Britzman, Deborah P. *After-Education: Anna Freud, Melanie Klein and Psychoanalytic Histories of Learning.* Albany: State University of New York Press, 2003.

Felman, Shoshana. *Jacques Lacan and the Adventure of Insight: Psychoanalysis in Contemporary Culture.* Cambridge, MA: Harvard University Press, 1987.

Freud, Sigmund. *The Standard Edition of the Complete Psychological Works of Sigmund Freud.* Edited and translated by James Strachey, in collaboration with Anna Freud, assisted by Alix Strachey and Alan Tyson. 24 vols. London: Hogarth Press and Institute for Psychoanalysis, 1953–1974.

———. "Three Essays on Sexuality." 1905. SE 7, 125–243.

———. "Analysis of a Phobia of a Five-Year-Old Boy." 1909. SE 10, 5–149.

———. "The Dynamics of Transference." 1912. SE 14, 97–108.

———. "Remembering, Repeating and Working Through (Further recommendations on the technique of psycho-analysis II." 1914. SE 12, 145–156.

_____. "Papers on Meta-psychology." 1915. SE 14, 105–216.

_____. "Some Character-Types Met with in Psychoanalytic Work." 1916. SE 14, 311–333.

_____. "Inhibitions, Symptoms and Anxiety." 1926. SE 20, 77–178.

Hinshelwood, R. D. *A Dictionary of Kleinian Thought.* London: Free Association Books, 1991.

Kant, I. "An Answer to the Question: 'What Is Enlightenment?'" In *Political Writings,* edited by Hans Reiss. Cambridge: Cambridge University Press, 1999, 54–60.

———. *On Education,* translated by Annette Chuton. New York: Dover Publications, 2003.

Klein, Melanie. "Development of a Child." 1921. In *Love, Guilt and Reparation and Other Works, 1921–1945.* New York: Delacort Press/Seymour Lawrence, 1975, 1–53.

———. "Early Stages of the Oedipus Conflict."1928. In *Love, Guilt and Reparation and Other Works, 1921–1945.* New York: Delacort Press/Seymour Lawrence, 1975, 186–89.

———. "Notes on Some Schizoid Mechanisms." 1946. In *Envy and Gratitude and Other Works 1946–1963.* New York: Delacort Press/Seymour Lawrence, 1975, 1–25.

Meltzer, Donald. *The Kleinian Development.* London: Karnac Books, 1998.

Phillips, Adam. *Terrors and Experts.* Cambridge, MA: Harvard University Press, 1996.

Steuerman, Emilia. *The Bounds of Reason: Habermas, Lyotard and Melanie Klein on Rationality.* London: Routledge, 2000.

Todorov, Tzvetan. *Imperfect Garden: The Legacy of Humanism.* Trans. Carol Cosman. Princeton, NJ: Princeton University Press, 2002.

Verhaeghe, Paul. *Love in a Time of Loneliness.* Trans. Plym Peters and Tony Langham. New York: Other Press, 1999.

———. *Beyond Gender: From Subject to Drive.* New York: Other Press, 2001.

CHAPTER 8

On Knowing and Desiring Children

The Significance of the Unthought Known

MICHAEL O'LOUGHLIN

Psychoanalysis has a long tradition of understanding that ignorance is an active refusal to know. Ignorance in psychoanalysis is understood as a desire not to know and can actually be considered an integral part of knowing rather than its opposite (Felman, 1987). My interest in this chapter is to explore the pedagogical and psychotherapeutic implications of working with these ignorances that Christopher Bollas (1987) refers to as "the unthought known" in the lives and desires of children—a latent subjectivity embodied in unconscious desires and ancestral memory. There is a rule of thumb in psychoanalytic practice which states that it is not what the patient says that matters; what merits attention is what the patient is *really* saying. A psychoanalyst pays relatively less attention to overt verbal utterances, listening instead for the unconscious communication that underlies the patient's words. The analyst gains knowledge of the patient from these communications and then returns this knowledge to the patient so that the patient can make use of it. Shoshana Felman, in *Jacques Lacan and the Adventure of Insight,* puts it this way: "... the analyst must be taught by the analysand's [patient's] unconscious. It is by structurally making himself a *student of the patient's knowledge,* that the analyst becomes the patient's teacher—makes the patient learn what would otherwise remain forever inaccessible to him" (1987, p. 83).

As any composition teacher who has helped a student to articulate "what you really want to say" in a piece of writing will readily recognize, the link between the analyst's task and school pedagogy is rather direct. Implicit in my discussion throughout this chapter is the idea that teachers err if they focus exclusively on rational, explicit, and memorable forms of knowledge. It is not in the ostensibly known and the to-be-known facts that creativity and desire are to be found. We ought to pay much more attention to the ignorance that lies beneath the façade of knowing because that which is ignored is also the source of unconscious desire and possibility. Felman asks: "What is the riddle I pose here under the guise of my knowledge?" (p. 96).

Psychoanalysis can provide us a way to explore why thinking *beyond* knowledge might matter in the classroom. Arguing that pedagogy and curriculum should grow not only from a child's own questions about the world and her or his place in it but also from knowledge present in the child's unconscious, I ask what it means to really listen to children. This is a question that positions the task of the teacher differently. Rather than assuming that the teacher knows ahead of time what knowledge is worth pursuing, I am proposing that the teacher, like the analyst, should learn to listen for the questions that matter to the child, and behind the questions, to hear the unspoken desires that animate the child's life. I believe that as teachers we need to learn to construct curriculum and pedagogy that supports children in identifying the things that they desire to know and be in the world. For me to do this meant first learning to listen to my own questions and desires.

Troubling Childhood

I had a troubled childhood. When I was an infant I suffered from severe projectile vomiting and therefore had to spend most of the first two years of my life in the local county hospital. There were occasional interludes when I was allowed home. I had two siblings, both toddlers themselves, only one and two years older than me. My dad worked all day and the whole family was perched precariously on the precipice of poverty. The little time I spent at home, my mother tells me was frenetic. When I vomited there were no spare linens and my mother had no running water, washer, or dryer. My illness caused serious domestic upheaval as well as lots of worry.

Meanwhile, at the hospital, my mother and father were advised to visit me as little as possible, as their presence invariably upset me, and times when they could actually hold me were strictly limited. My mother tells me that when she visited, she would peer longingly at me through the glass window. The hospital was so anxiety-producing for me that to this day, when I hear an ambulance, I experience anxiety. I have been left with an abiding sense of vulnerability.

My subjectivity has been constructed, then, through the absences, losses, anxieties, and dread that surrounded my tenuous grasp on life, as well as by my prolonged exposure to institutional "care." I was fragile. I was different. I was alone. Yet I also experienced myself as desired, and this was enough to inspire in me a struggle to live. This, of course, is not my past. It is very much my present. My anxiety in the company of strangers; my difficulty in putting myself forward in my writing (cf. O'Loughlin, 2005); my difficulty functioning in impersonal institutional environments; and my pleasure in working with children all have a plausible correlation with my earliest experiences. My childhood is not an historical remnant. It is very much who I am today. I live my childhood anew each day. As Rose (1992) noted in the context of a discussion of children's fiction: "The most crucial aspect of psychoanalysis for discussing children's fiction is its insistence that childhood is something in which we continue to be implicated, and which is never simply left behind. Childhood persists..." (p. 12).

In *Women Hollering Creek* Cisneros captures the notion of the embeddedness of childhood within us rather whimsically:

> What they don't understand about birthdays and what they never tell you is that when you're eleven you're also ten, and nine, and eight, and seven, and six, and five, and four, and three, and two, and one.... Like some days you might say something stupid, and that's the part of you that's still ten. Or maybe some days you might need to sit on your mama's lap because you're scared, and that's the part of you that's five. And maybe one day, when you're all grown up, maybe you will need to cry like you're three, and that's okay. That's what I tell mama when she's sad and she needs to cry. Maybe she's feeling three.
>
> Because the way you grow old is kind of like an onion or like the rings inside a tree trunk or like my little wooden dolls that fit one inside the other, each year inside the next one. (1991, pp. 6–7)

A popular view is that psychoanalytic psychotherapy is designed to help people transcend their pasts. I think not. I believe I need to embrace the forgotten or unnamed knowledge of my past, so that I may use it to express my desire more fully.

The idea of the enduring nature of childhood was greatly reinforced when I began to practice as a psychoanalyst. My initial determination was to confine my practice to adults. I had begun my professional life as a first-grade teacher, and I had spent much of my adult life visiting schools and writing and teaching about children's issues. Having reached middle age with my own children entering adulthood, I thought that perhaps it was time I worked with an adult population with whom I imagined I had a shared life experience. It was time I grew up. To my surprise, from the moment I began my clinical practice I was plunged into untangling the minutiae of childhood—the aspirations, losses, disappointments, hopes, attachments, etc. that constituted my adult patients' lives. I enjoyed this very much, and soon I decided to devote a significant portion of my practice to seeing actual children so that I could engage with children's unfolding subjectivities.

In working with children I am in many respects a child. I work childishly. I have a playful consulting room, labeled recently by a perceptive parent of a toddler as the "it's okay to knock the blocks over room." Yet, I am also the adult analyst intent on reading child's play as an expression of the unsymbolized aspects of a child's unconscious expression of desire. As Mathelin (1999) documents so unequivocally in *The Broken Piano*, children's desires are inextricably constructed in the matrix of parental desire. Thus, paradoxically, to have a child in therapy is clearly to have their parents in therapy too. In *History Beyond Trauma*, Davoine and Gaudillière (2004) take the argument further, suggesting that humans also embody unconscious memories of the unresolved trauma of their ancestors. The consulting room is a very crowded place indeed, and the separation of life into childhood and adulthood is troubled by these shadows of past-into-present and present-into-past.

In other words, parents impose upon their children not only their own wishes and anxieties but also the wishes and anxieties that were passed down to them from their parents and their parents' parents. Perhaps the most common challenge facing any child analyst is the fact that adults, sometimes consciously and often unconsciously, demand that their children perform identities, behaviors, and even desires that emerge not from the children's needs and wishes but from those of the adult. In *The Case of Peter Pan*, Rose (1992) cites adults' vested interest in proclaiming childhood innocence as an example. This insistence on seeing childhood as innocent, Rose argues, give adults a way of avoiding awareness of the complexity of their own identities. "If we do not know what a child is," Rose states, "then it becomes impossible to invest in their sweet self-evidence, impossible to use the translucent clarity of childhood to deny the anxieties we have about our psychic, sexual, and social being in the world" (p. xvii).

What makes *Peter Pan* such a controversial and interesting work is precisely the blurring of boundaries between the world of children and adults.

As Rose explains, J. M. Barrie, the author of *Peter Pan,* was far from a disinterested observer of children. His love of boys is well established. *Peter Pan* was originally penned as a tale within a larger story, *The Little White Bird* (Barrie, 1902). In that work the male adult character narrates the story of Peter Pan to a young boy as part of a seduction ploy. Rose's book is a study of how *Peter Pan* has been plucked out of this context and sanitized as the archetypal narrative of childish innocence. It is possible though, to trouble this putatively innocent tale, as Rose does, by raising the tricky question of desire:

> Suppose, therefore, that Peter Pan is a little boy who does not grow up, not because he doesn't want to, but because someone else prefers that he shouldn't. Suppose, therefore, that what is at stake in *Peter Pan* is the adult's desire for the child.... I am using desire to refer to a form of investment by the adult in the child, and to the demand made by the adult on the child as to the effect of that investment, a demand which fixes the child and then holds it in place. A turning to the child, or a circulating around the child— what is at stake here is not so much something which could be enacted as something which cannot be spoken. (pp. 3–4)

So, in constructing childhood as discrete from adulthood, and as innocent, the motives of adults may be suspect. The ascription of childhood innocence may represent a manic attempt to deny the unacknowledgable history of our own subjective experience and unnameable desires. It may also represent an adult projection of unnameable desires. We subject children to mixed messages. We want them to grow up, yet we tell them to act their age. We proudly celebrate childhood innocence, yet we live with a legacy of colonialism that continues to infantilize and inferiorize ethnically and racially different persons as *minor(ity).* We ascribe purity of motives to children, yet we create technologies of care and education that discipline their bodies and minds (cf. Rousmaniere, Delhi, and De Conninck Smith, 1997; Donzelot, 1979) and work to conceal from children the unconscious knowledges, especially unthought memories of trauma, that could allow children to name their histories and release their creativity. In what follows, I turn to my analytic practice to demonstrate the importance of helping children to symbolize their histories, their questions, and their desires.

Naming the Unthought Known

I am returned to an episode in therapy. "If this therapy isn't working," the father says, staring pointedly at me, "and if *you* don't do what I need *you* to do [now pointing an accusatory finger at his twelve-year-old son]

then I am going to send *you* away to boarding school like your brother."*
This father had placed me in an impossible bind. Speaking with me on
the phone before he ever brought his son for therapy he asked me how I
worked with children in therapy. I gave a brief explanation and added that
sometimes, if the child finds it helpful, one or both parents would become
partners in the therapy and participate in sessions with their child on an
as-needed basis. He replied tersely, "I don't think that will be necessary."
In any event, he allowed his child to enter therapy, but he intruded periodi-
cally when he felt that his son was not adjusting sufficiently to the demands
of family and school life. The bind for me of course continues to be figuring
out how to accomplish the "adjustment" goals the father demands, at least
sufficiently to allow the boy to remain in therapy, while simultaneously
liberating the child from excessive parental demand. What if, as is the case
here, the boy's inability to mourn his biological mother, who died many
years ago, is now emerging in the form of resistance to his father and new
stepmother? What if the father himself failed to mourn his dead wife, and
his son's rebelliousness constantly raises the specter that the wall he has
carefully constructed against his own emotions will come crashing down?
As Brenkman (1999) notes, in the introduction to Maud Mannoni's *Separation and Creativity,* contrary to psychiatric and educational approaches
which focus on symptom removal and behavioral adjustment, one purpose
of psychoanalytically informed therapy with a child is to engage the child
in understanding the process by which that child's desires have become
spoken for him or her through parental and/or institutional (for example,
school) demand:

> [W]hat can the child discover in the analytic dialogue about what
> it means, within his or her own psychic reality, to be in the eyes of
> others the bearer of a "symptom," "illness," or "deficiency" and to
> be treated with a mood-altering drug? The power of psychoanaly-
> sis lies in its specificity and even its limits. Its task is to expand the
> area of experience that can be articulated in the individual's own
> terms and own name, and therefore must leave open, case by case,
> how that project will mesh or not with the medical and educa-
> tional goals of normalizing children's behavior. (p. xx)

As Mannoni herself earlier noted, echoing Bakhtin's (1986) notion of
how the social ventriloquates through individual speech, "we must also
realize who is speaking, because the subject of the words is not necessarily
the child" (1970, p. 20). To the extent that Judith Butler (1997) is correct

---

* All names of child patients and family members have been changed, and details of their
lives have been altered in order to ensure anonymity.

that *subjectivity* may be synonymous with *subjection* because the child inherits the demands, desires, and language of parents and society, then the task of psychoanalysis is to liberate: to enable the child to name the unconscious external forces shaping his or her desires and thereby producing "symptoms," so that the child can then get out from under that yoke to experience creativity and possibility. As Mannoni (1970) stated, we need to help the child remove "the screens the adult erects to keep the child in a state of *unknowing*" (p. 27).

Framing psychoanalysis from a Lacanian perspective, Mannoni argues (cf. also Mathelin, 1999) that the symptom or presenting problem that brings the child to therapy needs to be understood as having been produced by circumstances. If all capacity for meaning is precluded for the child, then the emergence of the repressed desire through somatized illness is a likely consequence:

> The reality of the "illness" is never underestimated in psychoanalysis, but an attempt is made to pinpoint how the real situation is lived by the child and his family. It is then that the symbolic value that the subject attaches to the situation, reechoing a given family history takes on a meaning. For the child it is the words spoken by those around him about his "illness" that assume importance.... Whatever the child's real state of deficiency or disturbance may be, the analyst endeavors to understand the words that remain petrified in an anxiety or encased in a physical disorder. In treatment, the subject's questions will replace the demand or anxiety of parents and child, a question that is his deepest wish, concealed hitherto in a symptom or in a particular type of relationship with his surroundings. What will become clear is the manner in which the child bears the imprint not only of the way his birth was awaited, but also of what he is going to represent for each parent as a function of their respective past histories. His real existence will thus come into conflict with the unconscious projections of his parents, and this is where the misunderstandings arise. If the child gets the impression that every access is barred to a true word, he can in some cases search for a possibility of expressing himself in illness. (1970, p. 61)

So how does one reveal to the child the truth that others would unconsciously wish to conceal? Mannoni invokes Winnicott's notion of potential space, arguing that a play space opens up the possibility of truth and creativity. As Winnicott noted, "If there is no play and no maternal counterplay the transition from dependence to independence is impaired" (cited in

Mannoni, 1999, p. 4). Lacking the ability to "name the unnamable" (1999, p. 7), the child is encased within the shell of an imposed parental identity and remains trapped in an alienated and painful existence; as a result, Mannoni suggests, the child lacks the capacity for creativity and fantasy. Intergenerational trauma compounds the problem. If a child continues to lack the capacity to metabolize traumatic losses into adulthood, then there is a high probability that a similar silence about emotional loss will be bequeathed to ensuing generations. Speaking of those concentration camp survivors who were unable to express and transform their initial trauma, Mannoni notes: "What remains unspoken is a wound that is handed down from generation to generation, a wound of memory the effect of which is to rob the victim of pleasure in life" (1999, p. 31). Echoing Alice Miller (1997), Mannoni argues that parents (and, of course, early childhood professionals too) who attempt to repair their *own* childhoods by being excessively rule bound, dutiful, or achievement oriented, unconsciously impose similar values on their children and thereby deprive them of the *fantastic* space that would allow them to grow up as playful, creative beings, instead of the "slaves to duty" (Mannoni, 1999, p. 36) who end up all too well prepared for long-term incarceration in rule-bound schools and workplaces later in life.

"Creativity," Mannoni notes, "is motivated by a present event combined with what of the past can be transposed, recreated, on an Other stage" (1999, p. 65). It is to be noted that the Other that is the catalyst is a therapist, teacher, or other mirroring individual who has developed the capacity to speak truth with the child. The twelve-year-old boy mentioned above gets through life wearing a mask. He is a clown, a funny man. He laughs and jokes his way through school. He evades my invitations to speak about his emotions by being silly. In my office he plays with the toys my younger patients use. He is childish in resistance to the adult demand that he grow up *in a certain way*. I have made only one promise to him: I will take him seriously.

Analysts use the term *symbolization* to describe the process of assisting patients in transforming their feelings into truth. Mannoni describes the role of the child's coming to voice in this process:

> Shut off from communication with others, lodged in a retreat to the point of thwarting all personal development, the subject has trouble with speech: he lacks the words to say what is happening with his state of being.... [T]he aim of analysis is to give the subject access to full speech and thereby to a fuller authenticity, which can only occur through speech that has been loosened from its moorings. When the subject's speech is thus reworked in analysis, it becomes possible for him to recognize desire. (1999, p. 94)

Davoine and Gaudillière (2004) also approach the issue of silenced trauma from a Lacanian perspective. Their concern is with the intergenerational transmission of traumatic events that have been blanketed in silence through processes of dissociation. They argue that people we deem *mad* are the victims of just such processes of erasure of the historical origins of their suffering:

> These cases of trauma and madness are a challenge hurled at clinical treatment, since the analyst comes up against a piece of the Real [i.e., the *unconscious* in Lacanian terms]. Because signifying speech was lacking, nothing could be inscribed, on this point, in the unconscious. The customary tools of treatment are thwarted, since, in this regard, the subject of speech, even repressed speech, has not been constituted. What is at stake then, is precisely the coming into being of the subject, the subject of a history not so much censored as erased, reduced to nothing, yet somehow existing. (p. 47)

Davoine and Gaudillière suggest that at moments of trauma in a child's life it is vital that adults not get so caught up in the traumatic response as to forget to provide verbal reassurance to a child of the order of "Something serious has happened, but you are not responsible for this sudden upheaval. Trust us" (p. 72). If this kind of reassurance is not provided, they note, "the thread of speech may be radically cut" (p. 71), leaving the child with no way to name or metabolize the traumatic feelings. The unconscious trauma is thereby encased in silence and, if unnamed, it will be transmitted in mute form to ensuing generations. The solution, they argue, is to render the unsaid sayable:

> As the child psychiatrist Lionel Bailly puts it, when "children hear the voices of the dead" they are most often those who died without burial, without a rite. This brief illusion will cease as soon as it is heard by a therapist in whom the voices of the dead can resonate instead of remaining a dead letter. (p. 145)

If the encased trauma is not given voice, Davoine and Gaudillière note, "a seed of psychosis" (p. 145) is planted because the child is left on its own holding this "terrible knowledge" (p. 146).

Before looking at some clinical examples of these phenomena among children, one final point must be noted: A child does not necessarily need to be exposed to a concrete traumatic event in order to be left with the silent burden of unsymbolized experience. All it takes is for the parents to pass on their own unconscious, unmetabolized psychic pain to the child.

As Davoine and Gaudillière note, "a baby may be assigned the role of *therapôn*, keeper of the mind for its parents, the boundary of their irrationality, remaining welded to them by a bond that may prevent any other attachment" (p. 157). An example of this in Lacanian thought (e.g., Fink, 1997; Mannoni, 1999; Mathelin, 1999) is the situation where a child is confronted with one parent who is absent or passive and another who is emotionally engulfing. In such cases, the child may not develop the capacity to own or verbalize his or her own experience. The outcome is predictable. We can expect such children to exhibit deep silence, unsymbolized emotions, severe anxiety, or symptoms of somatized illnesses as a response to the unnameable burdens imposed on their psyches.

Symptomatology of Misdirected Desire and Unmetabolized Loss: Some Clinical Examples

Gabe—The Silent Scream

Gabe began seeing me when he was ten. He is an affable boy with a tremendous talent for mimicry. He bonded well with me and took with relish to playing card games, drawing, and telling tall tales. Despite having a flexible and accommodating fifth-grade teacher, Gabe began to refuse school. This happened only sporadically and with a little crisis intervention the moment passed. It was obvious, though, that Gabe was carrying a heavy emotional load. Any attempt to probe his emotions or offer an interpretation of his experience caused him to freeze. Sometimes he came to session and sat with his arms tightly folded for the entire hour, unable to speak or participate. He exemplified *The Silent Child* described by Danon-Boileau (2001) in the book of that title. He had an emotional crisis in sixth grade. What exactly precipitated this is unclear. The transition from the smaller elementary school, where he had a strong bond with a single teacher, to the larger and more impersonal middle school may have been a factor. More likely, escalating tensions in the home increased Gabe's need to scream, except of course he was unable to. His father is emotionally unavailable and *unreasonable*. In a recent altercation his father dressed him down verbally and left Gabe feeling emotionally devastated. His mom, who, as a child, had experiences with school refusal and emotional constriction that remarkably mirror Gabe's own symptoms, is anxious, depressed, and hopeless in the face of his resistance. Both parents are unable to provide a reconstitutive mirroring experience that might reassure him in the face of terror. Gabe now refused to go to school at all. I met with the school psychologist and Gabe's teachers. I found them to be empathic and emotionally supportive. Yet Gabe spurned all offers of help. He stayed home, ran out of the school building, or spent the day in the student support office under the eye of the psychologist.

He became increasingly depressed and angry. A crisis was building. He tore his room apart. He kicked the furniture in my office. He drew a series of self-portraits reminiscent of the ones in *The Silent Child* in which he depicted himself as terror-stricken, and with a series of bars drawn harshly across his mouth powerfully depicting his muted scream. In one picture, in addition to the barred mouth, he added layers of vibrating lines around his body as if he were in a state of shock. I have constructed an image of Gabe at home, both parents screaming at him to go to school, and his only method of voicing his trauma is refusal. This of course merely exacerbates their desperation and his flight from reality. Gabe eventually began voicing threats to himself and others. He ran away. He climbed out of his bedroom window and threatened to jump from the roof. He ordered most of his valuable possessions removed from his room. A child psychiatrist was consulted, and Gabe was placed on medication to stabilize his mood. He resumed school—for the most part. Gabe's affable self returned—more or less.

Yet, he is still struck dumb. Ironically, for a boy who can speak in so many other people's voices, his own voice is often muted. Just recently he left me in no doubt as to how he feels about my inability to name the pain that is tearing up his insides. He arrived at my office in good humor, carrying an adult briefcase. He opened it with a flourish and took out a toy gun and pointed it at me. "Bang. You're dead." True to form, he ignored my interpretation that he was expressing disappointment with me for failing to name his trauma. We played some games and he talked about events in his life, and then, before leaving, he offered to draw a picture. He took out the pistol again and traced its shape on the paper. He wrote the caption "19 caliber" on top of the drawing of the gun. Directly across from the barrel of the pistol he drew a stick figure with a look of terror on its face, and with blood pouring from its head and stomach onto a large pool on the floor. "You don't have to guess who this is," he told me amiably, as he wrote the legend "Mike O." underneath the figure. Then he left.

I have some urgent unfinished business with this young man. Fink (1995) describes Lacan's definition of psychosis thus:

> Psychosis, according to Lacan, results from a child's failure to assimilate a "primordial" signifier which would otherwise structure the child's symbolic universe, that failure leaving the child unanchored in language, without a compass reading on the basis of which to adopt an orientation. A psychotic child may very well *assimilate*, but cannot *come to be in* language in the same way as a neurotic child. Lacking the fundamental anchoring point, the remainder of the signifiers assimilated are condemned to drift. (p. 55)

His case is an agonizing reminder that, as Lawrence Langer (1991) illustrates so deftly in *Holocaust Testimonies*, sometimes a trauma cannot be spoken. Or, perhaps it is the case that the talking that takes place in therapy can never truly name certain traumas. Primo Levi's suicide, years after apparently working through his Auschwitz experience by writing *Survival in Auschwitz* (1996) and other memoirs, suggests that we need to be cautious about the reach of our influence or the power of the "talking cure." Is it always possible to use language to rescue somebody who is more spoken than speaking? Gabe will leave his local school this year to attend a psychiatric day treatment center.

Perry—Lacking Nom du Père

Perry is ten. The psychologist who referred him to me told me that she feared he was on the verge of a psychotic break. At our first session Perry presented as a precocious, adultified child who inserted himself readily into his parents conversations, finished his parents sentences, and like a Greek chorus, offered wise and cautionary coda to their remarks. I could hear the parents ventriloquating through Perry, better than I could hear either their own words or his voice. It felt like an orthopedic consultation in that they spent most of the session talking about Perry's physical fragility. Perry had indeed broken some bones and spent a few months in traction, but this whole family felt fragile—as if everybody could fall apart at any moment. His mother had recently completed hospitalization for a nervous breakdown, and the whole family looked like they were terrified of disintegration. Perry's drawings were stick figures of the kind a much younger child might draw—both parents were depicted with smiling but overpowering faces, and little else. At our second session he took a little stuffed tiger, removed it from the dollhouse, and placed it outside at the back of the house because it was dangerous. Then he built a large Lego containment fence. Having removed the menacing tiger, Perry arranged the figures in the dollhouse meticulously. He then took the baby and placed it in a clear space in the bedroom, and built a large Lego wall all around the baby to keep it safe. Suddenly, the tiger was roused from its slumber. It crashed through the fragile walls of its enclosure, tore into the house, and killed all the people inside. The following week the dollhouse went on fire and Perry marshaled his fire trucks to attempt a rescue. Perry's world was a fragile and dangerous place indeed.

Both parents agreed to come for consultations at a time separate from Perry's therapy. I soon learned that while his younger sibling would sleep over at a grandparent's home, Perry refused because he did not want to leave his mother. I had learned from my referral source that after dropping her children at school, Perry's mother often stayed in the school building or its vicinity all day as she could not bear to leave her children. It soon was evident that this mother had an overwhelming longing for her children and was using them to assuage some deep, unfulfilled need from her own childhood. She lay in bed with them for at least an hour each night before they went to sleep. She had resisted toilet training them and hence both her children were persistent bed wetters. When her husband traveled, quite frequently, both children slept with her, and when he was home, they displaced their father from the parental bed in the middle of every night and consigned him to the couch so that they could sleep with mother. She had projected her own needs so compellingly into her children that she was convinced that she was experiencing *their* needs. She felt lonely and abandoned, and she was convinced that this was what her children experienced. Her children needed to be babies to assuage mother's desire. When I explored this in session with the parents, Perry's mother told me that Perry's favorite activity was to curl up in her lap in the fetal position with a bottle of water. The recent death of her sister, who had been this mother's *de facto* caregiver, had precipitated a major psychotic break and hospitalization for the mother. The family sought me out immediately after she was discharged as the psychiatric team had advised her of the danger to her children, particularly Perry, whom they recognized as carrying an inordinate psychic burden.

Probing gently into his relationship with his mother, I asked Perry to depict his nighttime experience. He drew two bunk beds. His mom stood next to his little brother in the lower bunk, she was smiling beautifully while embracing his sleeping brother. Meanwhile, Perry, in the upper bunk, was standing fully erect, with his arms raised in supplication, apparently screaming for mommy. Perry then took a dark purple marker and created a dense colored scrawl that almost obscured his own figure entirely. Turning the paper over, he continued by drawing himself again, this time dwarfed by a very large ghost. He hastily reassured me that he knew ghosts weren't real. On another occasion Perry spoke with me about being in college. "Will you miss mom when you are in college?" I inquired. "Oh yes," he replied, "but I will call her every day on my cell phone and I will come back and sneak in at night when daddy isn't looking, and I will go into bed with mommy and stick my bi-i-i-ig penis in her." The obliteration of himself in his drawing, the shadow of the ghost, and the oedipal fantasy are all indicative of the awareness that this young boy has of the terrifying power he is being asked to wield in his family. This young boy was rushing headlong for a full-blown Oedipal victory with all of its catastrophic consequences.

The heart of the Oedipal crisis, Lacan tells us, is that children must come to understand that they can neither possess nor be possessed by their parents. While both children and parents may struggle with this reality, children must learn to turn to find comfort and engagement outside of the fantasy of remaining forever at the center of their parents' world. This reality is what Lacan named the *nom du père* (the Law of the Father). Neither Perry nor his parents had learned how Perry might name his own desires separate from those of his parents. In Lacanian terms, the Law of the Father had collapsed entirely in this family.

The most critical part of my work has been to reestablish this law so that Perry has the space and the invitation to leave behind the psychosis of his infancy—or more precisely, of his parent's infancy. The consequence of not doing so for Perry, the symptom bearer of his family (cf. Mathelin, 1999; Winnicott, 2002), is that he will have to continue to live the psychotic life of a baby in order to keep his parents sane. Perry and his parents have done well in therapy. In weekly parent counseling sessions, I have worked through the parents to engineer changes in the family dynamics by enabling them to become conscious of how their desires are manifesting themselves in Perry's symptoms and assisted them in creating emotional boundaries and rebalancing the distribution of parental authority and demand.

Lacan, Fink reminds us, "emphasizes the fact that patients' lives are determined by their 'purloined letters'—the snatches of their parents' conversation (that is, of the other's discourse), often not intended for their ears, that were indelibly etched in their memories and sealed their fate. Patients bring those letters to analysis, and analysts attempt to render them legible to their patients, to uncover the hidden determinants of their desire" (1997, p. 206). In therapy Perry has begun to deal with these issues in his transferential relationship with me. He acts out his rescue scenarios and uses me as a prop in his plays. As Mannoni would suggest, Perry is beginning to use fantasy and play in a way that he has never had the luxury of doing before. I provide him with vocabulary that names his struggle with enmeshment and names the battles against anxiety that are revealed weekly in his play. He strides into my office confidently, sits on my therapist's chair, and says "Mike, I think I know what we need to work on today." I become an instrument of his desire and he is master, at least of this microuniverse. His teachers report that Perry is also a lot more comfortable in his own skin at school (cf. Briggs, 2002). As Derek Wolcott, speaking of the fragmentation of the Antilles through colonial conquest, remarked in his Nobel acceptance speech, sometimes the vase that is shattered and rebuilt possesses a very special beauty: "Break a vase, and the love that reassembles the fragments is stronger than the love which took its symmetry for granted when it was whole. The glue that fits the pieces is the sealing of its original shape ... and if the pieces are disparate, ill-fitting, they contain more pain than their original sculpture" (1992, unpaged). Perry is beginning to piece together a life in which he can make meanings of the troubles he has experienced, naming his own desires while coping with a world not of his making.

Educators and the Unthought Known

Having considered in some detail the existential plight of children who have encountered obstacles to claiming their own subjectivities, it only remains to clearly enunciate the underlying purpose of adults who work in professional capacities with young children. As Fink (1995) notes, Lacan views trauma as a blockage in the child's capacity to symbolize, to turn unnamed experience, embedded in the unconscious real, into language. This, of course, can happen only through dialogue and symbolization. Felman defines dialogue as "the radical condition of learning and of knowledge" (1987, p. 83). Dialogue, here, however, has a special meaning. It refers to the capacity of the Other (teacher, parent, therapist) to bring into the symbolic realm aspects of the child's subjectivity that are unarticulated. The subject, paradoxically, can become a subject only through dialogue with the other. However, if this dialogue is of the catastrophic type often practiced by parents and teachers, in which their own demands are forced on the child, then it will produce only alienation. This, Fink reminds us, occurs because the focus is on the Other's demands (e.g., for achievement, conformity, duty) rather than on the kind of desire that will bring into being the child's subjective sense of self. To elicit desire the analyst must take care not to offer too much understanding or clarification even though the patient demands it. Feeding demand only leads to the negation of the kind of desire that leads to creativity and the growth of fantasy. As Fink noted, "[t]he more you try to understand, the less you hear—the less you can hear something new and different" (1995, p. 149).

In my clinical practice, I have worked against imagining that I can know ahead of time what a particular child needs and have rather devoted myself to listening for the child's desire and to trying to understand my own desire in relation to the child. I believe that it is possible to likewise construct a school curriculum and a pedagogy wherein children might engage in play and learning that would create the potential for them to articulate and bring forth their inner desires and fantasies. Such a curriculum could provide the space to name and unlock traumatic knowledges that can lead to crippling inferiority and an inhibition of the child's subjective possibilities.

Play (cf. S. Fraiberg, 1996; L. Fraiberg, 1987, Paley, 2004), open ended and emotionally grounded conversation, and the use of children's literature allow children to experience the multiple dimensions of their subject selves and to get in touch with their "unthought knowns" through encountering openly evocative emotionality (cf. Bettelheim, 1989; Coats, 2004; Sendak, 1970, 1988). These practices have the capacity to assist children in symbolizing their unconscious knowledges and releasing their imaginations.

A major obstacle to radically creative teaching that values fantasy and play is the emotional baggage that adults bring to their work with children. If adults are to nurture freeing dialogue with children, then the adults must first free themselves from barriers to their own feelings so that they avoid restricting the child's creativity with excessive demand (cf. Field, Cohler, and Wool 1989; Jersild, 1955/2000). Psychoanalysts commonly refer to this as the problem of countertransference. Mannoni (1970) argues that in an ideal world all teachers would experience psychoanalysis so that they might better get in touch with the traumas and blockages of their own inner child and thereby be more open to emotionally freeing dialogue with the children in their care. Phenomenologist Max Van Manen, for example, argues in *The Tone of Teaching* that adults need to approach children with tact and thoughtfulness to bring forth each child's unexpressed possibility. As Van Manen notes, children bring us the gift of "experiencing the possible" (1986, p. 13). We merely have to allow ourselves to be free enough to receive that gift and reciprocate, a point that Buddhist thinkers have repeatedly made (cf. Epstein, 1995).

This, of course, is an unabashedly romantic notion of pedagogy as freeing children—and adults—to explore their inner beings in an unfettered manner. In *A Child's Work: The Importance of Fantasy Play,* Vivian Paley (2004) brings us back to reality with a harsh reminder of the drastic decline in fantasy play in early childhood curricula in the past decade in the United States. Paley's text offers powerful illustrations of the emotions that fantasy play elicits in children and the ways in which through natural storytelling processes children move from emotional expression, through language, to symbolization of their experiences and the construction of empathic learning communities in early childhood classrooms. In the analysis of young children's fantasy play that has emerged from decades of acutely attuned eavesdropping, Paley arrives at a startlingly psychoanalytic observation: "Had I listened more closely," Paley notes, "I would have heard among other secrets, that when one is young almost every story begins with and returns to a mother and child." (p. 18). Paley delightfully describes how she and her children "use fantasy to calm our anxieties and reassemble ourselves along promising paths" (p. 19), and laments greatly the academicization of early childhood education, a movement that denies children the opportunity to become the subjects of their own experiences: "The potential for surprise is largely gone. We no longer wonder 'Who are you?' but instead decide quickly 'What can we do to fix you?'" (p. 47).

What then of the great progressive tradition of educators as guardians of the possibility for children to live whole lives, unrestricted by either the demands of parents or the sociopolitical limitations of our societies? I spoke just today with the kindergarten teacher of Vanessa, a beautiful five-year-old patient of mine who is suffering acute stress. Vanessa gouged her arms with a scissors at school, and when her teacher denied her access to scissors, she alternately chewed or scratched her arms to shreds. This little girl lives in an intolerably stressful situation at home—so much so that if she were a little older she would be considered at risk for suicide. Her sole refuge is school. Her teacher told me that Vanessa, who can barely write, leaves a stream of notes on the teacher's desk every day telling her teacher how much she loves her. Just this week, the teacher told me through her tears, Vanessa asked if she could come live at the teacher's home. School ends in three weeks, and we both fear for this beautiful child when she says goodbye to one of the few anchors in her unstable world. The love this teacher offers is inspiring, as is her capacity to see beauty and possibility in this mute and truly vulnerable little girl. In my estimation, it is our ethical responsibility as educators to offer our students spaces in which to name and realize the *unthought knowns* that are pathways to their desires. The corollary of this, of course, is that we have to be prepared to stoutly resist initiatives that are designed to erase children's desires and limit their imaginations.

References

Bakhtin, M. (1986). *Speech genres and other late essays.* Austin: University of Texas Press.

Barrie, J. M. (1902). *The little white bird.* London: Hodder & Stoughton.

Bettelheim, B. (1989). *The uses of enchantment: The meaning and importance of fairy tales.* New York: Vintage.

Bollas, C. (1987). *The shadow of the object: Psychoanalysis of the unthought known.* New York: Columbia University Press.

Brenkman, J. (1999). Introduction. In M. Mannoni, *Separation and creativity: Refinding the lost language of childhood.* New York: Other Press.

Briggs, A. (Ed.). (2002). *Surviving space: Papers on infant observation.* London: Karnac.

Butler, J. (1997). *The psychic life of power: Theories in subjection.* Stanford, CA: Stanford University Press.

Cisneros, S. (1991). *Women hollering creek and other stories.* New York: Vintage.

Coats, K. (2004). *Looking glasses and neverlands: Lacan, desire, and subjectivity in children's literature.* Iowa City: University of Iowa Press.

Danon-Boileau, L. (2001). *The silent child: Bringing language to children who cannot speak.* New York: Oxford.

Davoine, F., & Gaudillière, J. (2004). *History beyond trauma.* New York: Other Press.

Donzelot, J. (1979). *The policing of families.* New York: Pantheon.

Epstein, M. (1995). *Thoughts without a thinker.* New York: Basic.

Felman, S. (1987). *Jacques Lacan and the adventure of insight.* Cambridge, MA: Harvard University Press.

Field, K., Cohler, B., & Wool, G. (Eds.). (1989). *Learning and education: Psychoanalytic perspectives.* Madison, CT: International Universities Press.

Fink, B. (1995). *The Lacanian subject.* Princeton, NJ: Princeton University Press.

Fink, B. (1997). *A clinical introduction to Lacanian psychoanalysis.* Cambridge, MA: Harvard University Press.

Fraiberg, L. (Ed.). (1987). *Selected writings of Selma Fraiberg.* Columbus: Ohio State University Press.

Fraiberg, S. (1996). *The magic years.* New York: Scribner.

Jersild, A. (1955). *When teachers face themselves.* New York: Teachers College Press.

Langer, L. (1991). *Holocaust testimonies: The ruins of memory.* New Haven, CT: Yale University Press.

Levi, P. (1996). *Survival in Auschwitz.* New York: Simon & Schuster.

Mannoni, M. (1970). *The child, his "illness," and the others.* London: Karnac.

Mannoni, M. (1999). *Separation and creativity: Refinding the lost language of childhood.* New York: Other Press.

Mathelin, C. (1999). *The broken piano: Lacanian psychotherapy with children.* New York: Other Press.

Miller, A. (1997). *The drama of the gifted child.* New York: Basic Books.

O'Loughlin, M. (2005). On losses that are not easily mourned. Under editorial consideration.

Paley, V. (2004). *A child's work: The importance of fantasy play.* Chicago: University of Chicago Press.

Piontelli, A. (1992). *From fetus to child.* New York: Routledge.

Rose, J. (1992). *The case of Peter Pan: Or the impossibility of children's fiction.* Philadelphia: Pennsylvania University Press.

Rousmaniere, K., Delhi, K., & De Coninck Smith, N. (1997). *Discipline, moral regulation and schooling.* New York: Garland.

Sendak, M. (1970). *In the night kitchen.* New York: HarperCollins.

Sendak, M. (1988). *Where the wild things are.* New York: HarperCollins.

Van Manen, M. (1986). *The tone of teaching.* Portsmouth, NH: Heinemann.

Winnicott, D. W. (2002). *Winnicott on the child.* New York: Perseus.

Wolcott, D. (1992). *The Antilles; Fragments of epic memory. The Nobel lecture.* New York: Farrar, Straus & Giroux.

INTERLUDE **V**

Curriculum and the Erotics of Learning

Film: *Ma Vie en Rose*

Paired Chapters: *Romantic Research: Why We Love to Read* by
Madeleine R. Grumet
Reading, Writing, and the Wrath of My Father by
Jonathan G. Silin
*Love in the Classroom: Desire and Transference in
Learning and Teaching* by Bertram J. Cohler and
Robert M. Galatzer-Levy

In this Interlude, we pair the film *Ma Vie en Rose* (*My Life in Pink*, 1997)
with three chapters by Madeleine Grumet, Jonathan Silin, and Bertram
Cohler and Robert Galatzer-Levy. Taken together, the film and chapters
speak to the fact that in psychoanalytic theory, learning is grounded in
erotics. As Jonathan Silin reminds us, for Freud, the drive to learn is a
drive to understand sex. Melanie Klein and Jacques Lacan offer somewhat
different versions of the child's curiosity; for Klein, what the child wants
to know is his or her mother's body; for Lacan, the child seeks to learn the
answers to fundamental questions—"Why did you have me?" and "What

do you require of me?" For both Klein and Lacan, these researches are often framed as questions about sex and sexuality and are driven by the child's need to understand his or her place in the family and in relationship between the parents. This is a need that arises, they tell us, with the child's loss of the first fantasy of perfect symbiosis with the primary caregiver. Learning, in other words, is founded in loss and as Grumet and Silin remind us, the need to overcome this loss is at the heart of the urge to learn. The child, now aware of separation and vulnerability, sets out to learn what is needed to secure the reassurance that she or he is wanted and will be loved and cared for. Along with Freud, Klein, and Lacan, the four authors writing in this section argue that in order to think about curriculum, we need to remember that early and ongoing needs to understand and express sexuality, relationship, and pleasure are the foundation for the child's larger curiosity about the world.

In Alain Berliner's *Ma Vie en Rose*, we are presented with seven-year-old Ludovic, a character with tremendous integrity and a powerful need to learn in order to make sense of his world. Ludovic is insistent in his conviction that his birth as a boy was a mistake. He pursues his desires without shame, losing himself in fantasy and the color-drenched world of Pam, a Barbie-like doll, and in his love for Jerome, his neighbor, who is also the son of his father's boss. Although Ludovic is able to articulate and engage his desire, he understands that this desire disrupts his relationships with his family and community. Given the rage of his father and siblings, the waning support of his mother, and the violence he endures from peers, Ludovic sustains losses of community that are quite real and present. He is expelled from school and because of his play with Jerome, his father loses his job and the family is forced to move.

Throughout the movie we see Ludovic working to understand and reconcile his position with his desire. With all the drive of the most passionate learner, Ludovic pursues one hypothesis after another to explain why his sex, his desire, and the desires of his family, peers, and communities seem to be at odds. Understanding that life would be easier if his sex matched his desire, Ludovic begins to insist that he will one day turn into a woman. He develops a sophisticated theory about the structuring of his desires. When God was giving out chromosomes, Ludovic explains, his second "X" was lost in the trash and he somehow got stuck with a "Y." As a result, he is a "girlboy" but, when he grows up, this mistake will be corrected and he will become a woman. In the meanwhile, Ludovic contends, it only makes sense that he should play with Pam, wear make-up and dresses, perform a mock marriage with Jerome, and kiss Jerome on stage during a school performance.

As this film makes abundantly clear, Ludovic's difficulties do not lie within himself—he has no conflict about his desire—but in the adults who surround him, attempting to force Ludovic's desires or at least his behaviors to match the required norms. This film uses fantasy, satire, and pathos to explore the responses of parents and communities when the desire a child expresses is not only controversial, but scandalous, and threatens common consensus about what it means to be respectable, educated, and sane. The film also proposes that the drive to respectability is motivated by the adults' need to deny that they are subject to the same unruly desires and passions that they condemn as abnormal in Ludovic. In one scene, we see Ludovic's parents admitting to a psychotherapist that in fact their desire had been for a girl. Running throughout the movie we see adults unconsciously responding to Pam and particularly to her theme song with the same dreamy desire that Ludovic feels. The hysteria of their condemnation of Ludovic can be understood, in other words, as their need to discipline their own half-felt desires.

The destructiveness of this need to discipline desire is a central theme in the chapter by Bertram Cohler and Robert Galatzer-Levy. Cohler and Galatzer-Levy tell us that the inevitable presence of teachers' and students' desires is immensely threatening to teachers. They propose that because we do not have a language that allows us to recognize and use the erotic investments we bring to raising and educating children, we actively repress and deny all passion in teaching, leading to emotionally sterile classes. As teachers we have no models for addressing the transferential and the counter-transferential material generated in relationships with our students and therefore our stances toward students are often reactive. Provocatively, Cohler and Galatzer-Levy argue that this is true for both the charismatic teacher, whose unexamined need is for the students' love, and for the authoritarian teacher whose need is for respect. In either case, fearing the messiness of real relationships, these teachers hold their students at a distance.

In Madeleine Grumet's essay, the need to control desire in the classroom grows from the need to deny the profound impact that the first relationship with the maternal object and the loss of that object has had on our lives and the life of our culture. Drawing on feminist theorists, Grumet portrays female teachers who repudiate their own interests as well as the interests of their students in the service of disavowing their early erotic attachments to their mothers and claiming that their loyalty is only to heterosexual desire. They are driven to see their role as teachers as the cultivation of reasonable subjects who carry out normative visions of reproduction belonging to civilization, tradition, and art, denying teaching as an erotic connection to the maternal and the emotional. In a striking incident in *Ma Vie en*

Rose, we see just such a scene. Ludovic's young and apparently progressive teacher has asked her students to bring into school and discuss their "favorite objects." This attempt at bringing the children's subjectivities into the classroom turns into a spectacle when Ludovic presents his Pam doll. We see the limits of the teacher's capacity to take the side of the child; in directing Ludovic to pursue a more reasonable toy for a boy—a plane perhaps—the teacher repudiates Ludovic's truth and desire in favor of claiming her place as defender of normalcy, rationality, and civilization.

This civilization, as Jonathan Silin reminds us in his autobiographical narrative, is often relentlessly heteronormative. As a boy in school, Silin lacked the ability either to name his desire or to find his desire in school texts or expectations of his teachers and he struggled to make subjective connections to the curriculum. It was not until late in his adolescence and largely on his own that Silin was able to begin to see and feel the world he desired and to begin to put the school demands of reading and writing to use for his own purposes. While it is not possible to know how as a boy he would have responded to another kind of curriculum, Silin argues that teachers have the opportunity to provide more than what he found in school. Effective teaching, Silin says, honors student imagination and authentic engagement, and creates space for difficult questions.

Grumet addresses the question of teaching by proposing that through the pedagogy they practice and the curriculum they value, teachers have the opportunity to point children to a world beyond their first world. Curriculum has the potential to offer children remediation for their losses through discovering new meanings, relationships, and sources of pleasure and engagement. Children can and do passionately attach to the world of ideas and the skills that are needed to enact their desires and to make and maintain emotional bonds with peers and adults. Meaning and connection can be constructed in many ways, in explorations of the beauty of children's literature, the magnificence of the solar system, the magic of numbers, or the histories and cultures of people with whom we share this planet. This is less likely to happen, Cohler and Galatzer-Levy suggest, in classrooms where teachers actively manage their anxieties through denying the importance of engaging passionately and intimately with their students and with learning as a relational, collaborative, and dialogic undertaking.

CHAPTER 9

Romantic Research

Why We Love to Read

MADELEINE R. GRUMET

Reading is an essentially romantic process, for it invites us to mingle our thoughts, visions, and hopes with someone else's. Nevertheless, like most romantics, we avoid close scrutiny of why we love to read. Fearing that our scholarly attention will spoil the affair, we prefer to study aspects of reading that we care less about rather than end up brokenhearted.

"What's love got to do with it?" has been a question that I have been asking since the early seventies when I was thirty-three, had three kids, had spent seven years at home with them, and returned to graduate school for a Master's degree in English education. What I had remembered from teaching were very strong emotional experiences—that boy in the back of the room scowling and sulking as I taught poetry to section after section of high school seniors. I was haunted by the image of his resistance, of his sitting there, with his head thrust back, knees stuck out, heels dug in, his legs punctuating the aisle with the angles of refusal. And I also remembered how hard it was for me, as I felt this resistance radiating from this one boy in the back of the room, how hard it was not to focus on his refusal, forgetting the considerable, if not passionate, interest of most of the thirty students who shared that space with us. Teaching had not been cool work for me, and I had hoped that graduate study would help me understand some of the love and dread that had drawn me into the work of teaching and into parenting as well.

I was fortunate to study with Bill Pinar, who was working to find ways of using humanities scholarship to elucidate educational experience, moving away from the quantification of social science research, which so often ignored the issues that interested me because they could not be isolated and measured. We turned to autobiographical texts of educational experience for data and worked to develop methods of reading and interpreting these texts that would reveal their ideological underpinnings as well as the motives, desires, and commitments that their authors brought to them (Pinar and Grumet, 1976).

When I would bring this work to national conferences, I discovered that curriculum researchers and theorists still labeled a topic in education that someone really cared about as subjective—thus, trivial. At that time only the conditions that framed the labor of men were deemed important enough to merit research and analysis. People who pursued this important work all wore leather jackets and talked about reproduction theory, which basically asserted that children were workers, created by the assimilation of schools to the culture of industry: a neomarxist version of the immaculate conception. It was a process of reproduction that left out both women and children: schools reproduced the norms of material production.

If you attended the meetings of the American Educational Research Association in those days you rarely heard children mentioned in discussions of curriculum theory. No one ever confessed to having been a child, and in presentations no one even admitted knowing a child. Of course, if you spent time in the coffee shops, all your colleagues ever talked about were their children: over breakfast, over coffee, over lunch, over dinner, at table after table after table.

Clearly, love has a great deal to do with learning and I began to wonder how we could introduce this knowledge contained in the domain of the private, the familial, the domestic into the conversation that shaped public education. What did the experiences of reproduction have to do with education? What did it mean to be parents? What did it mean to have been children? How did the experiences of having been children and parents influence the education we constructed for other people's children? We worked to bring those conversations from the coffee shops to the podium.

This project to have our public knowledge incorporate the wisdom of experience that habit and tradition had consigned to the secrecy of our private lives was also the motive that inspired me to write *Bitter Milk: Women and Teaching* (1988). The title, *Bitter Milk,* was drawn from a presentation by anthropologist Gananath Obeyesekere (1981). He described the severe separation anxiety, called the dark night of the soul, experienced by some women in Sri Lanka as they leave their families to get married. Obeyesekere was interested in studying collective rituals that seem to have real psychological efficacy for the person who goes through them. The ritual to cure these women requires them to drink bitter milk, a mixture of milk and crushed margosa leaves, the same fluid that their mothers had put on their nipples to wean them when they were babies. I was fascinated by the tension of attachment and separation that pervaded the ritual and its cure, and by the ceremony of alienation that was required to effect this separation of mother and daughter, and I appropriated this metaphor for my study of women and teaching.

It seemed to me that the fact that there are so many women in education was significant and that working with other people's children when you yourself had been a child and you yourself may also have children would affect how, as a teacher, you would make sense of curriculum and instruction. My version of bitter milk explored our gendered experiences of reproduction and their relations to our systems of knowledge and education, which we use both to distance ourselves from children and to claim them. Often those agendas, however contradictory, are simultaneous.

Basically, what *Bitter Milk* argues is that "what is most fundamental to our lives as men and women, sharing a moment on this planet, is the process and experience of reproducing ourselves" (1988, p. 4). You can imagine that in the seventies that statement was not too popular with anybody. Men who did not know how to make careers out of that thesis did not like it, and women who embraced feminism as having liberated them from obligatory childcare did not like it. We were all so eager to disassociate ourselves from the powerlessness of children and the women who cared for them that I had to clearly distinguish reproduction from its cultural baggage:

> The fundamental is suspect if it suggests a single way of addressing the project and process of reproduction. To be a gendered human being is to participate in the reproductive commitments of this society, for reproduction is present as a theme in human consciousness without providing a norm for human behavior. (Grumet 1988, p. 6)

Let me repeat that phrase because I think it declares an important distinction: reproduction is a theme in human consciousness without providing a norm for human behavior. That distinction reminds us that if we do not have kids, it does not mean that the reproduction of the species and that our own gendered existence as people capable of reproduction are not significant themes in our lives:

> Male or female, heterosexual, homosexual, bisexual, monogamous, chaste or multi-partnered, we each experience our sexuality and attachments within a set of conditions that contain the possibility of procreation. Our identities incorporate our position relative to this possibility. They encode our assent or refusal, our ambivalence or our desire, our gratification or our frustration. Whether we choose to be parents or to abstain from this particular relation to children, the possibility of procreation is inscribed on our bodies and in the process of our own development. Even if we choose not to be a parent, we are not exempt from the reproductive process for we have each been a child of our parents. The intentions, assumptions, emotions, and achievements of educational practice and theory are infused with motives that come from our own reproductive histories and commitments. What is fundamental is not the nuclear family of an orange juice commercial enjoying a suburban breakfast in the family room. What is fundamental is that although there is no one way of being concerned with children, we cannot deny our responsibility for the future, whatever form our projects of nurturance assume. (Grumet 1988, pp. 6–7)

The theoretical foundation for this material came from Dorothy Dinnerstein's book, *The Mermaid and the Minotaur* (1976), and from Nancy Chodorow's book, *The Reproduction of Mothering* (1978). These texts provided language that linked epistemology—relationships between subject and object—to the language of psychological development. The words "subject" and "object" work in both domains. In epistemology, subjectivity is consciousness and anything we think of provides the objects of that consciousness: Brentano's postulate. In object relations, derived from Freudian psychoanalytic theory, the object also receives the active energy of the subject, so anyone who matters to a child is an object of her love as well of her cognition or intentionality.

The primary parent is, in most cases, the first object of a child's notice, attention, and affection. Phenomenologists and psychologists have argued that a child must first become the object of another's love before it can become a subject: "the you is older than the I." Let me quote Stephen Strasser (in Grumet 1988, p. 7):

> My affirmation of the "you" must transcend all doubt for me, it must be characterized as the "primordial faith" upon which all my further cogitos rest. For the nearness of the "you" is a primordial

presence, one that makes me believe that relations with other beings also are meaningful. My turning-to a "you" is the most elementary turning-to, one that causes my intentionality to awaken. In short, only the "you" makes me be an "I." That is why, we repeat, the "you" is older than the I.

It is in relation that children both discover the world and develop a sense of themselves. However, we imagine that in the beginning the distinction between the subject and the object is not very clear. I have to use the word "imagine" because we have no way of interviewing one another or our children about the experiences of consciousness set at a presymbolic level. In an essay entitled "The Egg and the Sperm," Emily Martin indicates how we have projected our own gender politics onto our very first emotions and interactions. She cites biological texts that describe the egg as large and passive: "It does not move or journey, but passively 'is transported,' 'is swept,' or even 'drifts' along the fallopian tube. In utter contrast, sperm are small, 'streamlined' and invariably active" (Martin 1991, p. 489).

She later cites another text that describes the egg as Sleeping Beauty: "a dormant bride awaiting her mate's magic kiss, which instills the spirit that brings her to life" (p. 490). If this imagery sounds old-fashioned, Martin cites a recent 1987 research report from Johns Hopkins, which provides a much more active role for the egg. "The innermost vestment, the zona pellucida, is a glycoprotein shell, which captures and tethers the sperm before they penetrate it" (p. 494). Martin notes that as soon as the egg gets into the act, it is presented as an aggressive sperm catcher, and she thinks that we have moved again to replicate the old division of the virgin and the whore: the passive, pure innocent egg, or the voracious, devouring, castrating egg. Now if we have difficulty talking about eggs and sperms without dressing them up in the costumes of our own romantic wardrobe, anything we are going to say about children and parents—about people—is going to be drenched in this drama. Thus everything that I shall say is suspect.

Object relations theory investigates a child situated within a field of relationships of which the child is a part. It shifts the focus from drives to the social field that surrounds the infant, offering relationships that anchor the infant in the world. Object relations theory does not assume that the Oedipal crisis is the only significant moment of psychosexual development. This theory pays attention to pre-Oedipal development, the years before kids are six or seven. It shares the emphasis on social interaction that shapes Vygotsky's work, and works to describe the social field that grounds the process of development as he describes it: "Any function in the child's cultural development appears twice on two planes. First it appears on the social plane and then on the psychological plane. First it appears between people as an interpsychological category and then within the child as an intrapsychological category" (Vygotsky 1981, p. 61).

Reading books with other people is part of the continuing process through which relations between people are transformed into psychological possibilities within a person. Furthermore, reading books with other people reverses the process, permitting the psychological possibilities provoked and experienced by the text to become enunciated and negotiated in social reality, thus creating the social interaction and sanction that may eventually move possibility from the realm of fantasy and aesthetics to the realities of daily existence. I do not think that we have grappled sufficiently with why we read books with other people—which we do endlessly, constantly in classrooms, and theaters, and churches and mosques and synagogues, in courtrooms and clinics. Rituals of reading are analogues for the social structure within which we develop selves and society. Through the interpretation of text, reading permits communications that may also significantly change social structure. This was Dewey's point: In the interaction of the child and the curriculum it is not just the child who develops, but it is also the curriculum. It's not just people who change; knowledge does also. We are speaking about the interaction of two dynamic systems.

Therefore, what I want to suggest is that we love to read, and that we also read in order to love. Now, as easy as that sounds it is a little facile. The symmetry of the phrase can mask its problem. Some of the psychoanalytic theory that addresses the relationship between language and love can give us cause for worry. Our colleagues have had reason to leave love out. In the work of Jacques Lacan and in the work of Julia Kristeva, it is the absence of the beloved that creates the space that texts fill.

The experience of space first comes to us in the space that opens up between us and the one who first nurtures us. It appears in the gap left by our first separations from those we have loved and identified with. Object relations theory suggests that our first object is continuous with our sense of self, and that intimations of our mother's separateness are accompanied with a sense of loss of some part of ourselves. Kristeva describes all those games we play with babies as we hold them and carry them, and she reminds us of the nervous giggling of babies that declares their tension and anxiety as they are tossed up in the air by a playful or hostile parent. Kristeva focuses on that moment when the baby is experiencing the sense of distance and space from the parent. It is in that space that communication has to happen for the baby to feel continually connected. It is in that space that we hear the melodies of "weeeeeee" and "up we go." It is in that space that we say, "where's mommy?" and "peek-a-boo." It is in that space that we say, "once upon a time" and "in the beginning was the word." We are still negotiating that space.

Lacan gets a little gloomy about this. He maintains that as we separate from the mother we give up our original sense of self because it had incorporated her, and the only way we get it back is in the mirror image of how we look in her esteem. And Kristeva also maintains that what we give up in order to become separate we always miss. She calls this category of missing person "the abject." An example of the abject would be all those body fluids that we let go of: spit, urine, feces, and mucus. Now when you are a baby, it is okay to let all that stuff hang out. And for those of us who have raised babies it is amazing how continuous that environment of their fluids and our bodies becomes. It is difficult to select the accurate preposition for the relation: in our bodies, of our bodies, on our bodies, with our bodies?

Lacan and Kristeva remind us what we give up as we close up. Lacan argues that language is a bridge we construct to connect us once again to that part of ourselves we surrendered when we separated from her. Language is something that we throw ahead of us to gather up what we have left behind. As we throw it beyond us to bridge the gap, we recuperate our losses through communication, through texts. Lacan suggests that we cannot ever really pull ourselves together with language, because this wordy material of history and culture is inadequate to symbolize and express that original sense of connection. More optimistically, Kristeva argues that language is not just symbolic, not just a collection of diacritical signs. Its melodies, rhymes, and sounds, its pauses and gestures constitute a semiotic strata of communication: a residue from the time of babbling, whining, and cooing when we giggled in the space that opened up as we were tossed in the air. She tries to suggest that through language, even as adults speak and write it, runs an underground stream that sings our early emotions, relationships, and sense of connection. Her intuition is extended into our sense of literacy that emphasizes the expressive, playful aesthetic elements of communication in which the semiotic is richly figured.

Texts serve to mediate the distance between self and other for their meanings, both externally produced and internally sustained, providing the bridging quality that object relations theorists recognize in transitional objects. In *Nourishing Words,* Atwell-Vasey (1998) brings object relations theory to the study of language-arts education:

> Winnicott explains that the infant assumes rights over the object, and the object is affectionately cuddled as well as excitedly loved and mutilated. This object never changes, except by the infant's will, and it must survive loving, hating, and perhaps aggression. "It must seem to the infant to give warmth, or to move, or to have

texture, or to do something that seems to show it has vitality or reality of its own." (Winnicott, 1971, p. 5, in Atwell-Vasey, p. 101)

Winnicott describes how children use blankets and teddy bears as transitional objects, those things we kept dragging around with us when we were little. I think I still use my purse that way. It took a long time before I could bear to give up my giant and favorite bag that I carried everywhere, hanging on my right shoulder. I had to wait until my fifth lumbar vertebra protested before I could bear to give it up for the little pouch I squeeze my stuff into now. It was clearly a transitional object for me. I liked to have it close to my body at all times. "It must seem to give the infant warmth, or to move, or to have texture, or to do something that seems to show that it has vitality and reality of its own." All those times when I can never find my keys have convinced me that it has "vitality and reality of its own."

The notion that the object has some reality of its own is important. Atwell-Vasey explains Winnicott as stressing that although a transitional object may be symbolic of the breast, "To the baby the transitional object does not seem as if it comes from without as it does from the observer's perspective, nor does it come from within like a hallucination" (Atwell-Vasey 1998, p. 101). Psychologically, the infant takes from a breast that is part of the infant, and the mother gives milk to an infant who is part of herself. Atwell-Vasey explains that when a mother adapts to the infant's needs, there is not really interchange between mother and child, so much as an "overlap of experience."

When I first read this phrase, "overlap of experience," in Atwell-Vasey's text I thought of Iser's (1989) phenomenological studies of reading that describe a sense of the text as alive, as something you can really get into, feel close to. Yet, what the text offers us, that even the best mother cannot provide, is eternal symbiosis. It is one of those transitional objects that Atwell-Vasey has described as never changing, except by the infant's will; it must survive loving and hating. Now even though stalwart mothers have been known to survive our tantrums and sulks, they do, occasionally, escape our will and go through a few changes themselves. But the book is always there: "I've got you." Why do we keep our books clustered around us, cluttering night tables, piled on counters, tucked in our pockets, loaded into our briefcases? I rarely reread them. But I cannot bear to move an office without having them there. Their presence, and the fact that they can be present and there if we want them, matters because they are witnesses to the development of our egos, they are an overlap of our own experience, and a lap that never disappears as its owner stands up and walks away. The well-read book provides an extraordinary sense of stability. It is the icon for an ego mediating the relationship between self and other. It fits this description of a third place: neither here nor there that Davis and Wallbridge present in *Boundary and Space*:

> For Winnicott the answer to the questions of whether or not the object is outside or inside is that we are neither inside the world of dream and fantasy nor outside the world of shared reality. We are in both places at once. So while the boundary between the me and the not me is of fundamental importance in the attainment of integration, health and indeed sanity, the potential space, the place where we live transcends this boundary. (1983, p. 168)

Now that space between the me and the not-me is not really a space that we have tried to bridge in education, for all our talk of community. We have focused on separation. Do your own thing. Individualism. Do not look at his paper. Is this your own thought? We admire autonomy. We admire thinking that is decentered, concepts uncluttered by the complexities of particular contexts or relationships. And to the degree that education privileges separation over and over again, it replicates male-gender development.

For there is another theme of loss in object relations theory that comes through strongly in the work of Chodorow and Dinnerstein. They ask the question: How come if mothers are the primary parents of boys and girls, and infants of both sexes identify with and love their mothers, boys turn into boys and girls turn into girls? And the story constructed to answer this question is, again, one of loss. The story tells us that what the boy has to do in order to be a man, to feel like a man, to experience the world like a man, is to repudiate this earliest sense of connection. Basically, to be male is to be not like her. Unfortunately, repression is not very neat. It is pretty hard for the little boy, who by the age of three is pretty clear that he is a little boy, to say, "I'll put away the stuff that's like her, but I'll keep all the other stuff going." So for the little boy that period of time when everything hangs out, when all those fluids are leaking and dripping and slurping and bubbling, and he feels continuous with the world, must be repudiated in order to achieve the relational stance of male identity: Things must be kept apart. Those of you who are statisticians might recognize this theme in the skepticism of the null hypothesis, which starts by assuming no relationship.

On the other hand, what the boy gets to sustain as a heterosexual male is his desire for someone like the person he once identified with. There are two aspects to this early relation to the primary parent: identification and also love. So for the male, heterosexual romance provides a kind of reunion, some recuperation of what he has relinquished in his own identity.

The process of genderization permits a woman to continue to feel identified with her mother, and maybe if we have not had to repress this early identification, as our brothers have, we still have some access to all those loose and leaky limes. Maybe that is why we cry more easily, maybe that is why we are more expressive. Nevertheless, as we grow older, that identification threatens our sense of ourselves and we confront the problem of how to feel separate when we still feel essentially and eternally connected.

Able to retain identification with the female primary parent, the woman achieves heterosexuality by repressing the desire that she has felt for her first love and transferring that need and emotion to a man. Loves that are repressed do not conveniently disappear. We work at keeping them away. We maintain our heterosexuality by denying our love of other women. If the overlap of experience that is our early love and identification with our mothers is echoed in our relationship with text, it may feel like an illicit intimacy, and if we find women complying with rigid and alienating reading curricula, we may find the motive for their compliance in their homophobia. When we look at schools, at school districts, and see thousands and thousands of women being bossed around by three men, we must ask ourselves, how can this be? Is sexism that effective? Why has this talented and educated multitude not organized so that their own experiences of nurture, family, and knowledge are salient in curriculum and in the social and political structure of schooling?

I think we have to consider the kind of homophobia that frightens women away from identifying with each other. They fear that by identifying with each other, they will be stuck at home; they will always be girls or marginalized with the other ladies. It is as if feeling grown up and real relies on male recognition.

Now when I first read this material (and I do this all the time with psychological literature), I said, of course, that is me, that is me, and I went through a couple of years of reading Chodorow, worrying a lot. But then I also recognized that it also was not me. My confusion was a consequence of the generalization of such theories. These theories are schemas: they cannot describe any one of us. If we are female, if we are male, we are somewhere on this continuum that stretches between identification and separation, heterosexuality and homosexuality that these theories describe. Theories of gender development are disrespectfully reductive:

> This story of palpable presence and shadowy absence, of turning
> to and turning away, is and is not my story. Over and over again,
> it contradicts the intimacies of my own childhood. It obscures my

mother's energy and activity in the public world, just as it erases my father's attentiveness and care. He walked with me in the dark morning hours when I would not relinquish the world for sleep. She gave speeches and came home late after the meeting, her eyes glowing, showing me that beautiful pin that she had been given to recognize her achievement. The theory fails to notice the photo in our album of my son, sleeping on my husband's chest, and the presence of their father's humor and inflections in our daughters' voices. These moments of familial specificity achieve meaning for me as they both confirm and contradict the relations that Chodorow describes. My father's participation in my infant care, my mother's leadership were both achieved in opposition to the politics of separation and connection that Chodorow presents. Furthermore, the meaning of their actions cannot be separated from this contradiction, for it was in opposition to these norms that my mother talked and my father walked. And sometimes the actors themselves, located somewhere between connection and separation, lose their grasp of their own experience. My mother puts my father on the phone to talk to the landlord. My father never talks about his business at home. My son asks about my work and reads my papers, but he is careful not to mention that the research that he is citing in his college classroom was written by his mother. (Grumet 1988, p. 14)

Our relationships to sexual stereotypes or to the narratives that constitute object relations theories are complicated. They don't describe us fully, and yet they describe us a bit and our culture enough that we are constantly interacting with them: sometimes absorbing them, sometimes confronting them, sometimes repudiating them. Winnicott may say that the transitional field gives us the opportunity to choose our world, but what I want to suggest is that it is not so easy to choose that world. When Tina Turner sings that love is a secondhand emotion, she may be referring to transference or more generally to its cultural determination. Clearly it is a hand-me-down.

Studies of infant/parent interactions may help us to see how this world is handed down to us from the people we love. The figure/ground gestalt that adults take for granted must be constructed for the developing child, and that process starts almost as soon as the child can focus. "See the doggie"; "Look, there's grandma." The pointing finger literally indicates the world worth seeing. Later, imitating animal sounds and car horns, performing laughter and mock weeping, we teach the infant to listen for sounds that we consider meaningful.

As we direct children's gazes, we introduce them to the world we care about, and so their notice of the world and ultimately the world they see is the one we care to bring to their attention. Babies just do not seem to know what is important, as any grandparent who has spent a significant sum on a gift for a toddler who ignores it, drawn only to the wrapping paper and ribbon, can testify.

Children do not get the world from just opening their eyes and looking around, and similarly, children do not get texts from just opening their eyes and looking around. Sometimes we get taken up with ideas about the writing process that suggest that we can pursue literacy without curriculum, which is the directing force, the pointing finger. Children cannot get literacy without curriculum, just as children cannot get the world without someone who points to a world worth seeing.

When we select a story to read to a group of children, when we choose texts for a curriculum, we are extending this process of identifying what parts of the world, what relationships, creatures, and events are worthy of their notice. Current debates about the canon are really our own debates about distinguishing the world that matters to us from worlds that do not. If we lived in a culture isolated from all others, then we could tell children only the stories that animate the immediate world we share with them. Religious myths, stories of ancestors, and stories that point to important events in the natural and cultural world would adequately constitute our curriculum. Even when our world became more complex, and we were fully aware of other cultures, we believed that we had the luxury of relegating stories of other worlds to exotica, a dilettante's tour through *National Geographic*. But as national economies and technologies have surrendered to international trade, nuclear power, and environmental dilemmas, it has become clear to us how difficult it is to subordinate one part of the world to another, to say this is important, but not that. Furthermore, we have come to admit that designating the immediate world we share with children becomes a normative and prescriptive activity when the children we meet daily come from homes with rich and various cultures and histories.

The task of pointing out the world is dangerous. If we point to everything, we relinquish order. Those who insist on the canon, or at least on some canon are often fearful that abdicating that distinction will ultimately dissolve all figure/ground salience, plunging the children we teach into cognitive, emotional, political, and aesthetic anarchy. If we point to a very clearly delineated and logically ordered world, like the Dick and Jane readers that introduced so many of us to worlds of red wagons and spotted puppies, we risk pointing to a world that children do not recognize as the place where they live.

Nevertheless, pointing out the world is not just a one-way process, with the adult doing all the pointing. Daniel Stern, studying the interaction of mothers and their infants, has observed that infants are much less passive than we have said they were in our child-development theories; they express their presence or lack of interest by interrupting their gaze or abruptly directing it elsewhere. Often parents follow their child's gaze, naming the world as the child scans it. Often the initiation and selection of the meaningful world then switches from one to another, as first the parent, then the infant directs their mutual gaze to the object to be named.

Stern describes this infant's response to an excessive ordering of her world:

> She determined which toy Molly would play with, how Molly was to play with it ("Shake it up and down—don't roll it on the floor"), when Molly was done playing with it, and what to do next ("Oh, here is Dressy Bessy. Look!"). The mother overcontrolled the interaction to such an extent that it was often hard to trace the natural crescendo and decrescendo of Molly's own interest and excitement.... Molly found an adaptation. She gradually became more compliant. Instead of actively avoiding or opposing these intrusions, she became one of those enigmatic gazers into space. She could stare through you, her eyes focused somewhere at infinity and her facial expressions opaque enough to be just uninterpretable, and at the same time remain in good contingent contact and by and large do what she was invited or told to do. Watching her over the months was like watching her self regulation of excitement slip away. When playing alone she did not recover it, remaining somewhat aloof from exciting engagements with things. (Stern 1985, p. 197)

Here, loss is occasioned by presence rather than absence, as Molly loses herself and the world in mute resistance and defiance, Molly's shutting down and avoidance is something we see in class when attention is overdirected and excitement is excessively monitored.

How can we rescue reading and research on reading from the sad romance of broken hearts? I am not saying that we do not suffer from a primordial separation, that the rest of life does not always feel a little lonely, but I suspect that we have overestimated the dyadic quality of our original experience of connection. Women may seem privileged by being so salient in these stories of human development, but we have paid for that privilege. When women serve as the primary caregivers to infants, it is assumed that because the neonate is preverbal preconceptual, and presymbolic, the nurturing woman is too. In the theories of Marx and Freud, only men have second nature; women and babies are caught in firsthand emotions. Now women do not become babies just because they care for babies; nevertheless, we write manuals for elementary teachers as if they were six years old.

We must remember that the nurturer is a complicated adult engaged with the world. That same woman who is babbling with the baby, relishing the nursing, and changing the diapers may also be writing books, working a trick shift in a factory from midnight until six o'clock in the morning, and managing many other children as well as complicated relations with other adults.

Bonnie Litowitz argues that we must change our research model if we are to liberate children, their parents, and teachers from notions of learning and development that are excessively individualistic and romantic:

> We have widened our studies to include two persons—a mother and child dyad—(or three, mother, father, child, triad).... Yet we study these dyads as two individuals: one whole, the other an incomplete part on its way to spinning off as a separate whole. This basically embryological model ... proposes the mother as context for the child until that time when the child can be context-free. But a new focus would examine the matrix in which both child and mother (and child and others) are embedded such that the child can participate in, initiate and control increasingly complex contexts of activity. (1989, p. 323)

We are always looking only at the child, as if the child's development did not in turn affect the development of the adults who care for him or her. We rarely look at how the teacher is developing while working with this child, just as we rarely look at how the child's mother or father or siblings change and develop. We look only at the child's movement as if everybody else in the child's world were static: completely developed, all finished. This is a strangely alienated way of being interested in somebody. Yet it is very comfortable for us, for in our interest in the *child* we excuse ourselves from probing scrutiny.

In her research, Atwell-Vasey shifts the focus to the context for development and the adults who control it. She explores the processes and rationales through which teachers of literature turned their own experiences of reading into the curricula that they brought to their students. Using autobiographical method, she asked these teachers to write about their own experiences of reading in all the contexts where it was important to them. Then Atwell-Vasey observed what these teachers were doing in their classrooms and used object relations theory to interpret the striking contradictions that she noted between their own reading experiences and the experiences they designed for their students. The difference was not merely a product of external control or interference. Avoidance of the intimacy and of the feelings that motivated their own reading experiences was at least as significant as the principal's intrusion or the constraints of testing.

Some time ago I spoke with a teacher who refused to teach the book *Summer* by Edith Wharton. The teacher had such a strong revulsion to the protagonist's oppression that she did not want to present the text to students as a model for their own experience, as if they would themselves turn into the character she pitied and despised. Here again we hear a sense of people turning into texts, of being lost in texts, overwhelmed by that with which they identify. The defense against that fear is the radical separation that speaks of a text as if it were a body to be dismembered. Things must be brought together; things must be kept apart.

Litowitz challenges us to move away from false individualism. "What methodology," she asks, "will enable us to explore one individual as psychologically part of another?" (1989, p. 323)

> All the notions of external-internal relations which have been used in our explanatory the ones to explain both motivation and learning may be ultimately attributable to a trompe l'oeil; that individuals ever become separate, bounded by their persons; and that cognitive and linguistic competence ever exists in a person's mind. We would cease to ask how psychic, cognitive or linguistic structures are built up; how individuals grow up to be separate, mature adults, who "know" formal operations and the full grammars of their languages. Rather, we would begin to ask: How do activities engaged in by a child and mother—or a child and teacher—change, with participation becoming more symmetrical; what are the continuities and shifts in exchanges and relationships which give the illusion of autonomous functioning; what are the processes by which activities and means of exchange are culturally given yet created anew. (p. 324)

The romance of reading invites us to recuperate our losses. As we enter into the fictive world and emerge from it, we experience the opportunity to reconsider the boundaries and exclusions that sustain our social identities. For Winnicott, the world of the text links each of us to those parts of ourselves from which we have separated. The text serves (as do other forms of art) to mediate the distance between self and other, for its meaning is both externally produced and internally sustained. This wonderful narrative of learning to read, written by Kathy Farrar (personal communication), portrays the ways in which reading blurs the boundaries that have separated us from others and from all the selves we might have been:

I was probably five years old when I first learned to read and write a word. I didn't experience this first educational step at school, or even at home. My reading lesson took place in an old farm house which stood empty except for a desk and file cabinet which allowed it to fulfill its role as office for the man who owned it and the homes and pastures nearby. My parents didn't read to me very often, but they made a practice of reading the Sunday comic strips to me. I have a very vivid memory of standing in the living room on a sunny Sunday morning while my parents remained hidden behind newspaper sheets for what seemed like hours. My memory is of losing patience with them for making me wait so long for my treat. I finally punched in the sheet of newspaper which my father was holding and received a spanking (one of a very few which I clearly recall) for my action. I didn't often "backtalk" my parents, but I remember crying and telling them that I would just learn to read so that I could read the "funnies" myself. I was as dead serious as a small child could be, and I buttonholed everyone I knew to try to get someone to teach me to read.

As a five-year-old growing up in St. Louis County in 1954, I was not sent to kindergarten. The local community had not planned for the post war "baby boom" which hit its schools, causing kindergarten classrooms to be needed for upper grades. There was even some dispute about which school I could attend because we lived in a distant corner of the county at a Junction called "Shoveltown" and the nearest school was a lengthy busride away from my home. These circumstances hampered my progress in my campaign to learn to read.

The day when I first learned to read a word was, I imagine, in the autumn. I remember a cool, grey day, around suppertime. Everything about that late afternoon seemed softened. House, barn, sheds and cows in the distance were filtered through fading afternoon sunlight. My flannel-lined bluejeans had been laundered many times, giving them a softness which only old, familiar clothing can have. My father and I walked hand-in-hand down the oil-soaked gravel drive for about a quarter of a mile to where "Uncle Gus" kept his office.

Gus's office was in the front room of the one-story, white frame farmhouse. The entire front side of the house was faced with a low-slung roof which overhung a grey wooden porch floor. The back of the house opened onto a small hillside and faced the open pastures.

My father had stopped by to pass the time of day and was pleased to see another neighbor was visiting also. I can't remember why, but the two visiting men went outside to check on something, leaving me alone with "Uncle Gus."

Now Uncle Gus was not really my uncle, but some sort of distant relative, as were many of the neighbors nearby. It was just the custom where we lived to call men and women friends uncle and aunt instead of Mr. or Mrs. So-and-So. Gus always seemed old to me and always unchanged in manner and appearance. He was of German descent and spoke with the lilt and cadence of speech common to farmers in our area. If Gus is still alive he probably still looks today as he did over 30 years ago. Sweat-rimmed, soft grey hat (indoors or out), dark grey cotton work shirt (rolled to the elbows in summer) and denim overalls (worn as they were originally intended; for work, not style) comprised his wardrobe.

He must have been a little uncomfortable with just a small girl to talk to. He was more accustomed to speaking with his friends about their broken combines, the price of feed or weather conditions as they related to harvests. Gus managed to ask me the usual kinds of adult-to-child questions which no doubt rewarded him with monosyllabic answers. Finally he hit a responsive chord. "Do you know your ABCs?" he ventured. I replied that indeed I did and then shyly muttered something about wishing I could read.

A twinkle came into his eye as he leaned back in his creaky old oak chair and asked me if I thought I'd like to learn to read a very important word. I sidled up close to his chair and watched intently as he opened his center desk drawer and pulled out a hand-sharpened, soft lead, carpenter's pencil and a thick pad of blue-lined paper. I watched as he carefully drew the letters M—A, and he told me that it spelled Ma. He wrote the letters M—A again right next to the first pair and asked me if I could guess what that word was. I was delighted to be able to read the word Mama, and to feel that I had accomplished at least part of the task by thinking it out for myself.

I must have demonstrated my new skill for my father when he returned for me, and for my mother when we got home, but I don't remember that part of the day. However. I'll always remember my own thrill at being able to read my first word.

In Kathy's account the text is a barrier separating her from contact with her parents and with the world. They are her passage to the world but on this sunny Sunday, reading suspends both activity and presence. Her parents are hidden behind the sheets of the newspaper. She makes contact: punching and being spanked. The spanking is "received," and in this scene it may indeed be a gift of contact, visceral, engaged, at once humiliating and triumphant. Communication with her parents is a struggle against the text; her mother remains sequestered behind the papers, and only appears again through language as her father and then Gus give her the symbolic power to summon her mother's power to connect to the world as she learns to read and write the word, "MAMA." Text comes between mother and daughter, freeing them to connect to the men and to the World, and ultimately to reunite in literacy.

The absolute boundaries that the text presents in the first scene, violated only by the contact of bodies, are blurred in the second scene. The public school is closed to her. She walks to Gus's place with her father, holding hands. I note the reconciliation and follow her transference to Gus, who is neither the absent mother nor the spanking, hand-holding father.

It is Gus who offers to mediate between the child and the adults in her world. Gus is given the title of "Uncle"; he stands between stranger and family. Gus crosses all the boundaries. His space is both private and public, home and office. His clothing—soft gray hat (indoors and out)—transcends the division of nature and culture. Gus's place is the potential space in Winnicott's theory. With his carpenter's pencil he teaches her the word "MAMA" and gives her the symbolic power to create a transitional object that spans the distance between utter presence and total absence. He is the one who shows her how to encode the relation that has given her the world.[1]

Gus is a teacher. He does what teachers do when they offer us texts and bring us to them, helping us to develop the semantic and cultural competence to live in their symbolic worlds. Kathy's parents deliver her to him as we deliver our children to daycare centers, nursery schools, high schools, universities, and graduate programs, hoping that someone will give them the power to connect again to the world with the love and passion and energy that they brought to their earliest relations with us.[2]

Notes

1. An extended version of this narrative and discussion of the relation of gender to reading and teaching may be found in my essay, "On Daffodils That Come Before the Swallow Dares" (Grumet 1990).
2. Now Litowitz would probably have us go back to scoop up Gus, noting how his encounter with young Kathy changed his world. In materials that time and space will not invite to this text, Kathy finds connections between her

own reading experiences and the ways she has worked with a boy she tutored in reading in Chicago. (See Grumet [1990] for a study that explores the connection of this narrative to others in a sequence that addressed schooling and teaching.)

References

Atwell-Vasey, W. (1998). *Nourishing words: Bridging private reading and public teaching.* Albany: State University of New York Press.
Chodorow, N. (1978). *The reproduction of mothering.* Berkeley: University of California Press.
Davis, M., & Wallbridge, D. (1983). *Boundary and space: An introduction to the work of D. W Winnicott.* Harmondsworth, UK: Penguin.
Dinnerstein, D. (1976). *The mermaid and the minotaur.* New York: Harper & Row.
Dewey, J. (1964). The child and the curriculum. In R. D. Archambault (Ed.), *John Dewey on education.* Chicago: University of Chicago Press.
Grumet, M. R. (1988). *Bitter milk: Women and teaching.* Amherst: University of Massachusetts Press.
Grumet, M. R. (1990). On daffodils that come before the swallow dares. In E. Eisner and A. Peshkin (Eds.), *Qualitative inquiry in education: The continuing debate.* New York: Teachers College Press.
Iser, W. (1989). *Prospecting: From reader response to literary anthropology.* Baltimore: Johns Hopkins University Press.
Kristeva, J. (1980). Place names. In L. Roudiez (Ed.), *Desire in language.* New York: Columbia University Press.
Lacan, J. (1968). *The language of the self.* New York: Dell.
Litowitz, B. (1989). Patterns of internalization. In K. Field, B. Cohler & G. Wool (Eds.), *Learning and education: Psychoanalytic perspectives.* New York: International Universities Press.
Martin, E. (1991). The egg and the sperm: How science has constructed a romance based on stereotypical male–female roles. *Signs 16*(3), 485–501.
Obeyesekere, G. (1981). *Medusa's hair.* Chicago: University of Chicago Press.
Pinar, W., & Grumet, M. (1976). *Toward a poor curriculum.* Dubuque, IA: Kendall/Hunt.
Stern, D. (1985). *The interpersonal world of the infant.* New York: Basic Books.
Vygotsky, L. S. (1981). The genesis of higher mental functions. In J. Wertsch (Ed.), *The concept of activity in Soviet psychology.* Armonk, NY: M. E. Sharpe.
Winnicott, D.W. (1971). *Playing and reality.* London: Tavistock Publications.

CHAPTER 10

Reading, Writing, and the Wrath of My Father

JONATHAN G. SILIN

I have been thinking a lot about reading and writing these days. My own little back-to-basics movement has been prompted by two seemingly discrete events.

First, as codirector of research for a large urban school reform project, I have spent a good deal of time observing early childhood classrooms in a hard-pressed, low-performing district (Silin and Lippman, 2003). The pernicious insistence on measurable standards, high-stakes tests, and accountability has filtered down to even the youngest children and their teachers. In these classrooms every activity must contribute directly and visibly to teaching academic skills. The morning message, once written by teacher to students at the start of the day as a vehicle for encouraging discussion of past experiences or upcoming events, is now a formulaic exercise designed to teach letter and word recognition. When children are invited to bring in a favorite stuffed animal, the activity is rationalized with a measuring assignment during work time. The kindergartners must determine the tallest and shortest creatures brought from home. While reading storybooks, teachers emphasize the names of authors and illustrators, ask children to draw inferences from pictures, and direct attention to techniques of character and plot development. Seldom is a text left unanalyzed, and rarely are the author's words allowed to wash over the children, the meaning and structure seeping into their pores without articulation. There is little time for cooking and block building, for trips into the neighborhood, and visits from people who do interesting work. In these, as in so many classrooms around the country, literacy takes precedence over life.

Across the Hudson River, in New York City, in the hospital rooms and nursing homes where my nonagenarian father has spent much of the last three years, I am also prompted to reflect on the power and limitations of the written word. Here the throat cancer that my father had been battling for so long has finally cost him the last portion of his larynx. Too debilitated or simply too stubborn to master the electrolarynx, an appliance that allows many to communicate despite the lack of vocal cords, my father is wedded to the written word. Steadfastly refusing a simple instruction such as "milk" or "sweater," he turns every request into a paragraph-long treatise on his current health status or the climate conditions in his room. He takes obvious satisfaction in his carefully crafted sentences, which range in mood from playful and humorous to angry and demanding. When he finally hands me the yellow legal pad on which he scrawls his communications, his expression is one of pride and watchfulness. Will I laugh at the right place, grasp his double entendre, or appreciate his concerns? Although I often wish for the more rapid, more "natural" dialogue possible with the electrolarynx, I cannot help but be awed by his command of written language. Despite his numerous disabilities, he is still able to generate ideas, exercise control, and make himself known with paper and pen. My father teaches me about the compensatory pleasures of the text.

At first blush, the days in classrooms and the evenings with my father would appear to have little in common. Together, however, these experiences make me appreciate the potential of written language for sustaining life and producing social worlds as well as the difficulties of nurturing such an appreciation in the contemporary world. Both experiences send me back to childhood, to wonder about my own early struggles with reading and writing. These "re-searches" into the past lead me to argue that learning often involves unspoken forms of loss as well as the acquisition of new skills and ideas. Effective teaching, teaching that honors student imagination, seeks authentic engagement, and creates spaces for difficult emotions, works through hinting and pointing rather than naming and telling. Literacy, and by extension the curriculum as text, becomes pleasurable when it exceeds social utility, leaves behind the familiar and the well rehearsed, and moves into uncharted territories where loss, discomfort, playfulness—even sexuality—can be fully expressed.

A caveat is in order. Although in this chapter I address my history of reading and writing, I am not a literacy scholar but have been an early childhood teacher, teacher educator, and researcher for more than thirty years with a history of autobiographical contributions to the larger field of curriculum theory (Silin, 1995, 1997, 1999b, 2000). As such, I have struggled with realizing the promise of what Clifford Geertz (1983) referred to so long ago as "blurred genres." Beyond the seduction of the well-told tale, autobiographical research has the potential for moving our thinking past the traditional polarities of theory and practice, teacher and student, and reader and writer (Marshall, 1992; Miller, 1991; Pinar, 1994). Most recently, writing personal and professional narratives together has taught me the complicated ways in which I use my early childhood skills in caring for my parents—the importance of routines, transitions, relationship building—and they in turn have prompted me to rethink the early years of life, including the learning of language and literacy (Silin, 1998, 1999a).

Curriculum as Compensatory Text

I was what has euphemistically been called a late bloomer, although not as late as my older brother who did not begin to read until seventh grade. My emergence as an independent reader was slow and difficult. One incident stands out. I am seated at a table pretending to read a book that my second-grade teacher had enthusiastically given me a few days earlier. It is illustrated with gaudy pastel colors and has the toxic smell of fresh ink. The story involves some popular cartoon characters of the day in which I have absolutely no interest. Not even the active commerce in comics among my brother's friends—and I do eye their collections with envy—has seduced me into reading about imaginary animals or people. My own overactive fantasy life, crowded with figures from the real world, has no space for these intruders created by the pens of Walt Disney and the like. I turn the pages every few minutes hoping to appear gainfully employed.

My teacher, a tall, thin woman in her twenties, circulates through the room that contains a handful of students. She is a new, well-meaning teacher, as my mother explains to me on several occasions trying to secure my fuller cooperation in the teacher's attempts to teach me to read. But good intentions aren't enough to win my confidence or that of the small band of defiant second graders with whom I hang out. We never miss an opportunity to take advantage of her inexperience.

Now the teacher leans over me with her prominent nose, receding chin, and black-framed eyeglasses, and asks me to read aloud. I stumble over every word with more than three letters and cannot answer the questions that she poses about the story. This encounter, in which the novice teacher who cannot control the class meets the reluctant reader unable to decipher the words on the page, is indelibly etched in my mind. It is a painful

• Jonathan G. Silin

moment of truth in which my ignorance is unmasked and her authority is established. It is a moment that I carry with me as I visit classrooms today and imagine myself a "classified" child, one whose name is posted at the entrance to the classroom and who requires an individual education plan to be filed with the vice-principal.

I do not know what kind of training my teachers received during the 1940s and 1950s, or to what degree the best intentions of teachers I currently observe are constrained by the extensive testing and assessment they must conduct (Schwartz and Silin, 2004; Silin and Schwartz, 2003). I do know that a new consensus has emerged regarding the place of literacy learning in the early childhood curriculum (International Reading Association and National Association for the Education of Young Children, 1998). This consensus focuses on the "big picture," on the child's understandings concerning the functions and uses of literacy in the contemporary world (Purcell-Gates and Dahl, 1991; Vukelich, 1994). While staff development efforts and research and accreditation assessments may not always have kept pace with this changed view of literacy as a set of social practices rather than just a set of specific skills, it is certainly one that might have served me well as a child (Dickinson, 2002; Ure & Raban, 2001).

Looking back, however, it is Madeleine Grumet (1990) who has helped me to make sense of my early ambivalence toward the written word. Drawing on Lacan (1968) and Kristeva (1980), she described the innocuous utterances of adults at play with young children as the first use of language to bridge the physical distance between self and other. Talking all the while, the loving caregiver holds the infant high in the air or hides his or her face in the game of peek-a-boo. The adult voice offers a sense of safety and continuity. "I am still here even though you cannot feel or see me." The sounds sustain connection. They create what Grumet calls a "mediating space," a place in which we try to reconnect to the people from whom we have been separated, the things that we have lost, and later, the person we once were. As language develops and written texts play an increasingly larger role in our lives, they too become a mediating space. Here, Grumet suggested, Lacan and Kristeva part company. Lacan emphasized the abject, that which we have rejected or given up on the way to becoming independent, and he had a more pessimistic view of our potential for recuperating our losses. In contrast, Kristeva, with her emphasis on the semiotic aspects of language—expressive, playful, aesthetic—posited a more optimistic outcome. For Kristeva, language is something other than a kit bag of symbolic substitution. It resonates with first relationships and early emotions.

Grumet's originality lies in the way that she described the curriculum at large as a mediating space. She transformed psychological descriptions about how language spans the distance between individual infant and care-giver into epistemological insights for curriculum making. She understood the curriculum as a place in which the intentions of the teacher and student meet, a place in which the initial dyadic relationship of caregiver and child opens out to the world. Teacher and student come to know each other as they explore a reality outside of themselves—the local community or perhaps a far away place and time, a storybook or science experiment. Like an engaging text, the effective curriculum invites us to explore the boundaries and exclusions we have accommodated on the way to constructing our social identities.

Reading can likewise become an act of recuperation, a place in which to find satisfying substitutions for the inevitable losses endured as a part of growing. Like a disconsolate infant who does not accept the warmth of a favorite blanket or touch of a rag doll when a caregiver has departed, I resisted the compensatory pleasures offered by the text. For the longest time the word and the world remained equally mysterious and foreboding.

Learning and Loss

Miraculously I had acquired a few essential reading skills by fifth grade even though I seldom had the desire to open a book. My lack of engagement with reading was now revealed during our Thursday morning trips to the school library. I am always anxious and at loose ends during these sessions. A short, gray-haired woman, with a quick temper, bad teeth, and smoker's breath, the librarian is the butt of many a ten-year-old's jokes. Each week she impatiently questions me about my interests to hasten the selection of a book. But I have no ability to name my interests and therefore assume that I have none. How can you not have any interests, she demands incredulously. A person of no interests, an uninteresting person, I am mortified by this inquisition. Never doing well under pressure, I settle on a Hardy Boys mystery, consciously attracted by the cover drawing of two friends and unconsciously drawn by the promise of scenes depicting illicit intimacy between them. Will they have a sleepover and be forced to share the same bed? Will they unexpectedly end up at the town swimming hole without their bathing suits? When a quick scouting foray into the text yields none of the desired moments, I disappointedly check it out anyway. During the week I read so slowly and unenthusiastically that I cannot remember the plot, let alone finish the book.

Here I acknowledge my envy of the ten-year-old girls who were my classmates. Although whenever possible we divided ourselves strictly by gender, I often caught glimpses of "the girls" rapturously engaged in reading about a plethora of horses and horse farms, nurses and hospitals, families and family discord. I could not imagine that girls had reading problems. But was all this textual interest simply an innocent exploration of imaginary people and places or an indication of some unfathomable interior life? Was my own textual hesitance a fear of what I might find or not find in the larger world?

At age ten I would not have labeled my curiosity about other boys as "homosexual curiosity." Research confirms that some gay men experience a strong sense of difference from a very early age (Cantwell, 1996) and there is acknowledgment now of a far greater diversity of genders and sexual orientations than in the 1950s. The seven-year-old hero of the highly acclaimed film, *Ma Vie en Rose*, for example, understands himself to be a hybrid gender, a boy who will eventually become the girl he was always intended to be. Ludovic has no shame, no doubts, about the situation in which he finds himself. His researches into the distribution of X and Y chromosomes lead him to tell Jerome, the boy he anticipates marrying when he is not a boy, "I'm a girlboy. My X for the girl fell into the trash. It was a scientific mistake" (Britzman, 2001, p. 12). He must only wait for the return of his wayward chromosome to fulfill his destiny. Still my disappointment in the Hardy Boys mystery speaks in part to the gap between the official curriculum and the unofficial interests that powered my curiosity. I was not yet a proficient or committed enough reader to lend the book my life or to impose my own imagination on the text. That was a trick I discovered in adolescence, at the same time as I was more accurately able to name my desires. Only then did I seem to engage in the transformative processes that would protect and nurture the pleasures, sexual and otherwise, that I sought. While I do not take literally Northrop Frye's (1947) assertion that imagination creates reality, it does seem to me that often the world we desire is far more real to us than the world in which we actually live.

Following on Frye and Freud, Adam Phillips (1999) suggested that, at heart, children's curiosity is sexual curiosity, children's theorizing is sexual theorizing. Curiosity is itself a form of appetite that children continuously seek to satisfy through fantasy, story, and the creation of coherent fictions. Curiosity might also be viewed as a response to a sense of insufficiency, a desire for wholeness. From a cognitive point of view, Piaget (1952, 1968) suggested that children are curious when they become aware of a disparity between what they apprehend and their ability to make sense of it. We are driven to seek equilibrium, or wholeness, when our theories of how the world works are no longer consistent with our observations.

Beyond feeling autobiographically right, Phillips's discussion of curiosity is redolent with pedagogical implications. No matter the motivation, curiosity—the wish that things were otherwise—is to acknowledge a sense of loss. Wanting the world to be different is a sign of life. The more we give up—the coherent self, the omniscient parent, the caregiver's solace—the more sophisticated our representational strategies become. The development of language, and by extension reading and writing, is a central part of this progressive, linear story in which we are ever more civilized, skilled at managing the processes of substitution through which our "natural" instincts are managed. Those who are more comfortable with a social or political rather than psychological reading of what is given up or lost in schools need only turn to the literature on the experience of marginalized populations in classrooms (Delpit, 1995; McLaughlin and Tierney, 1993; Rodriquez, 1982).

While analysts such as Lacan, Winnicott, and Klein emphasize the child's helplessness and loss, Freud was more impressed by the child's resilience and imaginative plenitude. Similarly, Phillips argued that parents and educators need to honor the satisfactions of the unarticulated experience. Not a romantic eschewing the accomplishment of language, Phillips wanted to clear a space in which children and adults can move back and forth, a space that recognizes the value of linguistic incompetence as well as fluency, verbal insufficiency as well as communicative competence. For some, the rush to literacy, to fill the void with words and texts, reflects fears of a time when emotions were less modulated, bodily functions less well controlled, and desires less well socialized. Then, language represents the only way forward, and unarticulated experience is consigned to the past.

I don't know if my own reluctance to read was part of a strategy to remain in the past and therefore closer to preverbal ways of being in the world. I do know that as a teacher of young children I did not think that learning might involve loss. Or more accurately, I accepted that whatever the child left behind was of lesser value (that is, efficacy in responding to the world) and therefore of little interest. Steeped in stage theories of development, I believed that the acquisition of new skills and knowledge was to be placed only in the profit column. Along with parents I celebrated familiar milestones—a child learns to button her coat, tie her shoelaces, or walk home from school on her own. I did not imagine that in learning a new way of being in the world, a child might also give up an old way, one that had worked for him in the past—the physical intimacy that occurs when an adult cares for his clothing or the social connection he experiences when accompanied by a caregiver on the walk home from school.

In her insightful commentary on Freudian pedagogy, Deborah Britzman (1998) suggests that it is the ability to tolerate ambiguity, complexity, and uncertainty that teachers should seek to foster in their students rather than false notions of truth, knowledge, and linear paths to learning. I read

Britzman to mean that along with the more commonly accepted emotions of mastery and control, learning may also involve disorientation and dislocation. Indeed, both Phillips (1999) and Barthes (1975) argued that discomfort and conflict, along with the ability to lose oneself, are integral to the deepest human pleasures. Even so, students may defend against a loss and the sense of being lost. In response, teachers need to embrace resistance and the conflict it causes inside of students and with others. When learning itself is recorded in a profit and loss register, it can help us to understand student resistance to our best pedagogical efforts.

Suspended Performances

By the time I enter high school, the terrain of interpersonal struggle has shifted from reading to writing. My grammar and syntax are awkward, my paragraphs filled with non-sequiturs, and my spelling unrecognizable. Nightly responsibility for editing my homework alternates between my mother and my father, the former far more patient and the latter always insistent that I understand the principles underlying his corrections. I am impatient, easily frustrated, and unwilling to internalize the lessons they struggle to teach me. In the end, I am never quite sure who is the real author of these anguished collaborations. They reflect my deep ambivalence about being held accountable for my own words, my own life.

This reluctance to claim my ideas on paper, I now believe, was connected in some complicated and still incomprehensible way to my recalcitrant and unacceptable sexuality. The written word was both the medium that tied me to my parents in endless battles over periods, commas, and paragraphs and the medium that eventually allowed me to see myself as an independent agent with a unique story to tell.

Initially seeking confirmation of my burgeoning homosexuality in the words of others, I considered the pseudoscientific tomes of Edmund Bergler and Alfred Kinsey. But their case studies of tortured unhappy lives had nothing to do with the desires that coursed through my body. I was forced to create far more arresting representations to guide my future. Electrified by the touch of Marc's hand on my shoulder as we walked home from the museum, unnerved by Roger's invitation for a sleepover date that New Year's eve, mesmerized by the folds in Donald's electric blue bathing suit—I began to authorize my own life.

These brief, furtively written narratives transformed vague longings into particular moments, and previously unthought ideas spilled onto the page. Tortured, aroused, sometimes lost and sometimes getting it right, I was having a good time. I acknowledge that when Roland Barthes (1975) described the pleasures of the text, he does not limit himself to such concretely sexual scenes. Yet, for him as for me, the body is always present at the scene of pleasure. The most common pleasure is experienced when the reader encounters that which is comfortable, recognizable, and affirming in the text. The less frequent, more intense sort of pleasure is experienced when the reader meets that which prompts discomfort, a loss of self, or *jouissance* (bliss). For Barthes, bliss was not necessarily associated with the recounting of specific pleasures. It is not the erotic scene itself but its anticipation, not the actual moment of fulfillment but the preceding moments that the reader seeks to sustain. With limited life experience and literary skills, I certainly did not understand, as Barthes explained, that pleasure works through the figurative as well as the representational. Nor did I realize that the writer can point to pleasure, but attempts to name or define it always fall short of experience. Nonetheless, in adolescence writing had suddenly become a source of pleasure, a place of affirmation and "imaginative plenitude" in which the body took primacy.

Exhilarated by my discovery, naïve enough to want to take my new-found pleasure public and sophisticated enough to know that narrative scraps would need to be transformed into a more formal literary statement, I authored a homoerotic short story deeply indebted to my first reading of James Baldwin. Undertaken as a senior English project, this personal declaration of independence, no parental editing required, was ultimately returned by the teacher without a correction, without a comment of any kind.

How did I understand this resounding silence? Confused. Disappointed. Forewarned. While the lack of response hardly short-circuited my desires, it certainly made clear the gulf between my personal researches and the academic world. I had taken what felt like a huge risk only to find that my paper and I had fallen into an abyss.

Elizabeth Ellsworth (1997) says that teaching takes place on what Peggy Phelan (1993) describes as the "rackety bridge between self and other" (p. 174). Ellsworth emphasizes the impossibility of knowing another, our inability to ford the abyss that opens out between people. The best we can do, she argues, is stand beside one another on that rackety bridge and get curious about the "suspended performances each of us might make so that each of our passions for learning might be entertained here" (p. 159).

In retrospect, it seems clear that my English teacher was unwilling to step onto that rackety bridge, let alone stand by me as we peered into the unknown. At the same time, and very much to her credit, she neither referred me to counseling nor suggested that she knew some superior truth about sexuality. In this I am lucky, for, as Ellsworth suggested, traditional teachers understand their function as representational, to present the truth of their subject matter. In contrast, Ellsworth posited teaching as a performative act, at its best serving a catalytic function that incites students to construct their own meanings. Pedagogy is unpredictable, incomplete, and immeasurable in its impact. Like Phillips, Ellsworth valued the life of the body and emotions that are so often papered over with words. She celebrated our potential for becoming lost in the text, absorbed in ideas, not knowing who we are or where we are going.

Ellsworth's respect for the absolute otherness that separates student and teacher is at the core of her work. While her analysis leads to insightful criticisms of traditional pedagogy, it offers cold comfort to the teacher who faces students every day. In contrast, Grumet (1988) posited the text and curriculum as a place in which student and teacher can learn about, if not understand, each other. Rather than enter the bleakness of an abyss (Is it before us or between us? I am never quite sure), we can, together with our students, turn toward the world. Grumet insists that it is the teacher's responsibility to point to the world that matters to her. This pointing, this invitation to explore, is a critical form of valuing. It leads us out of the pedagogical cul-de-sac created by Ellsworth's search for an authentic student–teacher relationship and into a potentially rich curriculum.

Drawing on very different sources from those of Grumet, Eve Sedgwick (2003) reaches a similar conclusion about the value of pointing and hinting over naming and telling. Sedgwick is attracted to the undecided, uncertain ambiguity of Buddhist pedagogy. Like Ellsworth and Phillips, she honored the unarticulated, preverbal life that flows just beneath the surface of our daily activities. Like Grumet too, Sedgwick recognized that the central role of the teacher is to point to part of the world, identifying a problem or experience worthy of the student's attention. She was less sanguine, however, about the process entailed in such pointing or confident that we know what we are actually pointing at. That is the space which unfolds between language and experience, the object and its signifier, the means and the ends.

Learning takes place as students comply with teachers' instructions. There are skills to be acquired, facts to be memorized, and habits of mind to be assimilated. Learning also takes place at a deeper level as students transform the teachers' lessons into personally meaningful ideas. Teachers cannot predict what will be significant to students. They can provide ample opportunities for the transformative work through which students make knowledge their own, including the time and materials required for the imaginative representation and reconstruction of experience (Greene, 1995). Literacy instruction should preserve and nurture pleasure, the idiosyncratic interests that feed curiosity, that keep us wanting to learn. All education involves socialization and sublimation. Successful education finds a balance where official and unofficial curricula each have a place and where public languages are acquired in such a way that they do not subsume private lives.

Writing Private Lives into the Public Record

As I became a writer, I also became a reader. In his short but memorable essay "On Reading," Proust (1971) described the places and days in which he first became absorbed by books. What remains most vivid about childhood reading, he claimed, is not the text itself but the call to an early lunch when the chapter is not quite finished, the summer outing during which our only desire is to return to the book left hastily aside on the dining room table, or the secret pleasure of reading in bed long after all the adults have gone to sleep. While particular phrases titillate our curiosity and provoke our desire, Proust assured us that there is no truth to be found in words themselves, just the keys that help us to unlock interior rooms of our own design. Only in adolescence did the solitude required of the engaged reader become tolerable, dare I say attractive, to me. And only then was I able to set aside my own immediate interests to lend the book my larger life.

Although I favored long family narratives and bildungsromans with lots of character development and psychological complications, my tastes were eclectic. I was especially given to perusing my parent's bookshelves, which contained everything from Kafka's *Metamorphosis*, forbidden to my best friend by his more protective parents, to Ayn Rand's *The Fountainhead* and Oscar Wilde's *Ballad of Reading Gaol*.

Now, on the very same shelves, wedged in between books on Jewish history and biographies of Zionist leaders (my father's) and piled haphazardly atop an assortment of art books (my mother's) are the volumes containing my own essays on education. I have never become used to seeing them mixed in with the volumes of my childhood; they seem oddly out of context, misplaced fragments from the academic world. And what do these carefully proffered "gifts" mean to my parents anyway?

They are proud of my scholarly achievements, clearly unimagined when I announced my intention of working with young children thirty-five years ago. Of course, the books on early childhood find a more prominent place on their coffee table than those on queer theory. So not long ago I was surprised to learn how eager my father was to send a journal article on the impact of HIV/AIDS on the gay community to my cousin's lesbian daughter. Needless to say, he didn't read it himself, but the mere fact that he would traffic in once-contraband matter is an indication of how far he had come.

The year is 1979, ten years before my father's physical decline will begin. My life partner Bob and I have just eaten in a favorite Chinese restaurant with my parents and the four of us are walking across 86th Street in Manhattan. It's a broad thoroughfare, bustling with pedestrian traffic and lined with clothing shops, electronics-cum-Oriental-rug outlets, and discount drug stores. My mother and Bob are in the lead while my father and I trail behind.

I am eager and a little apprehensive about sharing my news with him. I have just published my first article in a radical gay newspaper, a diatribe against mainstream political organizations. Naïvely, I tell myself that any publication will help to legitimize my life in his eyes. It's an opportunity for dialogue and a chance to explain my world. More directly, I want his approval for a project about which he remains deeply disapproving despite his loving disposition toward me. My father listens carefully to my description of the article even as I see him become increasingly upset. "But why did you have to publish *there*?" he finally blurts out. My father hates the word *gay,* winces every time I use it, and would never refer to a "gay" newspaper. I explain my desire to speak to a particular audience, to the community of which I am a member, and to influence the direction of the political current. Then, his anger boiling over, he asks the question that goes to the heart of our muddled relationship, "And why did you have to use *my* name?" Of course, he is not really asking a question. He is launching an accusation of bad faith and telling me that I am not a separate, autonomous adult but a dependent child, an extension of his ego. My father seems to believe that he owns the family name and that my right to use it is qualified, conditional upon his approval.

While I anticipated his discomfort with my public identification as a gay person and the potential harm to which I might be exposed, I did not foresee my father's sense of personal injury and the shadow my gayness casts over his life. I am shocked to realize that he fears more for himself than for me. I did not realize that he would feel directly contaminated, perhaps threatened, by my gayness. Now I say the painful and obvious truth. We share the same name, and, proud of my article, I never thought about hiding behind a pseudonym. More practically, I remind him that *Gay Community News* is a small Boston paper and that if any of his acquaintances should read it, they are most likely gay themselves.

Our conversation is brief, but its impact long lasting. My father's desire to control my use of "his" name reflects the confused boundaries and emotional intensity that characterize our relationship. Once again, it is words that bind us together and keep us apart. My father's response also confirms what I have long suspected: my resistance to reading and my difficulties mastering the basics of composition mirrored an intuitive understanding that the written word would lead me to new places, on my own, away from the protective sheltering of my family. Easily succumbing to homesickness, I wanted neither to venture forth nor, once pushed forward by others, to be surrounded by reminders of the people and places that I had left behind.

As I read my literacy life, the most important lesson I take away is that for some children, learning may bring with it a loss of connection to people and ways of being that feel good and right. This suggests to me that teachers need to allow time and space for children to take responsibility for their own learning and the difficult emotions it may entail. I became an invested writer when words were connected to pleasures and texts reflected imaginative reconstructions of reality. Here I extrapolate that schools need to make a larger place for pleasure, for reading and writing texts that speak to and from the body about things that really matter to teachers and students, including sexuality. My experiences in classrooms and in reading about them teaches me that pointing and hinting rather than naming and telling are likely to prove more successful strategies for nurturing the imagination because they leave greater opportunities for children to insert themselves into the curriculum and to make it their own.

I know this is a tall order and in many situations an improbable one. I, in turn, can speak only as an educator for whom reading and writing still carry an emotional resonance tinged with fears of separation from and desires for my father's approval. For me, this resonance, the feeling of alienation and homesickness, has never been more powerful than now as I find myself—the child who resisted reading until the last possible moment and who fought so hard to create his own voice in letters—become the adult writer bearing witness to my father's silence.

References

Barthes, R. (1975). *The pleasure of the text.* R. Miller (Trans.). New York: Hill & Wang.

Britzman, D. (1998). *Lost subjects, contested objects.* Albany: State University of New York Press.

Britzman, D. (2001, October). The return of "the question child." Paper presented at the Reconceptualizing Early Childhood Conference, New York.

Cantwell, M. (1996). *Homosexuality: The secret a child dare not tell.* San Rafael, CA: Rafael Press.

Delpit, L. (1995). *Other people's children.* New York: New Press.

Dickinson, D. (2002). Shifting images of developmentally appropriate practice as seen through different lenses. *Educational Researcher, 31*(1), 26–32.

Ellsworth, E. (1997). *Teaching positions.* New York: Teachers College Press.

Frye, N. (1947). *Fearful symmetry.* Princeton, NJ: Princeton University Press.

Geertz, C. (1983). *Local knowledge.* New York: Basic Books.

Greene, M. (1995). *Releasing the imagination*. San Francisco: Jossey-Bass.

Grumet, M. (1988). *Bitter milk*. Amherst: University of Massachusetts Press.

Grumet, M. (1990). Romantic research: Why we love to read. In S. Appel (Ed.), *Psychoanalysis and pedagogy* (pp. 147–163). Westport, CT: Bergin & Garvey.

International Reading Association and National Association for the Education of Young Children. (1998). Learning to read and write: Developmentally appropriate practices for young children. *Young Children, 54*(4), 3–46.

Kristeva, J. (1980). Place names. In L. Roudiez (Ed.), *Desire in language*. New York: Columbia University Press.

Lacan, J. (1968). *The language of the self*. New York: Dell.

Marshall, B. (1992). *Teaching the postmodern*. New York: Routledge.

McLaughlin, D., & Tierney, W. (Eds.). (1993). *Naming silenced lives*. New York: Routledge.

Miller, N. (1991). *Getting personal*. New York: Routledge.

Phelan, P. (1993). *The unmarked: The politics of performance*. New York: Routledge.

Phillips, A. (1999). *The beast in the nursery*. New York: Vintage Books.

Piaget, J. (1952). *The origins of intelligence in children*, M. Cook (Trans.). New York: International Universities Press. (Original work published 1936.)

Piaget, J. (1968). *Six psychological studies*. A. Tenzer (Trans.). New York: Vintage Books. (Original work published 1964.)

Pinar, W. (1994). *Autobiography, politics and sexuality*. New York: Peter Lang.

Proust, M. (1971). *On reading*. J. Autret & W. Buford (Trans. & Ed.). New York: Macmillan.

Purcell-Gates, V., & Dahl, K. (1991). Low SES children's success and failure at early literacy learning in skills-based classrooms. *Journal of Reading Behavior, 23*, 1–34.

Rodriquez, R. (1982). *Hunger of memory*. Boston: Godine.

Schwartz, F., & Silin, J. (2004). Changing the Social Landscape of Early Childhood. *International Journal of Equity and Innovation in Early Childhood, 2* (1), 19-42.

Sedgwick, E. (2003). *Touching feeling*. Durham, NC: Duke University Press.

Silin, J. (1995). *Sex, death and the education of children: Our passion for ignorance in the age of aids*. New York: Teachers College Press.

Silin, J. (1997, May 28). Self-display or social engagement? Using personal narrative as vehicle for public education. *Education Week*, pp. 36, 38.

Silin, J. (1998, February 25). Revisiting childhood. *Education Week*, pp. 41, 43.

Silin, J. (1999a). Speaking up for silence. *Australian Journal of Early Childhood, 24*(4), 41–46.

Silin, J. (1999b). Teaching as a gay man: Pedagogical resistance or public spectacle? *GLQ, 5*(1), 95–107.

Silin, J. (2000). Real children and imagined homelands: Preparing to teach in today's world. In N. Nager & E. Shapiro (Eds.), *Revisiting a progressive pedagogy* (pp. 257–273). Albany: State University of New York Press.

Silin, J., & Schwartz, F. (2003). Staying close to the teacher. *Teachers College Record, 105*(8), 1586–1605.

Silin, J., & Lippman, C. (Eds.). (2003). *Crossing the river: An urban success story.* New York: Teachers College Press.

Ure, C., & Raban, B. (2001). Teachers' beliefs and understandings of literacy in the pre-school: Pre-school literacy project stage 1. *Contemporary Issues in Early Childhood Education, 2*(2), 157–168.

Vukelich, C. (1994). Effects of play interventions on young children's reading of environmental print. *Early Childhood Research Quarterly, 9,* 153–170.

CHAPTER 11

Love in the Classroom

Desire and Transference in Learning and Teaching

BERTRAM J. COHLER AND ROBERT M. GALATZER-LEVY

This chapter considers how desire shapes teaching and learning in classrooms ranging from early childhood through university. Not surprisingly, the question of how desire may be played out in classrooms is a sensitive one. The high profile of cases ranging from the alleged sexual predation of preschool teachers to the recent spate of reports on high school teachers seducing their students demonstrate widespread concerns in our culture about how desire may be manifest in teachers' sexual abuse of children and adolescents. Such concerns reflect the understanding that power inequalities between student and teacher increase the risk of coercion (Gabbard, 1996/2004). As Rich Johnson (1997) and Joseph Tobin (1997b) document in their research into "no-touch" policies in preschools, teachers and administrators are anxious to avoid any hint of sexual misconduct.

It is hardly surprising, then, that discussions of desire in teaching and learning provoke anxiety. Educational administrators and teachers, concerned with risk management, blanch at the mention of desire (Tobin, 1997a), and since all awareness of desire toward our students is suppressed in the classroom (Zachry, 1939), it is difficult and unusual to consider the role that desire plays in classrooms and learning. While psychoanalysts are familiar with having fantasies of love and erotics about analysands and have a well-developed conceptual framework for addressing them, educators almost always deny feeling any desire toward students. To be clear, we are in no way endorsing sexual behavior between teachers and students.[1] At the same time, we argue that a price is paid for this suppression of consideration of teachers' desires. Mistakenly believing that awareness of desire inevitably leads to bad behavior, we militate against any consideration of teacher desire, simultaneously searching for and guarding against any behavior that might hint at forbidden desire. Our argument, quite simply, is that such a stance can lead to unnecessarily sterile and dull classrooms dominated by efforts to prevent bad teacher behavior.

Silence and suppression do not mean that desire is absent. In taking up active suppression, we deny the possibility that we might use desire appropriately in enriching teaching and making learning more meaningful. When awareness of desire is tolerated, energy arising from it can stimulate teaching and learning. This perspective, together with a recognition of the subjective curriculum (the personal meanings students and instructors make of the subject matter), the impact of the classroom as a small group, and the concept of transference,[2] underlies a psychoanalytic educational psychology (Cohler and Galatzer-Levy, 1992; Jones, 1960, 1968). We are not ignoring teaching and learning as cognitive endeavors (Cohler, 1989; Zabarenko, 2000), but we maintain that understanding the complex relationship of teachers and students, including their erotic relationship, is critical to understanding education.

Psychoanalysis and classroom education are remarkably similar endeavors. Both rely on the emotional bonds to promote development. While the goal of the analyst–analysand relationship is primarily the renewed emotional growth of the analysand and the goal of the teacher–student relationship is primarily the student's intellectual development, many of the factors that contribute to these developments are very much alike. Students of education have tended to focus on the cognitive components of learning at the expense of understanding its emotional components. By its very nature, analytic work focuses on emotional issues, including the relationship between the analyst and the analysand. Educators can learn much about the nature of relationships that promote learning from the study of psychoanalysis. This chapter is structured with this idea in mind, and, to this end, we draw from psychoanalytic clinical practice to consider how issues of desire in the classroom might be thought about through insights gained from psychoanalysis. This chapter begins with a discussion of the taboo subject of desire (manifest as erotic transferences and countertransferences) as a central classroom dynamic in order to consider fully the impact of suppressing discourse about desire on teaching and learning. We then consider the potentially instructive situation of gay and lesbian teachers who are constantly forced to undertake the recognition and negotiation of desire in learning environments.

Recognition of Desire and Erotics in Teaching and Learning

Ken Bain in *What the Best College Teachers Do* (2004) notes that the best teachers love what they teach and love working with students. While the notion of "loving one's students" and "loving teaching" are commonplace in education, Bain, like most who use the word "love," does not discuss the foundation or erotics of love in teaching. What, then, do we mean when we talk about teachers' desires, their passions, their love of students, and the role of erotics in the classroom? Two pioneering collections take up this topic, Joseph Tobin's (1997) *Making a Place for Pleasure in Early Childhood Education* and Regina Barreca and Deborah Morse's (1997) *The Erotics of Instruction*. Stemming in part from recent contributions to feminist psychology, which focus on issues of relationships and personal concerns in social life, these collections show the importance of recognizing desire for engaging students of any age in learning.

Anne Phelan (1997), a contributor to the Tobin collection, defines the erotic in elementary classrooms in relation to movements toward community and pleasure. Phelan writes:

> Eros is the drive that impels human beings toward union. The desire for union and communion manifests itself in classroom moments of joy, laughter, and pleasure. A shift from the normal state of classroom order to that of erotic desire presupposes a partial dissolution of the binary opposition of teacher and student. During erotic moments, boundaries are blurred and established patterns of relations are disturbed; these are moments of exuberance and excess for teachers and students, moments that are unreserved, lavish and joyful. (p. 78)

What Phelan points to is not an enactment of sexual desire upon children but a recognition of the power of Eros to drive us to deeper connections and the more intimate relationships that are at the heart of good teaching. In other words, desire, driven by Eros, has many manifestations. As Phelan's description points out, one of these is the ability to understand, value, and conduct passionate relationships with our students.

Another manifestation is the recognition that passionate learning can lead to sexual desire. This is an issue explored by lesbian teacher Rebecca Pope (1997), writing in *The Erotics of Instruction*. Pope begins this piece by recalling the warm relationship she had with the instructor for whom she worked as a research assistant while in college. Her instructor was concerned with her life, invited her out for elegant dinners accompanied by wine, and engaged her in long conversations about life and love. Pope developed a crush on this teacher and recalls her stinging disappointment when her instructor, upon learning of Pope's feelings of desire, fled in terror; Pope reports feeling devastated by this abandonment. Now a university teacher herself, Pope writes of her awareness of both desire and power and can comfortably acknowledge that desire, including erotic desire, often moves between students and teachers. Pope recognizes that acknowledgment does not lead to the necessity of action, and in being aware of the desire and making an ethical decision in response to these feelings, she does not need to repeat the failure of her mentor by fleeing either the student or her feelings.

When educational discourse based in legal risk management considers desire between a student and a faculty mentor only as a problem, it rules out recognition and expression of desire, robbing teachers and students of potential closeness. Tobin (1997a, 1997b) notes that acknowledgment of desire in an environment of moral panic and litigation fears about teachers' sexual abuse of children, discussions of desire in the early childhood or elementary classroom are rare. Tobin describes the sorry consequences of this focus. To protect against allegations of child abuse, teachers are often told not to touch children or to be with children privately. Moral panic has led to sanitizing teacher–student relationships to such an extent that preschool and kindergarten teachers may decline to give hugs to their charges or let them sit on the teacher's lap. The result is a word-oriented, antisomatic classroom ethos. In a manner reminiscent of the "discipline" described by Michel Foucault (1978), preschool educators talk about the importance of correct times and places for the exercise of the body. Nap times, snack times, and recreational times are all carefully controlled. Bathroom times present particular challenges for teachers and children alike. But while children are taught to control their body, they are not taught to value or care about it. Life in classrooms focuses on the containment of desire and pleasure.

Tobin suggests that not only children, but also teachers are cautioned against even recognizing desire. One consequence of this caution about the expression of desire in teaching is a detached classroom in which students and teachers pretend engagement in learning. That is, the concern with protecting ourselves from the knowledge of our desires toward our students can manifest itself in a demand for emotional distance from students. Recognizing the intensity of emotional responses to students threatens teachers because it stimulates awareness of wishes and feelings about students, which are experienced as at best questionable and at worst reprehensible.

Despite the desire to avoid the implications of desire, erotized desire is evident in classroom from preschool through professional education. From Phelan's perspective, erotics are present whenever passionate and deeply engaged reciprocal teaching and learning is taking place.

According to Pope, children, adolescents, and adults all regularly develop devotion and crushes on their teachers. Similarly, Aina Barale (1994) questions whether student infatuation with an instructor can ever be prevented, and she does not see it as a problem; rather, she observes that there may be little practical distinction between being a role model and being the subject of a crush. Likewise, Barreca and Trimble, both writing in *The Erotics of Instruction* (1997), observe that most men and women can recall that as students they fell in love with instructors of both genders at one time or another. Barreca speculates that many who enter teaching as a career have sublimated their love for a beloved instructor into a love of the subject matter. Trimble illustrates this idea, describing falling in love with an instructor while in college and later adopting his love of poetry in her own teaching. Barreca observes that this erotic transference is fostered by the realization that the instructor is both available yet distant; it is safe to fall in love when there is no danger that the love will be directly reciprocated. Psychoanalysts understand and accept that desire and erotics play a central role in the analytic relationship and therefore have developed many important conceptual tools for working with these feelings in supportive and creative ways in the analysis. In the following section, we turn to a consideration of desire and erotics as a means to see how analysis might inform thinking about desire and erotics in classrooms and learning.

Relationship, Alliance, and Transference in Analysis

The psychoanalytic process includes a "triune construction" of three separate elements (Meissner, 2000, p. 512): the real relationship of analyst and analysand; the therapeutic alliance between analyst and analysand that fosters analytic work (Greenson, 1967; Zetzel, 1958); and the transference (called a "transference neurosis") (Freud, 1914a). The real relationship is the least controversial of this triune of psychoanalytic perspectives in understanding teaching and learning; it refers to the very humanness of this relationship. Both extrinsic factors such as social background and intrinsic factors such as the personality of each participant are a part of this real relationship. This real relationship and the generally good feeling between analysand and analyst and facilitate the work of analysis leading to the analysand's enhanced self-awareness and personal vitality.

The second element of the triune, the therapeutic alliance, (Meissner, 1996, 2000; Zetzel, 1958) refers to the elements of the relationship designed to foster change in the patient. Sometimes the irrational, emotionally laden elements of this alliance are obscured because the relationship can seem so reasonable and supportive (Freud, 1912a, 1915; Schlessinger and Robins, 1983). The analysand's interest in seeking help, the analyst's commitment to providing it, the sense of safety provided by the consulting room and the analytic situation, and the analysand's trust in the analyst, are all aspects of the alliance (Ellman, 1991). Many elements of the analytic situation that have been thought of as causing frustration in fact introduce greater safety into the analytic situation. For example, early discussion of the prohibition on physical intimacy between analyst and patient emphasizes that physical gratification would take away the motive for exploring the origins of the desire for such intimacy. While such fantasies are used as part of the analytic process, analysts also emphasize the loss of safety that analysands would experience if they thought their erotic wishes could be enacted. People cannot learn well when we feel anxious and distracted (Sullivan, 1953). The feeling of safety facilitates the work in analysis in which the analyst is attuned to the analysand's communications and able with a sense of tact and timing to proffer interpretations which increase the analysand's self-awareness (Wilson and Weinstein, 1996).

Sometimes it is difficult to distinguish between the second part of the triune, the therapeutic alliance, and the third part, the transference (Meissner, 1996). Alliance is a product of the relationship between the analyst and analysand and is intrinsic to the analytic situation. Transference is a product of factors extrinsic to the present situation in analysis and arises from the lived experience of each participant (Hargadon, 1966). The alliance and transference support each other.

Transference is the most intensely studied element of the therapeutic "triune" in psychoanalysis (Bird, 1972; Blum, 1982; Ellman, 1991; Meissner, 1996; Orr, 1954; Rioch, 1943). Desire in analysis is usually discussed in terms of transference—the meanings that analysands attribute to analysts—and countertransference—the meanings that analysts attribute to analysands. The meanings of the relationships that analysands and analysts make are based on experiences of living with others from the earliest years, across the course of life and into the present. Relational theory, including both object relations and self psychology, has extended the classical paradigm to include not only enactments of desire founded within the family circle of early childhood, but also those with others throughout one's lifetime. These transference-like enactments include the use of others as a means of enhancing self regard (Galatzer-Levy and Cohler, 1993; Kohut, 1984; Wolf, 1989). Transference presents a paradox: it is the dynamic underlying the analytic treatment, motivating the analysand's tie to the analyst, but it often leads to enactments of the analysand's experience of the analyst (repeating early life experience in the analysis) rather than remembering and working-through early experience. Understanding this transference is central to the psychoanalytic situation.

Freud emphasizes that psychoanalysis does not create transferences but only brings them to light. As he observes:

> What are transferences? They are new editions or facsimiles of the impulses and phantasies which are aroused and made conscious during the process of analysis; but they have this particularity ... that they replace some earlier person by the person of the physician ... a whole series of psychological experiences are revived, not as belonging to the past, but as applying to the person of the physician at the present moment. (Freud, 1905, p. 116)

The psychoanalytic situation helps to make these transferences visible, but transferences arise spontaneously and inevitably in all relationships (Freud, 1910a, 1916–1917; Rioch, 1943; Wallerstein, 1993). The transference emerging in psychoanalysis may be usefully thought of as reflecting the relationship between analyst and analysand (Gill, 1982; Hoffman, 1998b; Rioch, 1943).

Erotized (or erotic) transference refers to the analysand's conscious desire directed at the analyst. It is particularly important because erotized transferences can result in *enactments* that threaten to take the place of understanding and working-through (Freud, 1914a). Desire, expressed through the erotized transference, may be both a source of resistance *and* a means of impelling the analysand to participate in the analytic process (Freud, 1915; Mann, 1997.) That is:

> Love, then, is dual-edged. Yes, it can be a resistance and destructive, totally blind, prone to action rather than understanding; yet, surely this is not all? Love is also *transformational* and enriches the individual in a way with which few other activities compare ... love is blind, but it also leads to insights and greater understanding as the lovers seek to explore each other psychically as well as physically. (Mann, 1997, pp. 32–33, italics added)

Even by reporting erotic fantasies and dreams, "talking dirty," the analysand may be trying to seduce the analyst (Bollas, 1995). This attempted seduction is often the analysand's effort to gain the caring from the analyst missing in the analysand's childhood rather than mature love. Writing from the perspective of psychoanalytic self-psychology, Ernest Wolf (1994) understands an erotized transference less as a resistance to the work of analysis than as a reflection of the effort to restore an experience of personal congruity and integrity. In this view the emergence of an erotized transference signals the analysand's sense of disruption in relation to the analyst. This concern with the analyst's availability reflects the analysand's experience that parents were unresponsive and emotionally unavailable.

An example from clinical practice may help clarify these ideas. J., a middle-aged woman whose self-preoccupied parents had left her rearing largely in the hands of a long series of ever changing "helpers," had intense sexual and romantic fantasies about her analyst. She hoped to convince him that she was the perfect woman for him. Most of her thinking about the analysis focused on how to make him sexually interested in her through means such as seductive dress, telling erotic stories as part of her "free associations," and exploring the question of whether it was ethical for patient and analyst to marry after the analysis. These activities served as a profound resistance as they replaced any interest in self-exploration. They indeed engaged the analyst, who was sometimes quite aroused by them. The nature of the fantasies, largely focused on mutual soothing and promises of always being available, suggested that the underlying longing were for care such as is given to a more fortunate young child rather than mature sexual longing.

Countertransference

As the last example suggests analysands' strong feelings are likely to precipitate intense emotional responses in analysts. These responses, which are called *countertransference* in the analytic situation, are an amalgamation of the current situation with the analyst-teacher's experiences within the family circle of childhood and the various modes of coping the analyst-teacher has developed. Countertransference is simply the transference that the analyst forms toward the analysand. Since transference is an inevitable part of all human relations, countertransference is also inevitable. The question is how to approach it. Psychoanalysts have been struggling with this question for over a century and educators may learn from that struggle.

Freud (1910a, 1915, 1916–1917) viewed the analyst's response to the analysand's emotional material as an interference in the psychoanalysis. However, Freud lacked the experience of being analyzed, so he could not recognize that analysis is founded in a relation between two people, each of whom contributes to the psychoanalysis (Loewald, 1986). Schafer (1993) observes that Freud's (1915) prescription that the analyst must respond exclusively rationally is not only impossible but trying to follow it may deter analysis. Ronald Doctor (1999) observes, "... in every analysis there has to exist moments of love, of falling in love, because the cure reproduces the object relation of the Oedipal triad, and it is therefore inevitable (and even healthy) for this to occur" (p. 89).

While analysts working in the first half of the last century focused almost exclusively on problems related to the Oedipal situation, in the era following World War II, there was an increased awareness that many analytic patients dealt with problems arising in personality development across the first years of life. These problems were manifest in difficulties in reality testing and experiencing a coherent, vigorous sense of self. The psychoanalytic engagement of such problems was discussed under the rubric of "the widening scope of psychoanalysis." This led to an enlarged view of countertransference as encompassing the entire psychoanalytic situation including all the analyst's feelings about the analysand (Tyson and Renik, 1986). This view of countertransference recognizes psychoanalysis as a two-person relationship. The analyst cannot possibly be a neutral screen on which the analysand seeks in a disguised manner to satisfy personally and socially reprehensible wishes emanating from childhood (Kohut and Seitz, 1963).

The analyst's role beyond that of neutral screen and interpreter has been discussed by many investigators. Paula Heimann (1950) emphasized the analyst's emotional sensitivity and the capacity to understand the analysand based on access to the analyst's feelings and wishes. Likewise Robert Fliess (1953) emphasized that the analyst tastes or experiences the analysand's affects and anxieties and uses this tasting to understand the analysand's experiences. Good analytic listening is *not* characterized by lack of emotional responses but rather in the capacity to listen and respond emotionally *without being overwhelmed*. Heinrich Racker (1968) enlarged the discussion of this capacity to taste and to bear the analysand's dysphoric states. He distinguishes between *concordant identifications*, experiencing and using the experience of the analysand's feelings to guide empathic responses to the analysand, and *complementary identifications*, which reflect the analyst's inability to tolerate these troubling feelings because of unanalyzed elements in the analyst's personality. This leads to a withdrawal from the relationship with the analysand, which is experienced by the analysand as an empathic break (Kohut, 1977). Such empathic breaks lead to feelings of disappointment, depletion, and despair in vulnerable individuals, which in turn can be the subject of analysis.

Empathic breaks are examples of *enactments* in which the analyst acts symbolically rather than putting the situation into words. Theodore Jacobs (1986) uses this term to refer to interventions arising from the analyst's emotional responses to the analysand whereas Judith Chused (1991) uses it to refer to symbolic interactions between analyst and analysand, which have meanings for each participant but which may be outside aware-ness and outside explicit analytic focus. Enactments are often evoked by analysands' reports of feelings and wishes that resonate with the analyst's life experiences.[3] Irwin Hirsch (1994) views enactments as reflecting an intense emotional engagement, albeit an unconscious engagement between analyst and analysand. He suggests that enactments reflect a mutual trans-ference or a two-person interaction. These ubiquitous events are symbolic representation of the analyst's thoughts and feelings which have meaning for *both* participants in the analysis.

Just as desire enters into the transference, desire may enter the counter-transference. Unfortunately, some analysts are no more forthcoming than teachers in considering the meaning and the potential uses of desire in the relationship and rather view awareness of desire directed toward the anal-ysand as dangerous. Angry feelings about analysands are acceptable, but acknowledging sexual feelings is sometimes regarded as a potential source of ethical violations. However, as Michael Tansey (1994) observes, it is pre-cisely when erotic countertransference is disregarded that boundary viola-tions are most likely to occur. This is an odd situation since enactments are symbolic. They are different from acting-in or acting-out, which involve a shift from symbol to manifest reality in a way that violates the boundaries of the psychoanalytic situation. Indeed, it is the very recognition of erotic wishes that provides an opportunity to think about the situations and so to move against putting these wishes into action in the analysis (Mann, 1997; Tansey, 1994).

While erotic transference is well understood, erotic countertransfer-ence is a largely tabooed topic in psychoanalysis. David Mann (1997), writing about transference and countertransference in *Psychotherapy: An Erotic Relationship,* argues that this should not be so. He maintains that the emergence of loving and erotic feelings in the psychoanalytic situation has two sides. While an erotized countertransference may be destructive if translated into action, if examined through talk, it may also be transfor-mational, enriching and enlivening the relationship of analyst and analy-sand. Ronald Doctor (1997, p. 90) observes:

> the therapist may experience healthy erotic feelings and these may be useful in the analysis if the therapist deals with the desire appropriately; if the therapist remains unconscious of the desire and does not analyze it effectively, then the erotic feelings are more likely to bring an unhealthy distortion into the work.

Mann (1997) concurs, observing that both analysands and analysts often retreat from recognizing desire. He observes that if analysts cannot acknowledge and come to terms with desire it seems unlikely that analysands will be able do so. Looking at his own personal experience, Mann, a heterosexual male analyst, recalls working with a gay analysand, an intelligent man with a magnificent body and excellent taste in clothes. While shopping, Mann saw some tee shirts similar to those of his analysand and was pleased to discover that they fit him well. When later analytic material suggested the emergence of an erotized transference, the analyst quickly recognized it reciprocally to his own desire and appreciation for this analysand. With another gay man in analysis, Mann found himself entranced by his analysand's reports of orgies and recognized his own homoerotic fantasies. When the analysand made a bid for sex with the analyst, Mann declined the offer. His experience of his analysand's desire as a concordant identification gave him increased understanding of the analysand's search for a replacement for his recently deceased father. He could then help the analysand grieve this loss and develop more meaningful intimate relationships with men. Clearly, Mann's examples illustrate the importance of productive investigation of erotic countertransference.

Notwithstanding, analysis occurs within a larger social context. Today there is great concern about sexual exploitation arising from the abuse of power and our society is particularly harsh in its response to sexual misconduct of all types. With regard to therapy, sexual activity between therapist and patient is a criminal act in the majority of states and engaging in such activity puts the therapist's license at grave risk. Because sexual misconduct is regarded as so heinous, some analysts have recommended a stringent approach to avoiding it by coming nowhere near the "slippery slope" that might end in overt sexual behavior (Gabbard and Lester, 1996). Unfortunately, such warnings lead to ever more conservative standards for conduct since behavior that had been regarded as appropriate now becomes itself objectionable and questionably ethical, seen as a step on the "slippery slope." Also because of the seriousness with which society takes sexual misconduct, ethics and licensing bodies tend to act with a lower threshold for evidence than might apply in other matters. When analysts overtly describe sexual feelings about patients, they risk being seen through a "where there's smoke there's fire" lens with serious consequences. The question of how countertransference responses are to be used in analysis cannot be addressed without reference to these contemporary social realities. These same considerations apply, perhaps even more strongly to educators.

254 • Bertram J. Cohler and Robert M. Galatzer-Levy

Making Use of Transference and Countertransference in the Classroom

As in analysis, transference and countertransference are everywhere in teaching and learning (Hargadon, 1966) and in fact are often at the heart of the student's desire to engage and learn (Hargadon, 1966). Freud (1914b) himself gave a beautiful example in an essay written to celebrate the fiftieth anniversary of the founding of his secondary school (gymnasium):

> ... it is hard to decide whether what affected us more and was of greater importance to us was our concern with the sciences ... or with the personalities of our teachers.... [T]his second concern was a perpetual undercurrent in all of us, and that in many of us the path to the sciences led only through our teachers.... [W]e courted them or turned our backs on them, we imagined sympathies and antipathies in them which probably had no existence, we studied their characters and on theirs we formed or misinformed our own. They called up our fiercest opposition and forced us to complete submission; we peered into their little weaknesses and took pride in their excellences, their knowledge, and their justice. At bottom we felt a great affection for them if they gave us any ground for it.... [W]e were from the very first equally inclined to love and hate them, to criticize and respect them.... (p. 242)

Recognizing that the erotic countertransference reflects the complex transference–countertransference matrix of learning and teaching, it makes sense for educators to become as aware as they can of these powerful forces in the classroom; without explicit awareness of countertransference, educators, like analysts, may find themselves repeating rather than dealing with central emotional issues in the classroom—either putting unconscious fantasies into action or distorting their relationships to students in an unconscious effort to avoid such actions. These distortions can be seen both in charismatic teachers whose performance in the classroom betrays a desire to be loved by students and in authoritarian teachers whose desire is to be respected and feared. David Hall (1971) describes this as a conflict of the romantic and the realist perspectives in education. Glen Glavin (1997) portrays this tension in terms of two modes of instruction, either the seductive or the abusive, each of which reflects unacknowledged desire.

The abusive or authoritarian teacher, presumably focused on a realistic perspective, sets up an antagonistic relationship with students, bullying them into learning in what is supposed to be their own best interest. In the television series *Paper Chase*, a law school instructor chides, torments, and lambastes students to prepare them for the courtroom. Abusive, tough, and reality-centered teaching is found in classrooms from nursery school to professional education. We all remember with a mixture of awe and terror those authoritarian teachers who "brooked no nonsense" in their belief that teachers must educate students to reality. Glavin contrasts the abusive teaching style with the seductive or romantic teaching style in which the instructor is heroic, self-effacing, and self-sacrificing. "Mr. Chips," the ideal type of teacher in this romantic, seductive, approach to education, reappears again and again in films such as *Dead Poets Society* and *Stand and Deliver*. In the romantic vision, the teacher, in love with learning and teaching, inspires students to heights of learning by example.

Glavin sees both of these models as problematic. In each case, the teachers, lacking in self-awareness, express their desires in demands for a certain kind of recognition that they repeatedly make upon their students. Importantly, both fail to recognize teaching and learning as a collaborative, dialogic process in which the learning occurs through shared participation of students and teachers. Learning then becomes a performance of meeting the teachers' desires and demands rather than pursuing the questions that students and teachers can share. Glavin observes that "the crucial capacity to feel and to communicate enjoyment of the self ... separates the successful teacher from the bore" (p. 16). At least to some extent, the dull classroom is a consequence of the pervasive fear that acknowledgment of desire will lead to inappropriate relationships between students and teachers at all levels of education. Radical feminist and queer accounts of teaching and learning are more honest in recognizing desire in the classroom and more optimistic than much of academic pedagogy about returning desire to the classroom.

Acknowledging desire that we inevitably feel toward students is an important step in guaranteeing against acting on such desire. Once we bring warded-off and disavowed wishes into awareness, we are less likely to act on such wishes, either in psychoanalysis or in education.

Further, and important for fostering educational goals, such awareness contributes to life in classrooms and frees teachers to be creative and responsive in their work with students. Psychoanalytic study of child development has recognized the importance for the child's emotional development as well as a parent's ability to experience pleasure and enjoyment from holding and caring for their children (Stern, 1995). For example, Jonathan Silin (1997), writing in *Making a Place for Pleasure in Early Childhood Education* (Tobin, 1997), is able to recognize both children's erotic pleasures and his response to the erotics of the early childhood classroom. Appreciating that children seek erotic pleasure from others, he is able to respond in ways that facilitate rather than suppress the enjoyment that young children take from their own bodies and from the care provided by their teacher in ways that are appropriate and that enhance both the child's own emotional development and the teacher's pleasure in caring for young children. It is this ability to take pleasure from childcare that fosters creative caregiving, which in turn fosters the child's own sense of vitality and enjoyment in mastery. Indeed, at a time when both parents work and young children are often in extended daycare, it is ever more important that teachers be able to enjoy both the physical and emotional aspects of caregiving. This enjoyment is facilitated by recognition of love felt toward these children.

Good teachers have sufficient presence of self to be able to use student admiration and idealization as an added source of personal vitality (Galatzer-Levy and Cohler, 1993). However, this idea—that teacher and students use one another to enhance personal vitality—makes many teachers feel uncomfortable. Such an emotional interaction, they fear, will be misunderstood as seductive or as a misuse of the instructor's power. Yet, effective teachers permit themselves to feel enlivened by their teaching and work with students, just as students are optimally able to make use of their instructor's enthusiasm and admiration in their own learning. Problems arise only when instructors have a deficient sense of self and need constant replenishment of admiration and idealization in order to feel psychologically alive. These instructors depend upon their students for a missing sense of self. In the same way, some students are unable to tolerate their instructor's admiration of their work. These students may believe that the instructor must have misread or misunderstood their work, or perhaps not read it at all.

Anne Phelan (1997) observes that, while the classroom is most often seen as an objective situation in which students' feelings toward each other and their instructor are supposedly unimportant, in anonymous course evaluations students often report on such issues as the instructor's sex appeal. Teaching Freud's (1910a, 1916–1917) discussion of transference inevitably leads to discussion of the transference–countertransference matrix. A few older students catch on quickly and then uncomfortably wonder, "If students have feelings about their instructors, might instructors have feelings about students?" Even graduate students and analytic candidates (student psychoanalysts) become nervous when talking about this issue. However, these sexual fantasies among both instructors and students may become transformed as David Mann (1997) suggests, becoming motivation for learning. Nancy Boutilier (1994) observes that desire is a wellspring to creativity in the classroom.

Sexual Identity, Intimacy, and the Negotiation of Desire

As much as issues of teacher desire raise fears of an inappropriate exchange in the classroom, these issues become greatly complicated when the teacher in question is queer. An underlying assumption of the classroom is the presumed heterosexuality of the teacher and students alike, making the constructed discourse of the classroom primarily heteronormative. The situation of the queer instructor (or student), on the other hand, is more complex while at the same time rendered visible and central in a way that heterosexuality is not. In other words, homosexuality is discursively understood as simultaneously a "secret" and as that thing which is so profoundly written onto the body and the psyche of the gay or lesbian that it inevitably becomes a visible issue, for good or for ill, in the classroom. Notwithstanding the various consequences of this dynamic, it is quite useful to consider the negotiation of desire that lesbian and gay instructors are forced to undertake all the time.

Particularly if the instructor is not "out" in the classroom, there are bound to be rumors and innuendos. Anneliese Truame (1994) described her disappointment that her queer mentors in graduate school were unable to let themselves be a source of idealization and admiration for queer identified graduate students. All too often, these queer identified faculty undermined the confidence of their students, encouraging these students to "closet" themselves, perhaps out of envy that their students might begin their own academic career without having to confront the same degree of stigma that their own mentors had earlier suffered in the academy and the community. However, many queer faculty resent having to discuss their sexuality at all and find it annoying to have to deal with this aspect of their private lives. Any discussion of this issue raises the emotional temperature of the classroom (Chapkis, 1994).

Queer students report that contacts with self-identifying gay or lesbian teachers and mentors are very helpful in seeing that it is possible to be queer and a successful adult. But such discussion usually stops short of acknowledging desire. However, as Rebecca Pope (1997) suggests, there is inevitably shared desire in this relationship. Explicit acknowledgment of such desire among mentors might permit greater ease when working with their students; mentors could be able to acknowledge their feelings and to discover that they were not alone with such desire, just as in psychoanalysis such recognition of feelings regarding the analysand leads to enhanced empathy.

In a particularly evocative essay, one of the few written by a gay elementary school educator, James King (1997) reports on the experience of being a gay primary public school teacher. He maintains that teachers, and particularly teachers of young children, are supposed to be asexual and passionate, but only about children's lives. He reports his own discomfort when the boys in his class showed an effort to become close to him. While the Gay Lesbian Straight Education Network (GLSEN) has prepared educational materials for schools with queer students or staff, King responds to his worry that a queer reading of texts in literature (Tierney, 2000) may reflect his own lifestyle agenda and not be in the best interests of teaching; King (1997, p. 238) explains:

> It is precisely to mute passion and to reduce the relevance of our lives outside the classroom that silence becomes so necessary to schools. Silence is also effectively deployed to control teachers' lives both inside and outside of school. Teachers and students enter a no-talk zone where our passions are inappropriate. Yet we are encouraged to be passionate about education of our students. So passion, like silence, is selective and ambiguous. The ambiguity is contained by our silences. But silence that denotes absence can never fulfill its mission. A vacuum violates nature; when nothing is said, our desire, our passions fester. In effect, our silence acknowledges the expectation that our desire will, can, and do become manifest in schools.

While he remains silent regarding his sexual orientation, King maintains that change in our management of desire within the classroom is necessary. He suggests that male teachers represent an object of displacement in which educators and others deflect their own erotic passions because of the image in our society of the male sexual predator.

In the end, there may be no greater danger for education than silence. Harriette Kaley (1993), writing on psychoanalysis in education, comments on the impact of silence about desire in the course of working with student teachers. She observes that teaching, including the education of teachers, may require us to break this silence and to help educators to bear the shock of recognizing the unthinkable. The result of breaking these bounds of silence is increased energy and passion about teaching and learning (Silin, 2004). Silence regarding desire and love in teaching and learning perpetuates the idea that children and teachers alike are asexual in the manner of Victorian sensibilities, which Freud sought to change through his own work.

Aina Barale (1994) suggests that particularly among queer students, planned or inadvertent disclosure of the instructor's queer sexual identity inevitably fosters an erotized transference. These queer identified students are particularly likely to want to become chums with their instructor whom they imagine as suffering similar community stigma but somehow managed to deal with it. While she observes that these student infatuations may foster learning and increase the passion within the classroom, which makes for more engaged learning and teaching, she believes that it may become particularly difficult for queer faculty and students to manage to maintain appropriate boundaries, to feel comfortable with these boundaries, and yet not to let these boundaries get in the way of life in the classroom. Barale comments, "it is precisely our sensitivity to the discomforts we cause and, as a result, also experience that can make classroom erotics a tempting solution to academic alienation" (p. 23). She urges continued self-observation, working to create boundaries that are comfortable and safe in the negotiation of desire within the classroom without disregarding the power of desire to inspire learning and teaching.

It is not only the larger community that views gay–straight alliances, queer mentoring programs, and even recruitment of openly gay and lesbian faculty and self-disclosure of their sexuality by queer youth as problematic. Mentors themselves are often uncomfortable with their position. Many queer students idealize or mirror their mentors who seem to have negotiated the goals of their own queer identity with some measure of success. Other queer students may use their mentors as "pals" or friends. Finally, at least some queer youth fall in love with their mentors (Isay, 1986; Phillips, 2003). Herdt and Boxer (1996) portray this issue in their discussion of a drop-in program for queer youth in a community services center. Volunteer youth advisors deliberately spend much time talking among themselves regarding their sensitive position in the lives of youth who are seeking to understand their own sexuality. Perhaps because of their own earlier experiences, queer mentors appear to be both aware of desire in their relationships with their mentees and are therefore committed to the discussion of the emergence, meanings, and uses of desire associated with serving as mentors.

Conclusion

Psychoanalysis is unique among the human sciences in recognizing the importance of desire in all relationships. Desire is the foundation for all teaching and all learning, but discourse about it has been replaced by a demand for silence shared by teachers, students, administrators, and parents. Psychoanalysis has studied desire in the context of the transference–countertransference matrix. As Heinrich Racker (1968) emphasized, transference and countertransference represent an intertwined circle in which each element implies the other. Among the most puzzling of transferences is the erotized transference in which the analysand expresses desire for sexual engagement with the analyst. While this has most often been described as a resistance to change, more recent study suggests that the transformed erotized transference can also provide motivation for change (Mann, 1997). Parallel to the erotized transference, but even more problematic for the course of the analysis, is the analyst's own erotized countertransference. Understood as an enactment founded both on the analyst's empathic resonance in response to this two-person relationship and the analyst's own life-story, recognition of the erotized countertransference facilitates the course of the analysis.

Psychoanalysis too often regarded an erotized countertransference as a problem rather than as an inevitable and important element of the psychoanalytic situation, which is one of a relationship between two people, each of whom inevitably becomes important for the other. While the erotized countertransference has been viewed simply as a complementary identification founded on repetition of unresolved conflicts in the analyst's past, it may also be a concordant identification founded on the analyst's resonance with the analysand's life-story. Understood as an enactment that does not become action, as David Mann (1997) demonstrates, an erotized countertransference may provide important information about the course of the analytic relationship itself. There is considerable debate regarding the extent to which these concordant identifications, or desire experienced by the analyst, reciprocal to the analysand's erotized transference should be discussed with the analysand (Hoffman, 1998a). However, the reality of this desire is an inevitable element of every analyst working with an analysand over time. The task of psychoanalysis is to make explicit that which is implicit in the meanings that the analysand makes of the analyst. This discourse of desire fosters enhanced vitality and spontaneity. All too often, similar implicit desire arising in the instructor's relationship with a student is manifest only as silence and even as a disavowal of desire.

Desire also makes possible the authenticity, spontaneity, and excitement that is missing in much of education, and perhaps in much of psychotherapy as well. Even in humanities courses, where desire is prescient in the curriculum, pleasure in reading, writing, and the relationship of student and instructor is too often replaced by silence and emphasis on prohibition. Erotized transferences and countertransferences are expected to remain hidden as a silent accompaniment of life in classrooms. Remaining invisible, disavowal of desire interferes in the mission of education (Kaley, 1993). Understood as enactment, it is important that instructors and students attend to this silent element in the classroom and that desire be recognized and talked about. Plato recognized the importance of talking about desire. The dialogues are replete with discussions of love, including love evident in education. We need a return to the recognition that desire can facilitate the love of learning, which is the goal of education.

Notes

1. In fact, as we will argue later, awareness of desire and its meanings is an important first step in protecting against the need to act upon this desire.

2. Freud described transference as the way in which desire, particularly socially unacceptable wishes arising in the family, is partly satisfied by being disguised in a way that makes it acceptable in awareness (Kohut & Seitz, 1963). Transference as ubiquitous. We continually reenact the our relationships with significant people across the course of life—not just in clinical psychoanalysis, but also in intimate and other adult relationships, and in contexts like education and the workplace.

3. The term "enactment" is perhaps unfortunate and is used by analysts somewhat differently from the way it is used in ordinary discourse. The baseline activity of the analyst is to put things into words, "When you get angry at me you try to provoke my anger at you to make your rage appear more reasonable." But often the analyst is initially unable to do this and instead engages in an action that symbolically contains the information that would ideally be provided in an interpretation. In this example, the analyst might forget to tell the patient of an upcoming vacation in a timely fashion, thus acting aggressively toward the patient, enacting the scenario rather than describing it. But not all actions are driven by countertransference of enactments in the psychoanalytic sense. The analyst who simply becomes overtly angry at the patient in response to provocation would be "acting-in" on the basis of the countertransference but this would not be an enactment because it did not take a symbolic form.

References

Bain, K. (2004). *What the best college teachers do.* Cambridge, MA: Harvard University Press.

Barale, M. A. (1994). The romance of class and queers: Academic erotic zones. In L. Garber (Ed.), *Tilting the tower* (pp. 16–24), New York: Routledge.

Barreca, R. (1997). Contraband appetites: Wit, rage and romance in the classroom. In R. Barreca and D. D. Morse (Eds.), *The erotics of instruction* (pp. 1–11). Hanover, NH: University Press of New England.

Barreca, R., & Morse, D. D. (Eds.). (1997). *The erotics of instruction.* Hanover, NH: University Press of New England.

Blum, H. P. (1982). The transference in psychoanalysis and psychotherapy. *The Annual of Psychoanalysis, 10,* 117–137.

Bollas, C. (1995). *The new informants: The betrayal of confidentiality in psychoanalysis and psychotherapy.* Northvale, NJ: J. Aronson.

Boutilier, N. (1994). Reading, writing and Rita Mae Brown: Lesbian literature in high school. In L. Garber (Ed.), *Tilting the tower* (pp. 135–141). New York: Routledge.

Chapkis, W. (1994). Explicit instruction: Talking sex in the classroom. In L. Garber (Ed.), *Tilting the tower.* New York: Routledge.

Chused, J. F. (1991). The evocative power of enactments. *Journal of the American Psychoanalytic Association, 39,* 615–639.

Cohler, B. (1989). Psychoanalysis and education: Motive, meaning and self. In K. Field, B. J. Cohler & G. Wool, (Eds.), *Learning and education: Psychoanalytic perspectives* (pp. 11–84). New York: International Universities Press.

Cohler, B., & Galatzer-Levy, R. M. (1992). Psychoanalysis and the classroom: Intent and meaning in learning and teaching. In N. Szajnberg (Ed.), *Educating the emotions: Bruno Bettelheim and psychoanalytic development* (pp. 41–90). New York: Plenum Press.

Doctor, R. (1999). Understanding the erotic and eroticised transference and countertransference. In D. Mann (Ed.), *Erotic transference and countertransference: Clinical practice in psychotherapy* (pp. 89–98). New York: Brunner-Routledge.

Ellman, S. J. (1991/2002). *Freud's technique papers: A contemporary perspective.* New York: Other Press.

Fliess, R. (1953). Countertransference and counteridentification. *Journal of the American Psychoanalytic Association, 1,* 268–284.

Fosshage, J. L. (1995). Interaction in psychoanalysis: A broadening horizon. *Psychoanalytic Dialogues, 5,* 459–478.

Foucault, M. (1978/1995). *Discipline and punish.* A. Sheridan (Trans). New York: Vintage Books.

Freud, S. (1905/1953). Fragment of an analysis of a case of hysteria. In J. Strachey (Ed. & Trans.), *The standard edition of the complete psychological works of Sigmund Freud* (Vol. 7, pp. 7–124). London: Hogarth Press.

Freud, S. (1910a/1957). Five lectures on Psycho-Analysis. In S. Freud, *The complete psychological works of Sigmund Freud* (Vol. 11, pp. 9–58). London: Hogarth Press.

Freud, S. (1910b/1958). The future prospects of psychoanalytic therapy. In S. Freud, *The complete psychological works of Sigmund Freud* (Vol. 11, pp. 141–151). London: Hogarth Press.

Freud, S. (1912a/1958). The dynamics of the transference. In S. Freud, *The complete psychological works of Sigmund Freud* (Vol. 12, pp. 99–108). London: Hogarth Press.

Freud, S. (1912b/1958). Recommendations to physicians practicing psychoanalysis. In S. Freud, *The complete psychological works of Sigmund Freud* (Vol. 12, pp. 111–120). London: Hogarth Press.

Freud, S. (1914a/1958). Remembering, repeating and working-through (Further recommendations on the technique of psycho-analysis II). In S. Freud, *The complete psychological works of Sigmund Freud* (Vol. 12, pp. 147–156). London: Hogarth Press.

Freud, S. (1914b/1953). Some reflections on schoolboy psychology. In S. Freud, *The complete psychological works of Sigmund Freud* (Vol. 13, pp. 241–244). London: Hogarth Press.

Freud, S. (1915/1958). Observations on Transference-love (Further recommendations on the technique of Psycho-Analysis III). In S. Freud, *The complete psychological works of Sigmund Freud* (Vol. 12, pp. 159–171). London: Hogarth Press.

Freud, S. (1916–1917/1963). Introductory lectures on psychoanalysis. In S. Freud, *The complete psychological works of Sigmund Freud* (Vol. 15, pp. 15–16). London: Hogarth Press.

Gabbard, G. O. (1996/2004). *Love and hate in the analytic setting.* Lanham, MD: Rowman & Littlefield.

Gabbard, G., & Lester, E. (1996). *Boundaries and boundary violations in psychoanalysis.* New York: Basic Books.

Galatzer-Levy, R. M., & Cohler, B. (1993). *The essential other.* New York: Basic Books/Persus.

Garber, L. (Ed.). (1994). *Tilting the tower.* New York: Routledge.Gill, M. M (1982). *Analysis of the transference.* Volume I: *Theory and technique.* New York: International Universities Press.

Glavin, J. (1997). The intimacies of instruction. In R. Barreca & D. D. Morse (Eds.), *The erotics of instruction* (pp. 12–27). Hanover, NH: University Press of New England.

Greenson, R. (1967). *The technique and practice of psychoanalysis.* New York: International Universities Press.

Hall, D. (1971). A case for teacher continuity in inner-city schools, *American Journal of Education (The School Review), 80,* 27–49.

Hargadon, B. K. (1966). Transference: A student-teacher interaction. *The School Review, 74,* 446–452.

Heimann, P. (1950). On countertransference. *International Journal of Psychoanalysis, 31,* 81–84.

Herdt, G., & Boxer, A. (1996). *Children of horizons.* (2nd ed.). Boston: Beacon Press.

Hirsch, I. (1994). Countertransference love and theoretical model, *Psychoanalytic Dialogues, 4,* 171–192.

Hoffman, I. Z. (1998a). Poetic transformations of erotic experience: Commentary on paper by Judy Messler Davies. *Psychoanalytic Dialogues, 8,* 747–766.

Hoffman, I. (1998b). *Ritual and spontaneity in the psychoanalytic process.* Hillsdale, NJ: The Analytic Press.

Isay, R. (1986). The development of sexual identity in homosexual men. *Psychoanalytic Study of the Child, 41,* 467–489.

Jacobs, T. (1986). On countertransference enactments. *Journal of the American Psychoanalytic Association, 34,* 289–307.

Johnson, R. (1997). The "no-touch" policy. In J. Tobin (Ed.), *Making a place for pleasure in early childhood education* (pp. 101–118). New Haven, CT: Yale University Press.

Jones, R. M. (1960). *An application of psychoanalysis to education.* Springfield, IL: Charles C. Thomas.

Jones, R. M. (1968). *Fantasy and feeling in education.* New York: International Universities Press.

Kaley, H. (1993). Psychoanalysis in education, *Psychoanalytic Psychology, 10,* 93–103.

King, J. R. (1997). Keeping it quiet: Gay teachers in the primary grades. In J. Tobin (Ed.), *Making a place for pleasure in early childhood education* (235–250). New Haven, CT: Yale University Press.

Kohut, H. (1977). *The Restoration of the self.* New York: International Universities Press.

Kohut, H. (1984). *How psychoanalysis cures.* Chicago: University of Chicago Press.

Kohut, H., & Seitz, P. (1963/1978). Concepts and theories of psychoanalysis. In P. Ornstein (Ed.), *The Search for the self: Selected writings of Heinz Kohut, 1950–1978* (Vol. I, pp. 337–374). New York: International Universities Press.

Loewald, H. (1986). Transference-countertransference. *Journal of the American Psychoanalytic Association, 34,* 275–287.

Mann, D. (1997). Oedipus and the unconscious erotic countertransference. In D. Mann (Ed.), *Erotic transference and countertransference: Clinical practice in psychotherapy* (pp. 73–88). New York: Brunner-Routledge.

Meissner, W. W. (1996). *The therapeutic alliance.* New Haven, CT: Yale University Press.

Meissner, W. W. (2000). The many faces of analytic interaction. *Psychoanalytic Psychology, 17,* 512–546.

Orr, D. W. (1954). Transference and countertransference: A historical survey. *Journal of the American Psychoanalytic Association, 2,* 621–670.

Phelan, A. (1997). Classroom management and the erasure of teacher desire. In J. Tobin (Ed.), *Making a place for pleasure in early childhood education* (pp. 76–100). New Haven, CT: Yale University Press.

Phillips, S. (2003). Homosexuality: Coming out of the confusion. *International Journal of Psychoanalysis, 84,* 1431–1450.

Pope, R.A. (1997). Hayley, Roz, and me. In R. Barreca and D.D. Morse (Eds.) *The erotics of instruction* (pp. 28–51). Hanover, NH: University Press of New England.

Racker, H. (1968). *Transference and countertransference.* New York: International Universities Press.

Rioch, J. M. (1943). The transference phenomenon in psychoanalytic therapy. *Psychiatry, 6,* 147–156.

Schafer, R. (1993). On transference love: Revisiting Freud. In S. Person, A. Hagelin & P. Fonagy (Eds.), *On Freud's "observation on transference-love"* (pp. 75–95). New Haven, CT: Yale University Press.

Schlessinger, N., & Robbins, F. (1983). *A developmental view of the psychoanalytic process: Follow-up studies and consequences.* New York: International Universities Press.

Shay, J. (1994). *Achilles in Vietnam: Combat trauma and the undoing of character.* New York: Atheneum.

Silin, J. G. (1997). The pervert in the classroom. In J. Tobin (Ed.), *Making a place for pleasure in early childhood education* (pp. 214–234). New Haven, CT: Yale University Press.

Stern, D. (1995). *The motherhood constellation: A unified view of parent-infant psychotherapy.* New York: Basic Books.

Sullivan, H. S. (1953/1997). *The interpersonal theory of psychiatry.* New York: Norton.

Tansey, M. J. (1994). Sexual attraction and phobic dread in the countertransference, *Psychoanalytic Dialogues. 4,* 139–152.

Tierney, W. G. (2000). Undaunted courage: Life history and the postmodern challenge. In N. K. Denzin & Y. S. Lincoln (Eds.), *Handbook of qualitative research* (2nd ed., pp. 537–554). Thousand Oaks, CA: Sage.

Tobin, J. (1997a). The missing discourse of pleasure and desire. In J. Tobin (Ed.), *Making a place for pleasure in early childhood education* (pp. 1–38). New Haven, CT: Yale University Press.

Tobin, J. (1997b). Playing doctor in two cultures: The United States and Ireland. In J. Tobin (Ed.), *Making a place for pleasure in early childhood education* (pp. 119–158). New Haven, CT: Yale University Press.

Trimble, D. (1997). Making love to the gods: Four women and their affairs with education. In R. Barreca & D. D. Morse (Eds.), *The erotics of instruction* (pp. 147–165). Hanover, NH: University Press of New England.

Truame, A. (1994). Tau(gh)t connections: Experiences of a "mixed-blood, disabled, lesbian student." In L. Garber (Ed.), *Tilting the tower* (pp. 208–226). New York: Routledge.

Tyson, R., & Renik, O. (1986). Countertransference in theory and practice. *Journal of the American Psychoanalytic Association, 34,* 699–708.

Wallerstein, R. S. (1993). On transference-love: Revisiting Freud. In S. Person, A. Hagelin & P. Fonagy (Eds.), *On Freud's "observation on transference-love"* (pp. 57–76). New Haven, CT: Yale University Press.

Wilson, A., & Weinstein, L. (1996). The transference and the zone of proximal development, *Journal American Psychoanalytic Association, 44,* 167–200.

Wolf, E. S. (1989). The psychoanalytic self psychologist looks at learning. In K. Field, B. J. Cohler & G. Wool (Eds.), *Learning and education: Psychoanalytic perspectives* (pp. 377–394). New York: International Universities Press.

Wolf, E. (1994). Narcissistic lust and other vicissitudes of sexuality. *Psychoanalytic Inquiry, 14,* 519–534.

Zabarenko, L. M. (2000). Psychoanalysis and learning. *Psychoanalytic Psychology, 17,* 264–293.

Zachry, C. B. (1939). Contributions of psychoanalysis to the education of the adolescent. *Psychoanalytic Quarterly, 8,* 98–107.

Zetzel, E. (1958/1970). Therapeutic alliance and the psychoanalysis of hysteria. In E. Zetzel, *The capacity for emotional growth* (pp. 182–196). New York: International Universities Press.

About the Contributors

Margaret E. Barber is Assistant Professor of Educational Leadership at Lehigh University, College of Education. Her work focuses on the preparation of school leaders and the psychodynamics of organizational change.

Gail M. Boldt is Assistant Professor in the Ph.D. program in Language, Literacy, and Culture at the University of Iowa. During her 2003–2004 developmental leave, she was a visiting scholar at the Chicago Institute for Psychoanalysis. Her research and graduate teaching focuses on studies of identity, childhood, and schooling from poststructural and psychoanalytic perspectives.

Deborah P. Britzman is Professor of Education at York University in Toronto and author of *Practice Makes Practice: A Critical Study of Learning to Teach* (1991); *Lost Subjects, Contested Objects: Toward a Psychoanalytic History of Learning* (1998); and *After-Education: Anna Freud, Melanie Klein and Psychoanalytic Histories of Learning* (2003), all from SUNY Press. Britzman is a candidate in training with the Toronto Institute for Contemporary Psychoanalysis.

Bertram J. Cohler is the William Rainey Harper Professor, the College and the Departments of Comparative Human Development, Psychology, and Psychiatry and the Committee on Interdisciplinary Studies, The University of Chicago. He is on the faculty of The Chicago Institute for Psychoanalysis and works as a clinical psychoanalyst.

David L. Eng is Associate Professor of English at Rutgers University. He is the author of *Racial Castration: Managing Masculinity in Asian America* (Duke University Press, 2001). He is also the coeditor, with David Kazanjian, of *Loss: The Politics of Mourning* (University of California Press, 2003), as well as the coeditor, with Alice Y. Hom, of *Q&A: Queer in Asian America* (Temple University Press, 1998). Most recently, he coedited, with Judith Halberstam and José Esteban Muñoz, a special issue of *Social Text,* "What's Queer about Queer Studies Now?" He is currently completing a manuscript titled "Queer Diasporas/Psychic Diasporas."

Robert M. Galatzer-Levy, M.S., M.D., is a training, supervising, and child and adolescent supervising analyst on the faculty of The Chicago Institute for Psychoanalysis. He is a Lecturer in Psychiatry at The University of Chicago. His professional interests include clinical psychoanalysis, nonlinear dynamic systems theory, and applications of psychoanalysis to social issues including law and education.

Madeleine R. Grumet is Professor of Education and Communication Studies at the University of North Carolina, where she has served as Dean of the School of Education. Prior to her appointment at North Carolina, she served as Dean of the School of Education at Brooklyn College, City University of New York. A curriculum theorist, specializing in arts and humanities curriculum, Professor Grumet has published many essays that interpret curriculum and teaching through the lenses of feminism, psychoanalysis, and the arts. She is the author of *Bitter Milk: Women and Teaching* (University of Massachusetts Press, 1988), a study of gender and the relationship of teaching and curriculum to experiences of reproduction.

Michael O'Loughlin is an Associate Professor at Adelphi University, New York. In the School of Education he teaches courses on child development and classroom management. At the Derner Institute of Advanced Psychological Studies he supervises doctoral students in clinical psychology and teaches courses on psychoanalysis, trauma, and cultural difference.

Alice Pitt is Associate Professor of Education and Associate Dean of Preservice Education at York University, Toronto. *The Play of the Personal: Psychoanalytic Narratives of Feminist Education* (Peter Lang, 2004) explores themes of psychical resistance and attachment to knowledge and psychoanalytic frames of research methodology. With Deborah Britzman, she has done research on difficult knowledge in university teaching and learning ("Speculation on Qualities of Difficult Knowledge in Teaching and Learning: An Experiment in Psychoanalytic Research," 2003, *Quali-*

tative Studies in Education), and is currently exploring the paradoxes of autonomy and issues of influence in professional life and learning.

Linda C. Powell is Senior Fellow at the Robert Wagner Graduate School of Public Services at New York University. As an organizational consultant and psychotherapist, she has been working with groups and individuals on issues of power and change for 30 years. Powell is specifically interested in issues of authority and social identity, and how these two interact in the routine challenges of organizational life and leadership. Her teaching, research, and advocacy efforts bridge Powell's personal, political, and professional interests in the importance of the individual in large-scale change.

Paula M. Salvio is Associate Professor of Education at the University of New Hampshire. In addition to serving as Guest Editor and Section Editor for the *Journal of Curriculum Theorizing,* Professor Salvio has published extensively in books on curriculum theory and in journals such as *Cambridge Journal of Education, Journal of Cultural Studies, Curriculum Inquiry, Journal of Teacher Education,* and *English Quarterly.* Her current research and teaching interests center on the rhetoric of performance and oral traditions, both of which are reflected in her investigations of feminist performance practices, women's storytelling, and adolescent's experiences of literacy in and out of school. Her book-length project, *Teacher of Weird Abundance: Essays on the Teaching Life of Anne Sexton,* is forthcoming with SUNY Press.

Jonathan G. Silin is a member of the Bank Street College of Education Graduate Faculty. He is the author of *My Father's Keeper: A Gay Son's Story* (Beacon Press, 2006); *Sex, Death, and the Education of Children: Our Passion for Ignorance in the Age of AIDS* (Teachers College Press, 1995); and coeditor with Carol Lippman of *Putting the Children First: The Changing Face of Newark's Public Schools* (Teachers College Press, 2003).

Peter Maas Taubman is Associate Professor in the School of Education at Brooklyn College, where he served as Assistant Dean from 2003 to 2005. His previous writing has focused on social identities and the work of Jacques Lacan. Currently he is writing a book about the deleterious effects of the National Council for the Accreditation of Teacher Education on teacher education.

Index

271

Plunkett, Eugenia, 68
Ponette (film, 1996), 161–164
Pope, Rebecca
    The Erotics of Instruction (1997),
        245–247, 257
Poverty, 46
    anxiety about, 48
    urban schools and, 47–48
Powell, Linda C., 5, 13, 14, 45
Private sphere
    globalization and, 137
Projection, 27–28
    education reform and, 42
    splitting and, 28
Proust, M.
    "On Reading," 237
Psychoanalysis
    alliance in, 247–250
    binary oppositions and, 4
    child, 168–171, 189–200
    countertransference and (*see*
        Countertransference)
    curriculum and pedagogy and, 186
    desire and, 248, 252–253, 259
    empathic breaks and, 251–252
    the Enlightenment and, 171
    film and, 9–11
    identification and, 145–149
    love and, 3, 249
    object relations and, 89
    prophylactic, 178
    relationship in, 247–250
    resistances to, 170
    transference and (*see* Transference)
    triune construction in, 247
    in the United States, 2
Psychoanalysis and education, 169, 244
    desire and, 258
    love and, 1–2
Psychoanalysts
    role of, 251
    as teacher, 185–186
Psychoanalytic theory
    interpellation and, 149
    narcissism and, 154–156
Public Conversations Project, 50
Public education
    American identity and, 46

capitalism and, 40
conflict between competing systemic
    forces and, 38–41
dual system of, 39–40
the institution in the mind, 41–42
privatization of, 53
race and class and, 39–40
reform, 34 (*see also* Urban education
    reform)
segregation and, 33–34, 39–40
stakeholders of, 46
standardized curricula and
    pedagogy, 39
Public policy
    educational reform and, 51 (*see also*
        Urban education reform)
Public sphere, 137
    withdrawal of government from, 46

R

Rabbit Proof Fence, 107–110
Race, 6
    anxiety about, 48
    desire and, 152–154
    education and, 39–40, 51
    identity demands and, 143–44,
        151–153
    as passionate attachment, 147–149
    politics of, 109
    transnational history of, 119
    urban schools and, 47
Race relations
    black–white, 120
    black–yellow, 121
Racial fantasies
    whites and, 152, 154
Racial formation, 119
Racial identification, 147–149
    group acceptance and, 148–149
    parents and, 153
    power and, 148
    social privilege and inequity and,
        148
Racial melancholia
    Asian Americans and, 115, 125–126
    communal nature of, 126
    transnational adoption and, 115